Praise for
The Elements of Narrative Nonfiction

*A true story told by a great writer becomes history,
because stories are how we remember. Rubie has written
a thoughtful and useful introduction to the art of nonfiction
storytelling. I wish I had had this book thirty years ago,
when I started out.*
> —Mark Bowden, author of *Black Hawk Down:
> A Story of Modern War*

*The Elements of Narrative Nonfiction is an invaluable
resource for anyone grappling with a nonfiction project.
It's smart, cogent, and comprehensive.*
> —Betsy Lerner, editor turned literary agent and
> author of *The Forest for the Trees: An Editor's
> Advice to Writers*

*In a publishing market where "narrative nonfiction" is looked
on not just as a genre but as the holy grail, Peter Rubie steps
forward to do what no one else has done before—define the
craft and lay out precepts for new bestsellers.*
> —John Silbersack, former HarperCollins
> vice president and senior vice-president,
> Trident Media Group

*Really excellent—by far the best (most informative, most
readable and just the most useful) advice I've read on writing
and selling narrative nonfiction, the "novel of true events"
(I love that phrase!).*
> —Leslie Sharpe, author, editor, and professor
> of creative writing and journalism at
> Columbia University

The Elements of Narrative Nonfiction

How to Write & Sell the Novel of True Events

By
Peter Rubie

Fresno, California

Published by Quill Driver Books
an imprint of Linden Publishing
2006 S. Mary
Fresno, California 93721
QuillDriverBooks.com

Quill Driver Books/Word Dancer Press, Inc. Project Cadre:
Doris Hall, Linda Kay Hardie, Christine Hernandez, Dave Marion, Stephen Blake Mettee,
Kent Sorsky

Quill Driver Books and Colophon are trademarks of
Linden Publishing, Inc.
Printed in the United States of America

Original Title: *Telling the Story*. Revised and retitled for this edition.
Front cover design: Jason Heuer

Quill Driver Books' titles may be purchased in quantity at special discounts for educational, fund-raising, business, or promotional use. Please contact Special Markets, Quill Driver Books, at the above address or at 559-233-6633.

To order another copy of this book, please call
1-800-345-4447.

135798642

Library of Congress Cataloging-in-Publication Data
Rubie, Peter.
  The elements of narrative nonfiction : how to write & sell the novel of true events / by Peter Rubie.
    p. cm.
  Includes bibliographical references.
  ISBN-13: 978-1-884956-91-1
  ISBN-10: 1-884956-91-2
  1. Reportage literature--Authorship. I. Title.
  PN3377.5.R45R83 2008
  808'.02--dc22
                                                    2008039433

Contents

The profession of book writing makes horse racing seem like a solid, stable business.
                    —John Steinbeck

Introduction

It's all storytelling, you know. That's what journalism is all about.
—Tom Brokaw, NBC News

Most authors don't get the opportunity to revisit past glories, so the opportunity that Stephen Mettee at Quill Driver Books offered me to go back over this book and try and make it better is a rare one, and it is much appreciated.

It's been more than seven years since HarperCollins first published this book, and what fascinates me most is how relevant it still seems to be. Narrative nonfiction books not only remain popular, but in some ways this style of writing is more appealing than ever to both readers and authors, especially journalists. Yet, despite the hundreds of books that tell you what to write, how to write, and when to write, this style of journalism is virtually unsullied by books offering concrete advice on how to tackle the writing within such a deceptively difficult genre.

Writing a novel is a little like being a woodcutter who goes into a forest, chops down a bunch of trees, and then transforms himself into a cabinetmaker to turn that raw material into elegant furniture.

Writing nonfiction is even more prosaic: You need to know your subject intimately, be able to explain it clearly, offer great advice that will not encourage people to hurt themselves or others, and have enough of a profile as an expert in your field that those interested in your book's subject will actually go out of their way to stick their hands in their pockets and shell out however much it costs to buy *your* book and then actually *read* the thing.

The successful writer of narrative nonfiction has to do even more: She needs to combine both the skills of being a novelist and being an expert in a particular subject with the integrity and insight of a journalist. She must extract a compelling, emotionally gripping story from the wealth of sometimes contradictory facts she has researched and interviewed people about, while retaining a reporter's integrity about the truth of what happened and who it happened to and making a compelling case on the page for why the rest of us should care about this story (think of Laura Hillenbrand's book *Seabiscuit* as the demonstration of the successful application of these skills). It's an awesome task to undertake and if done properly utilizes the sensitivity of a literary novelist like Annie Proulx and the skills of research-rich and insightful historical writers such as David McCullough or Mark Bowden.

When I was a teenager about to enter college, I once said to an older (working) actor friend of mine, "I'm thinking of becoming an actor." And he said, "If you're thinking about it, don't do it." The point of that story is that, rather like my actor friend, in the past I've been criticized for underscoring how difficult writing can be, rather than encouraging and inspiring writers. Considering how much of my life is spent willingly mentoring people, such criticism makes me grumpy because the real complaint is that I'm not spoon-feeding enough answers to students to make things easier for them.

But these critics are missing the point. Who says you deserve to be published? Who says just because you want something badly enough, or you practice hard enough you deserve to succeed at it? Effort and intent are not enough, though, of course, they certainly count for something, You need to be smart and aware of your potential audience. The two simple questions any prospective writer of nonfiction needs to answer honestly and objectively are, "Who's going to buy my book?" and "How many people can I get to buy it?"

Go to any Barnes & Noble megastore and look around the bookshelves at the thousands of titles stacked there. Why on earth should anyone in their right mind publish another one? This is a major obstacle any writer must overcome if he wants to be published—let alone sell well—and spoon-feeding students, even if it were possible, is never going to help them tackle *that* problem successfully.

This book is inspirational in design, as well as practical in nature. My job is both to challenge you and to suggest some ways you could shape things when there seems to be chaos; I try to make you think about what you're doing and how you're doing it, not because my way is the best way, because it clearly isn't, but because in adapting or rejecting what I suggest you will or should develop your own answers. And when you have developed enough technique and confidence to analyze what you're doing when you get into trouble with your material (and we all do at some point or other), you'll have some tools to figure out not only what is going wrong but how you may be able to fix it.

The truth is that *any* art form worth mastering and perfecting is difficult. If it weren't, it wouldn't be worth doing. And I don't need to inspire you, do I? You're already inspired; that's why you're reading this book!

The Rise of Narrative Nonfiction

In Cold Blood, All the President's Men, Dispatches, The Perfect Storm, Jarhead, and *Into Thin Air* are just some of the narrative nonfiction books that have been recent huge bestsellers and they have one thing in common: They read like novels, but they are true stories.

The success of books such as *Longitude* by Dava Sobel, the story of the invention of the sea-going chronometer, *The Perfect Storm* by Sebastian Junger, a modern-day twist on an old-fashioned Jack London-esque adventure-cum-science story of a sea storm of the century, and Jon Krakauer's *Into Thin Air,* an account of climbing Mount Everest that ended in disaster, have given publishers pause when considering what sells best, and therefore what interests the average American most. Back in the 1960s, 1970s and 1980s, bold, brassy fiction from writers like Harold Robbins, James Michener, James Clavell, Danielle Steel, and so forth made up the bestseller lists. And certainly, brand name authors of fiction still sell well, as the John Grishams, Tom Clancys and Stephen Kings of this world demonstrate.

However, a casual examination of other recently success-ful books include a growing number of narrative nonfiction titles such as *Black Hawk Down; A Bright and Shining Lie; Walking the Bible; The Soul of a New Machine; The Professor and the Madman; Greed and Glory on Wall Street; Indecent Exposure; Barbarians at the Gate; Den of Thieves;* and *A Civil Action,* to mention but a handful.

A Bottom-Line Business

While some in the publishing industry have long bewailed the de-mise of the "mid-list" novel, considered by many to be the "nice" quiet novel of manners and observations of the human condi-tion, today most major publishers are certainly more focused on "blockbusters"—those novels that can "breakout" and sell in large quantities. Publishing always was, and continues to be even more so these days, a bottom-line business. Numbers of books sold count, and the author who cannot move copies of his book will not last long in the major leagues of publishing. This reality may infuriate many and it's not one I defend, but it's nevertheless a commercial fact that one must face. Raging about how things "should be" does nothing to change how they are.

As the mid-list novel has been challenged by the Internet or the DVD or the GameBoy as a source of distracting popular entertainment, the success and appeal of narrative nonfiction books has infused publishing with fresh blood. The books pounce on an untold or barely told incident and pry it apart, search-ing for a way to understand through the microcosm of the story more about the macrocosm of our world—who we are and why we do the things we do, while at the same time giving us a rattling good yarn.

Narrative nonfiction has also given readers and publishers a much-needed respite from new regurgitations of the predictable "same-old, same-old" that book publishing accountants demand in order to satisfy the insatiable appetite of the tyrannical bottom-line approach to big time publishing. It allows experimental books of nonfiction to be marketed and sold in a predictable way, which keeps the bookstores happy, and yet allows some authors to indulge in experimental writing that would otherwise prove to be very hard to sell on a commercial scale.

Take, for example, Dave Eggers' *A Heartbreaking Work of Staggering Genius.* Eggers' book (not unlike the man himself) is defiantly unconventional. It is an angry, witty, coming of age memoir that is almost self-consciously inventive. As he describes the deaths of his parents and his attempts to care for his younger brother, Eggers deliberately comments on his inability to do justice to the story he is telling, in a disarming (some would say disingenuous) attempt to outpace any conceivable criticism. Eggers book is an example of why some experimental works, like Edmund Morris' *Dutch* or James Frey's *A Million Little Pieces,* remain in print despite their suspected lack of worth and obvious problems. The authors were at least trying to do something new and different in a form that encourages, or at least tolerates, more idiosyncrasy than do many other forms.

At a Harvard panel discussion about narrative nonfiction in May 2000, during a culturally complacent period from which we were rudely jerked by the events of 9/11/2001, Walter Kirn, contributing writer to *Time* and literary editor of *GQ,* said this about narrative nonfiction and its impact on popular culture: "We don't live in a very experimental time, literature-wise in fiction.... The 1960s and 1970s were times of invention of meta-narrative. We had Goddard films that took everything, cut it up into a million pieces, and threw it up in the air. [Now] we live in a very conventional time, aesthetically, when it comes to storytelling. I've noticed this in novels, and I think it's probably true in nonfiction. . . .

"I think we live in a fairly politically and culturally complacent and quiescent time. I don't think those edges or borders are being pushed yet.... A lot of this is a feature of not having great stories to tell. There is not a Vietnam War going on. You have to seek far and wide to find some of these stories now."

The events of 9/11 dramatically changed this, of course, creating a new cultural landscape where we have been forced to confront such profound issues as individual freedoms and rights to privacy versus the government's need to protect its citizens, as well the free press' mandate to make those in power account for their actions versus what some might call an unhealthy recent attempt by government to keep everything it does secret and hidden from the public it is sworn to protect.

Many creative writing programs around the country have moved away from teaching the art of the short story, and instead they now often focus on a type of self-awareness writing (some critics might call it "self-involvement"). Memoir and the concept of the reporter as a participator in a story, not a removed, objective observer, is becoming the norm. The courses try to teach the art of reconstructing pithy dialogue, writing in the first person, using the present tense, setting a scene and so forth. It has become an academic institutionalization of what Gay Talese termed New Journalism, whose guiding principle is, "to seek a larger truth than is possible through the mere compilation of the facts."

Some trace the beginnings of this New Journalism to Norman Mailer's 1960 *Esquire* piece about Jack Kennedy's nomination, and to Murray Kempton's columns for the *New York Post* in the 1950s. Some argue it can be traced as far back as Nathaniel Hawthorne's 1862 dispatches for the *Atlantic Monthly* magazine from the front lines of the Civil War, making his work the progenitor of that of George Orwell, Ernie Pyle, John Steinbeck and others.

Contemporary book-length narrative nonfiction is usually considered to date from Truman Capote's remarkable 1966 book *In Cold Blood,* considered by many the "grandfather" of present-day narrative nonfiction, though it was oxymoronically described at the time of its publication as a "nonfiction novel." (A novel by definition is a fiction, that is, an invention, while nonfiction by definition is its opposite—*not* fiction but truth.) Capote's book became the inspiration for literary true crime, as a successful sub-genre of narrative nonfiction, although it eventually led to the excesses of Joe McGuinniss' 1993 book *The Last Brother,* a fictionalized biography of the still-living Ted Kennedy that invented his thoughts rather than quoting him directly, and of Edmund Morris' *Dutch* (1999), the authorized biography of President Ronald Reagan, which bemused everyone with its fictional narrator and imaginary characters. But McGuinniss and Morris are certainly not alone. Meyer Levin wrote *Compulsion,* a novelistic account of the Leopold-Loeb murders, and before him Theodore Dreiser based *Sister Carrie* on a real case that tried to illustrate the difficulties of women struggling in newly industrialized America.

The point of this book is to discuss some ideas about how best to carefully meld journalistic research with fictional techniques. *The Elements of Narrative Nonfiction* has grown out of my early experiences as a journalist and then a publishing house editor, and my later experiences working with authors and editors as an agent who for over 20 years has specialized in representing journalists and books of narrative nonfiction.

The writer of a piece of narrative nonfiction has to be an investigative journalist, adept researcher, interviewer, and skilled novelist. That's a tall order to ask of someone who has not done one or more of these things professionally.

One of the dangers of writing guides like this is that they can become opinionated and filled with rigid rules. I am not in favor of writing as a form of mass-produced, homogenized factory literature, but in order to discuss issues of technique and analysis it's important to have a structure and a language of technique to refer to, if only to eventually reject it in favor of something that works better for you. Following the "rules" in this book won't help you write a best seller. However, if you are an "Infant Innocent," this is as good a place as any to start, and hopefully it is better than most. This book is intended as a tool kit, and a map and compass to help you find your way around a deceptively tricky genre of writing, one that is, as Paul Dickson, an award-winning journalist and author of *Sputnik: The Shock of the Century,* once described as "possibly the most fun you can have with your clothes on."

Narrative Nonfiction: The New Genre

I got this idea of doing a really serious big work—it would be precisely like a novel, with a single difference: Every word of it would be true from beginning to end.
—Truman Capote, on *In Cold Blood*, (quoted in the *Saturday Review*, Jan. 22, 1966)

Just before I started writing this book, I found myself traveling for a month with my wife. Now, I hate to shop. My wife loves the hunt of it (she's from the South and came out of the womb with a baking spatula in one hand and a credit card in the other). Anyway, during our travels, while my wife went trolling for bargains, I found myself haunting bookstores, as was my usual habit when on my own in a strange place. Some were independents, and some were part of chainstores (and, by the way, both types can be great places to have a cup of tea and rest up with a book while awaiting the return of the southern huntress, triumphant with her spoils).

While I waited, I decided on a whim to search for books that could be classified as "narrative nonfiction." It was an instructive experience: As a separate and unique genre, narrative nonfiction doesn't really have a bookshelf place in most book stores in the United States, Canada, and England. Yet we all seem to know what we mean by it: "factual writing that reads like a good novel."

A Gathering of Genres

Narrative nonfiction is really an umbrella term for a collection of genres that are found in every bookstore. Narrative nonfiction can be broadly divided into sub-genres, but what gathers them together is more a style of writing than a type of writing and each can be considered "a novel of true events." Adventure, biography, history, military, memoir, travel, and true crime, to mention but a handful of genres, can shade into each other (for instance, travel and adventure can interrelate, as in *Riding the Iron Rooster: By Train Through China* by Paul Theroux, or history, biography, and military can combine, as in *Band of Brothers* by Stephen Ambrose or *John Adams* by David McCullough).

Regardless of a precise genre definition, all good narrative nonfiction books share the commonality of being well written, literate stories, with characters, scenes, and a narrative arc, as well as being digests of connected facts.

Richard Preston's bestselling *The Hot Zone*, for example, might seem at first blush to clearly be a book about popular science, but it shades into adventure because of the dramatic, novelistic style that Preston uses to tell his story. At its heart, *The Hot Zone* is the inside take on the little-known story of what happened when one of the world's most virulent viruses, the ebola virus, broke out in a laboratory near Washington D.C., and how it was contained. The story is told through the limited viewpoints of a couple of characters, including the author himself, and it becomes emotionally compelling because we come to care about these people, worried that our principal characters will fail in their stated ambitions, and exuberant when they win through against catastrophic odds.

During a panel discussion at Harvard about narrative nonfiction, Robert Vare, senior editor at *The Atlantic Monthly*, made the following insightful comments about narrative nonfiction:

> "I think [narrative nonfiction]... is essentially a hybrid form, a marriage of the art of storytelling and the art of journalism—an attempt to make drama out of the

observable world of real people, real places, and real events. It's a sophisticated form of nonfiction writing, possibly the highest form that harnesses the power of facts to the techniques of fiction, constructing a central narrative, setting scenes, depicting multidimensional characters and, most important, telling the story in a compelling voice that the reader will want to hear.

"Nabokov...had the most illuminating remarks about narrative. He wrote, 'The term narrative is often confused with the term plot, but they're not the same thing. If I tell you that the king died, and then the queen died, that's not narrative; that's plot. But, if I tell you that the king died, and then the queen died of a broken heart, that's narrative.'

"...narrative nonfiction bridges those connections between events that have taken place, and imbues them with meaning and emotion."

Random House executive editor Peter Gethers told me that for him, "[Narrative] nonfiction is not a genre, it's a style. It simply means that nonfiction is told in a compelling way with an emphasis on story." Farrar Straus & Giroux publisher and editor-in-chief Jonathan Galassi agreed: "Readers buy books for many reasons, but I don't think the author's [predetermined stylistic] approach to his or her material is primary among them, though it may have a powerful effect on a reader's enjoyment of the book."

Little did Walker & Company publisher George Gibson know what he was starting one day in 1994 when he called up a magazine writer named Dava Sobel to talk about turning one of her magazine articles into a book. The subsequent book *Longitude* was to become more than merely the history of the invention of the chronometer; it was also to become the intriguing story of the man who invented it. The book was published in 1995 and Gibson hand sold the book to bookstore buyers at every opportunity he found. Slowly but steadily, it took off in the United States, eventually spending 18 weeks on the New York Times bestseller list. Even then, when Gibson tried licensing the rights to the book in the United Kingdom, it was turned down by over a dozen publishers before Fourth Estate added the title to its list. It then hit the bestseller lists in England as well. The unexpected, though hard-fought success of Longitude was, in its own way, as important a milestone in the promotion of narrative nonfiction as a "hot" genre as was Capote's *In Cold Blood.*

The British edition of *Longitude: The True Story of a Lone Genius Who Solved the Greatest Scientific Problem of His Time* was released in August 1966. On both sides of the Atlantic, the book's success started a "gold rush" among publishers looking for similar books, a gold rush which has yet to abate. We have seen the rediscovery of books such as Ernest Shackleton's 1914 classic *South*, a tale of remarkable survival and endurance at the South Pole, and esoteric stories such as *Fermat's Last Theorem*, with at least two other major books on the subject at about the same time, one by Simon Singh, the other by Amir D. Aczel, which tell the story of the struggle to solve a seventeenth-century mathematical puzzle. Another recent narrative nonfiction success was Janet Gleeson's *The Arcanum*, about the invention of porcelain.

Derek John, a director of A.P. Watt, the British literary agency, was quoted as saying that the demand for such "compact, exquisitely written books is partly due to people having shorter attention spans in an overloaded culture."

Random House executive Peter Gethers doesn't agree: "I don't think writers like Junger and Krakauer have challenged conventional notions. They feed into a centuries-long tradition of nonfiction storytelling. I actually think a book like *The Perfect Storm*—which I loved—is quite an old-fashioned book, in the absolute best sense. For what it's worth, I was recently having a conversation with someone, bemoaning the state of the world. We tried to come up with things that are better now than they were 50 years ago. We came up with only three things: food, baseball stadiums, and nonfiction books. I think there's a thirst for books like Krakauer's and Junger's because there's a thirst for anything that's actually good these days. We thirst for good politicians, good movies, you name it. It's just that narrative nonfiction actually seems to deliver the goods lately."

Editors at publishing houses, however, were not about to use the oxymoronic term "nonfiction novel" which some marketing maven, clearly trying to finesse the un-finessable, had coined to define Truman Capote's 1996 true-crime story *In Cold Blood*. Instead, publishers quickly began to use the term "narrative nonfiction"—fact-based books that read like fiction.

All narrative nonfiction affords the reader a story, engaging characters, the promise of adventure and controversy, the revealing of secrets, and the opportunity to peer backstage and behind the curtain. Recall the ill-fated boat ride (*A Perfect Storm*), the illicit taboo of an adult love affair with a missing father (*The Kiss*), or the going into battle during a modern war (*Black Hawk Down*) as examples of the vicarious experience of true-life events. However, every time a journalist turns a real person into a "character" and puts thoughts into his mind, every time a reporter recreates dialogue for scenes that weren't recorded and at which the writer was not present, no matter how scrupulously those thoughts and dialogue are based on extensive interviews, the writer enters a gray zone between fact and fancy. Just how "true" are these stories? How much can I trust what I read? Does it really matter?

These questions are the heart of this book.

Why Stories?

We use "stories" as a way of making sense of the world around us. We grow up with them, and we crave them like a fix. They are reassuring and comforting in some strange way, perhaps because of their structure and order and their predictability. As children we often want to be read the same story again and again in an almost hypnotic fascination. But as we approach puberty it slowly dawns on us that like Santa Claus and the Easter Bunny, many stories are inventions. Despite this apparent "betrayal," despite "real life" slowly impinging on our shrinking world of fantastic possibilities, we still want to believe in stories. That's why the con artist is so successful. He doesn't really sell us a bill of goods—he discovers what it is we want, and then he helps us sell ourselves by telling us a story we want to hear. We want to believe his story, and we help him shape it to our needs. The best litigators are not those who discover and assemble the "truth" for juries—the best litigators are those advocates who manage to spin the most convincing story from the same facts his or her opponent is using to tell a different story.

When the novel originated in the eighteenth century, the novelist often presented himself not as an author of untruth but as an editor of a true history, rather a scoundrel, in effect, passing himself off as something other than he is. Daniel Defoe's *Robinson Crusoe* (1719), for example, considered by many to be the first novel, tries to present itself as nonfiction by being written in the form of a journal by a supposed real-life character. The author played sort of a game with his audience, who at the time knew no difference between a journalist and a satirist. Defoe was a well-established journalist, and his novel is remarkable for its journalistic attempt to present the story and its details as true. (The novel was partly based on the memoirs of Alexander Selkirk, who was marooned on Mas a Tierra in the Juan Fernandez Islands off the coast of Chile as a punishment for insubordination. Selkirk spent four years and four months on the island; Crusoe spends 28 years as a castaway.)

Almost 300 years later, it could be argued that the novel has become a creature of artifice with fabulist qualities, for the most part locked into a genre mentality in order to be marketable to modern audiences. So-called non-genre fiction (and, it can be argued that "literary fiction" is as much a genre as "mystery" or "romance"), such as Alice Sebold's highly, and rightfully, acclaimed *The Lovely Bones*, has become the antithesis of Crusoe. It is written as magic realism, or allegory—forms that shout from the rooftops, "I am a lie." A novelist is a prince of liars, but because he is forced to admit he lies, he somehow manages to reveal truths that narrative nonfiction (and journalism) can not always reveal, being devoid of the novelist's "mask."

Jack Hart, former managing editor of *The Oregonian* newspaper, said: "I think [high-brow] literary fiction has fallen prey to [intellectual] campus navel-gazing and has lost touch with ordinary humanity. And it has the [lack of] audience to prove it."

Farrar, Straus, and Giroux publishing executive Jonathan Galassi counts both Thomas Friedman (*The World is Flat*) and Jonathan Franzen (*The Corrections*) among his authors. He says, "I think a lot of fiction today tends toward autobiography (a very problematic development and in many ways a sign of weakness of imagination). Narrative nonfiction uses fictional strategies and tools to forward the development of an idea. I'd say the convergence between fiction and nonfiction is quite notable.... Recent successes in fiction, most notably Franzen's *The Corrections*, indicate a swerve away from post-modernism ... in some ways a return to the heroics of nineteenth-century realist fiction, particularly in the Russian vein, where the narrator's sensibility is not the sieve through which reality is strained." Ironically, but pertinently, the novel and the work of narrative nonfiction appear to be converging, gradually, but inexorably.

Narrative nonfiction books have themes that tend to the historical, but certainly not completely. The reader learns something by tracing the "story" of an arcane object, event, or phenomenon, rather than just absorbing the life events of an historic figure or the episodes of an important political development. In Hart's view, nonfiction has a ready advantage over much introspective mid-list fiction published today. "I like Tom Wolfe's explanation," he says. "Narrative nonfiction 'enjoys an advantage so obvious, so built-in, one almost forgets what a power it has: the simple fact that the reader knows all this actually happened.'"

Is Reality Really Real?

Once upon a time, in the early 1960s, the art house movie documentary *Mondo Cane* was shocking—a "behind the scenes" look at the "real" brutal face of the world that the networks considered "unfit" to broadcast. Turn on the TV nowadays and *Mondo Cane* has been replaced by its sociological "grandchildren"— the antics of desperate human lab rats, their lives and failings willingly dissected before millions by Dr. Phil, Oprah, Jerry Springer, or the invasive camera lenses of *The People's Court*, MTV's *The Real World*, *Big Brother*, *Survivor*, *Fear Factor*, and myriad other shows, each one progressively nastier than the last in an attempt to be more "real" than its predecessor. How long before we reach the world of Stephen King's novel *The Running Man* where televised audiences watch a condemned man flee for his life while executioners chase him? And, our contemporary reading tastes are marching right alongside our viewing tastes.

Instead of enjoying novels about the trials and tribulations of the rich and powerful as we did in the 1960s, 70s and 80s, in the novels of Jackie Collins, Harold Robbins, or Sidney Sheldon, the best-selling memoir of recent years for St. Martin's Press has been Emma McLaughlin and Nicola Kraus' *The Nanny Diaries* which combines a "real life" memoir with a salacious exposé of the weakness and foibles of the self-involved monied classes that novelists previously reveled in writing about. *The Nanny Diaries* is to the twenty-first century what *The Great Gatsby* was to the early twentieth century, but lacking Fitzgerald's insight or skill as a writer. *The Nanny Diaries* relate material that is more effective and delicious for contemporary audiences because we believe it is not just drawn from real life, but it is real life (though if you care to make the search, there are signs and clues that, of course, like all such material the episodes have been "improved upon" in order for the book to "read better"). The appeal of *The Nanny Diaries*, as an example of a contemporary expose, is that we less-privileged masses can momentarily feel superior to those who often act as though they are superior to us.

Craving Stories

The danger with this obsession with "reality" is that we may be creating a society that novelist Doris Lessing describes as having "a reluctance of imagination." If not reluctance, then it is at least a kind of cultural "fatigue of imagination." We grow tired of the familiarity and predictability of the fiction we are offered, when we can just as easily enjoy the "crack cocaine" high of watching the consequence-less violence of revenge stories in many of our films, video games, and TV shows. No thinking is encouraged or allowed in many cases. *The Wild Bunch,* once shocking, is commonplace compared to *The Hills Have Eyes,* or *Saw I* (through whatever the latest sequel number happens to be).

Our fictional reading tastes crave stories that involve us emotionally, not just stimulate our imaginations. These days we want to become intimately acquainted with what is possible and what is extraordinary by examining "true" examples of those who have dared and overcome and pushed the envelope of human experience. In effect, we're tired of the theory fiction suggests, and we want to watch the reality of life in action instead. The truth is, in today's marketplace it seems commercially more viable to write a memoir of growing up as the third generation of men in one family convicted of murder than to write a novel on the same subject.

George Gibson, publisher of Walker & Company, is not convinced, however. "I disagree with Lessing," he says. "I...don't agree that a lurid memoir is more commercial than a novel."

Jack Hart feels that, "[frankly,] I'd rather read the true experiences of a third-generation criminal than a novel on the same subject."

I know how he feels because I feel similarly, though I also recognize that this is in part a reflection of the fact that there are few novelists in print at the moment who could carry off such a story with more insight and elan than a talented and careful journalist. As much as I believe that *The Hot Zone* or *Black Hawk Down* are superb examples of involving narrative nonfiction, I don't believe either author could produce a nonfiction book about murder as involving as Albert Camus' *The Stranger,* though the appeal of Truman Capote's *In Cold Blood* is exactly that comparison.

But Capote's "nonfiction novel" [Ugh!] turned out to be more fiction that we first believed precisely because of the difficulty the nonfiction writer faces in retaining the integrity of keeping nonfiction "real" but making it read like a novel. Add Norman Mailer's Pulitzer prize-winning *The Executioner's Song* about the murders by and capital punishment of Gary Gilmore, and it's relatively easy to see what the limitations of narrative nonfiction are even in the hands of masters of the art of writing when compared to what the novelist can achieve using pure invention.

However, the brutal truth is that not only does the reading public clamor for such true-life material, it's "easier" for journalists to write "true stories" well and sell them than for novelists to write insightful fiction that sells well.

For the moment, the memoir seems to be playing itself out as a "hot" sub-genre of narrative nonfiction. How many more incidents of confessed, intimate faux pas lovingly crafted for public consumption can we stand? With some notable exceptions it is generally a literature of narcissistic self involvement revealing stories involving more and more tasteless taboo breaking and exhibitionism as each new book is encouraged to top the revelations of the one before. Blake Morrison, in his British collection of essays *Too True* (Granta, 1998), said, "Confessionalism is masturbation [but] ... with art ... it become[s] empathy."

Where the novelist has to construct a fictional world and then make strenuous efforts in her writing not to jerk us out of what John Gardner calls "the fictive dream," the author of narrative nonfiction is given more leeway by a reader "because it's true." If a thing happens and seems to be unbelievable or a fortuitous coincidence in a novel, the reader might well dash the book across the room in disgust at such clumsy writing never to return to the story (or the author) that somehow betrayed him; in nonfiction, a thing may be equally outlandish but we comfort ourselves with the thought that "after all, it's true." We read on, falsely secure in the arms of the narrator, trusting in his narrative re-creation, often excusing clumsy storytelling and poor writing when we shouldn't.

Making It Live

What's important in writing nonfiction is the content: the idea, the new paradigm, or the question-and-answer the work presents. Narrative nonfiction adds the dimension of story.

I gained a certain insight into writing narrative nonfiction while working as an editor for BBC Radio News. Radio is a wonderful medium for a writer because by and large everything spoken is scripted. In writing news for the "Beeb," it was important to state facts, but in a bold, colorful sentence or two that also created word pictures that would make the people and places involved in the story come alive for the listener. These days, writers of narrative nonfiction are wise to do at least this, to use some of the tools of fiction, such as narrative spines with beginnings, middles, and ends, characterizations, suspense, and even surprise. Through the use of these types of fictional devices, "truth" becomes refracted, like light through a prism, and takes on an "other" quality, although it is still "the truth."

Some of the most successful classical novelists, whether Defoe or Dickens, Tolstoy, Thackery, Austen or Eliot, have relied on "real" events and "real" people on which to build their fiction. So what is the real difference between a novel that features, say, the battle of Waterloo (Thackery or Tolstoy), and *The Killer Angels* by Michael Shaara, about the battle of Gettysburg? The answer used to be that the novel answers the question "why" and gives us the emotions of the people involved, putting us inside the minds of the key participants. However, Truman Capote's *In Cold Blood* daringly struck out in a new direction for nonfiction by usurping these fictional tasks, claiming them for what has come to be known as narrative nonfiction. Along with *Longitude*, which reinvigorated the genre, it is the most influential of modern narrative nonfiction works, at least on a technical level.

The Saga of *The Lovely Bones*

Some argue the novel has been forced to become either more extreme or imaginatively surreal (such as Alice Sebold's *The Lovely Bones*) in order to survive. Perhaps, as the mania for "reality" based entertainment continues to ratchet up the stakes, the truth about the need for stories that are true but read like fiction is that fiction has been so trivialized by the emphasis on genre expectations that the whole form has become devalued in some way.

As a result, American novelists who wish to hit bestsellerdom (and that's practically everyone) hesitate to try to write stories that deal with the more profound philosophical questions of life (such as: "Who are we? Why are we here? What is our purpose?" etc.) and readers increasingly shrug off fiction as superficial, as an unchallenging, almost comforting, invention. Art and commerce need to be in balance, yet commerce seems to be undermining art these days.

The outstanding success of *The Lovely Bones* might seem to contradict this idea, because it owes its success at least in part to an audience that suddenly both recognized that it had been starved of challenging and worthwhile fiction to read, and appreciated the sheer accomplishment of the author's heartfelt but not preachy ability to tackle profound issues. It was named a Book of the Month Club main selection. Barnes & Noble included the book in its Discover program, highlighting new writers, and Sessalee Hensley, the chain's fiction buyer, placed an initial order of more than 10,000 copies, instead of the 3,000 to 5,000 copies that was standard for that program.

Anna, a Book-of-the-Month Club judge, told a TV audience on NBC's *Today* show, "If you only read one book this summer, read *The Lovely Bones*."

There was also an unfortunate, although serendipitous, timing to its publication: An outstanding novel about a murdered child who narrates her story from heaven, it was published while several wrenching stories about missing children, finally found murdered, played in the national media for weeks. The fiction, in a way, became an insight into the nature of truths we can not fathom unless we have had the misfortune to experience them. Advertisements boasting of its success created more success, and, like a snowball headed downhill, it gathered its own momentum.

The Lovely Bones was also a case of bold publishing. The publisher, Little Brown, originally anticipated a modest 10,000 copy print run, but had enough insight to print and ship many times that number after the book drew attention, so that when readers asked for the book in the store it was available.

It's worth remembering, however, that Sebold's first book was a nonfiction account of her rape in 1999 called *Lucky*, which was published by Scribners. "Rape is one of the subjects people have a knee-jerk reaction to," Henry Dunow, Sebold's agent, is reported to have said. "A number of publishers expressed distinct misgivings." By late 2002, *The Lovely Bones* had been number one on the *New York Times* fiction list for several weeks, knocking Stephen King's *From a Buick 8* to number two, while *Lucky* was dragged back from the dead and became number two on the *Times* nonfiction paperback list.

What's the lure of the narrative nonfiction story? Gibson thinks it's because "people love good stories, especially those that educate them at the same time or take them to places they'd never otherwise go, which is what great fiction does." Gethers is more pragmatic: "There are still plenty of mid-list novels being published. But I do think that one of the reasons for the rise of narrative nonfiction is that television seems to have taken the place of a lot of novels. People watch *The Sopranos* to get their fiction fix."

Despite all this, commercial sensibility is vital in the final stages of polishing publishable material. One of the first questions an editor or agent asks of a manuscript is, "What genre is it?" Without knowing that, the editor does not know where to place the book on the house's marketing agenda or in the house's catalog and the bookstore owner does not know where best to shelve the book in the bookstore, and the sad truth is, few bookstores place books in two different places at the same time (say, putting *The Physics of Star Trek* by Lawrence Krauss in both the science section, and the science fiction section). In her book *Thinking Like Your Editor*, literary agent Susan Rabiner, the former editorial director of Basic Books, explains that in a meeting with book buyers for Barnes & Noble she discussed this very issue: "Over coffee I raised my complaint. Failure to stock *The Physics of Star Trek* in the Star Trek fiction section as well as the science section would cost thousands of sales for both of us. Couldn't they at least shelve the book in both places? To my amazement, the answer was no, they couldn't."

The reason? Bookstores like Barnes & Noble have buyers who buy books in certain fields. So the buyer for science titles might stock *The Physics of Star Trek* but he or she has no involvement with the science fiction buyer, who stocks the SF shelf where Star Trek books belong. Depending on the store and the buyers, the same book could appear in either section of the store, but rarely both at once.

Categorizing Books—a Marketing Conceit

On average, some 50,000 trade books a year are published in the United States. Some are hardcover (sometimes called cloth), although many more are paperback, both mass market (the small-sized books that fit in your pocket) and trade (the larger-sized ones that almost look like hardcovers). All of these must be categorized in some fashion.

The development of genres came about as a marketing necessity. Category and genre are marketing terms that mean, more or less, the same thing. Their purpose is basically to help the potential book buyer more easily find what he's looking for. Categories are also guidelines that let you know, generally, what you can expect to find in a certain book. The writer of narrative nonfiction, because it attempts to recreate a "real" set of circumstances, is allowed more experimental latitude in technique than the novelist these days, which appeals mightily to authors interested in writing popular experimental literature.

While genres are being constantly reinvented, it's important that a prospective author become familiar with both the classics of a genre as well as the latest published books in the genre to get a sense of what readers expect. A writer should be aware that a genre can be "hot," then quickly become overbought, and, as a result, become hard to sell into for a while. There are a number of websites and newsletters that can help you figure out if the kind of book you are writing is either "hot" or "cold" in the publishing world. Two of the most well known are *Publishers Weekly* (the online version as well as the magazine itself) and Michael Cader's *Publishers Marketplace,* which costs approximately $20 a month, though he produces a free weekly version that includes less detail. Then there are sites such as Media Bistro and any number of blogs by editors and agents that are worth consulting.

When your book comes out, you're not really competing with all the other books in the store. You're only competing with all the other books in your genre. So, without diverging too much from what's expected, you ought to be thinking about how you're going to make your book different from others like it. Discovering that difference comes from knowing your genre well enough that you can spot a "hole," or good idea.

Know your audience. One of the biggest differences between books and other media forms is that movies and TV don't discriminate by age and gender. In general, books are written with a specific audience in mind. Adventure and travel books, for example, which are often man-against-nature types of stories, are bought and read mainly by men. Only those books that become huge sellers typically transcend the limitations of appealing only to specific audiences.

Artistic Categories

All forms of art employ categories. In music, for example, you can write an opera, a tone poem, a symphony, a concerto, a folk song, or a pop song. A composer is guided by the form of a particular genre, be it the sonata form, the fugue form, or the AABA melodic structure common in popular music.

Musicians often mix genres, coming up with what is called a "cross genre." Gershwin and Bartok for example, borrowed heavily from other genres such as folk music, spirituals, and gospel music, while jazz greats Duke Ellington and George Russell worked in the opposite direction, borrowing from classical forms. Each composer also influenced the work of others.

Because narrative nonfiction is character driven, it has a structure that echoes fiction and can be divided into a number of sub-genres. Its narrative spine should either give us the "why" of a situation (as is the case in *Into Thin Air* or *Black Hawk Down*), or track the story of an idea (as is the case in *The Professor and the Madman*, the story of the creation of the Oxford English Dictionary and the codification of the English language, or *Longitude.*)

What follows are a series of thumbnail notes on the broad sub-genres of narrative nonfiction. Many edge into each other, but it's important when you submit a book that you choose a particular genre and only refer to that genre to describe it. (Remember Susan Rabiner's story about attempting to place a particular book in two different areas of a bookstore, which was mentioned earlier.)

Adventure

The true adventure story is an amalgam of travelogue, memoir, and old-fashioned man-against-nature or man-against-beast kind of story, popular in the late nineteenth and early twentieth century. As a growing part of the population is drawn to more and more extreme activities to pursue for pleasure, so we are also drawn to read more and more extreme and dramatic adventures about ordinary people in extraordinary places and circumstances who often risk life and limb, whether deliberately or not. *Into Thin Air* and *The Perfect Storm*, books that evoke the works of Jack London, Robert Louis Stevenson, and Joseph Conrad, are good examples of the adventure genre, as well as the earlier book *Kon Tiki*, Thor Heyerdahl's story of trans-Pacific anthropology and seamanship on a balsa wood raft.

Travel Books

This genre breaks down into narratives of adventures a protagonist has in getting from point A to point B, but it also includes elements of travel and destination guides. A travelogue will often include lyrical descriptions of faraway places and be aimed at an audience known as "Armchair Travelers."

These books often lift the curtain and peer under rocks, and non-narrative books often provide mundane but important information on hotels, restaurants, places to go, interesting sights to see, and so forth. Travel guides are non-specific-destination books that tell you how to travel in a particular way, such as by donkey across Tibet or by train across China, as in Paul Theroux's *Riding The Iron Rooster*, or just staying put and experiencing something new and "other," such as Peter Mayer's *A Year in Provence*. Again, *Kon Tiki* might fit here, or *Into Thin Air*, even though these books are also considered adventures.

Biography

Historian Doris Lessing says that "The past is not simply the past, but a prism through which the subject [of a biography] filters his own changing self-image."

The subject's life should have had a profound effect not only on the people who came into contact with him or her, but some shadow of it should also touch the reader of the biography as well.

Biography is a popular category if you can find a suitable subject, but to carry it off the writer must become an expert on that subject. The same kind of investigative, analytical attention to detail used in writing true crime is of foremost concern in writing exceptional biographies, such as A. Scott Berg's *Max Perkins: Editor of Genius*; *John Adams* by David McCullough; and *Spy: The Inside Story of How The FBI's Robert Hanssen Betrayed America* by David Wise.

Biographies take several forms. Many use the work and life of the biographical subject to delineate and define the subject's inner and external world. The three types of biography all try to reveal the essence of the subject: 1) Interpretive, where the events of a subject's life lead us to a better understanding of the inner person and how that person fit in with his world; 2) Objective, which gather facts and documents how the subject lived; and 3) Dramatic, which uses fictional techniques to recreate the subject and his or her times.

Dramatic biographies, such as *Eleanor of Aquitaine: A Life* by Alison Weir or her earlier *The Life of Elizabeth I*, use known facts about the subject and her time, facts which are interpreted by the biographer's imagination, in an effort to reveal the intimate qualities of the subject.

The controversial Ronald Reagan biography *Dutch* falls broadly into this category. Edmund Morris' biography of ex-President Reagan involved the author creating himself as a fictional character in order to tell the former President's story, and he attracted a lot of criticism for this approach.

In general, a biography has to have a theme, and its subject has to fit into the context of the times the subject lived in. More than that, the subject of a biography should also be a symbol of some sort for the spirit of his age. The book should bring out some thematic element of that culture. Broadly, a good biography is one that illuminates and shows the times as much as the person.

The dangers of biography are inaccuracy and hero worship. The biographer needs to cultivate an objective eye that fits his subject into the world, albeit with compassion. Most biographies treat their subjects as one of three things: an example, a victim, or a source of wisdom.

Biography depends on two things, public and personal papers and sources and living witnesses. Of course, in the case of the long-dead, you're stuck with only one of the two.

Biography is also a demanding form of writing, requiring that the author come to know the subject intimately, live with the subject for a long time, somehow make peace with the subject's flaws yet obtain necessary permissions from those relevant people who are living, and ensure any quotes are accurately related and sourced.

The biographer must have the skills of a storyteller to construct an insightful, compelling narrative, the skills of a diplomat to deal with the many witnesses who can shed light on the subject's life, the skills of a detective to dig out facts and research on the subject. The biographer must be devoted to his subject and yet objective enough to explore the dark nooks and crannies of the life in question, and the biographer must possess the literary and psychological brilliance to create a book that the subject could honestly admit was an accurate portrayal of who they are or were and what they are or were. Unless you are a skilled writer, and someone with a strong analytical background, biography is going to be a tough genre with which to break into publishing.

History

Biography and history, as well as current affairs, often edge into each other. To succeed, both the narrative work and the more scholarly element have to be written by a recognized scholar, or by someone with credentials of some sort, for example, a Ph.D. You can have other credentials, though. A parish priest could write a major work on religion and get it published; a teacher could write a book about the history of education; a journalist could do a book about almost anything if he got his sources lined up; a parent of a sick child could have research all there is to know abut his child's disease and then write about it. You need to have some edge, however small, beyond your interest in the topic, though. In general, those who are passionate about something also tend to have studied it a lot and are often experts by default.

The appeal of the historical story is the chance to meet real people as they really were. The historical writer also strives to maintain the customs, culture, and knowledge of the period. In a time of political correctness, it is sometimes difficult to maintain the integrity of portraying cruelty, ignorance, and hardship that clash heavily with contemporary values. Like the biography, the historical narrative has relevance because of what the past has to tell us about the present. Arthur Miller's play *The Crucible,* about the Salem witch trials, was written in the early 1950s, but it was also an allegory about the McCarthy House Un-American Activities Committee witch hunt for communists. Most historical stories tell us something about who we are now, or cast light on events that we thought we knew but discover we have been deceived about or have misinterpreted in some way.

Military

This genre is really a subset of both history and biography. Good examples of successful military books in recent years are *The Killer Angels* and more recently *Black Hawk Down* and *Jarhead*. Others include, *Band of Brothers: E Company, 506th Regiment, 101st Airborne from Normandy to Hitler's Eagle's Nest* by Stephen E. Ambrose; *Reason Why/the Story of the Fatal Charge of the Light Brigade* by Cecil Woodham-Smith; and *Trafalgar: The Nelson Touch* by David Howarth.

These genres blur as history becomes more subjective and historians use the techniques of fiction to facilitate a deeper understandings of the past and its influence on the present.

How does one define or distinguish history from fiction, from historical fiction, or from fictionalized history? How do the interpretations and biases (read: "politically corrected" attitudes) of the present "infect" our understanding of what was really going on in the past? These are all issues the historian, or military historian, must tackle.

Memoir

Memoir is a somewhat tainted genre these days, and it has blossomed from the pure recounting of a specific life to incorporate a personal account of almost anything. For example, the excellent *Into Thin Air* by Jon Krakauer is considered an adventure book, but is described by the author as "a personal account of the Mt. Everest disaster" of 1996. It is, in other words, a memoir. James Frey's *A Million Little Pieces* on the other hand, purports to be a memoir, not because of its facts—most of which just aren't true—but because it's true to its spirit of outrageousness, which is a far more dubious claim. "My mistake," Frey wrote in an explanatory note to the current edition on sale, ". . . is writing about the person I created in my mind to help me cope, and not the person who went through the experience." Oh please!

Discussing the phenomenal success of memoir as a sub-genre during the 1990s, Robert Winder, deputy editor of the British literary magazine *Granta* wrote, "Bookshops ... groan with [the] confessions [of] criminals and addicts, abuse victims and sports fans, war heroes and domestic saints (or sinners) [who] queue up to get their lives off their chests."

Memoir is a demanding genre to write well. A big fuss was made of Kathryn Harrison's book about incest, *The Kiss*, and also Frank McCourt's memoir of a childhood cursed with drink, violence, and poverty, *Angela's Ashes*, because they were so intimate and revealing of these terrible experiences. But they also "upped the ante" for the average writer of memoir because not only were the books well written, they had a "salacious" quality that has set the bar higher for writers of commercial memoirs.

Nowadays, commercially successful memoirs are about traumatic events in a writer's life that a writer of exquisite skill can transform into a universal experience we can all share. It is the nearest thing to poetry a writer of prose can do. Read Isabelle Allende's moving book, *Paula*, about the sickness and coma her daughter suffered.

Memoirs are about a child's sickness, a father's death, a loss of honor or career. We become engrossed with another's pain because the writer's sensibility allows him or her to extract from a dreadful personal experience powerful universal emotions that illuminate our own lives. Editors who buy memoirs do so because the writer has successfully transferred the experience to the page in a strong emotional way, and in so doing, like the alchemists of old, has transmuted the experience from base lead into gold.

When a memoir such as Peter Mayle's *A Year In Provence*, which is not about personal pain but about a growing and learning experience, succeeds, it often edges into another genre. In this case, adventure and travel.

True Crime

The model for true crime books—and the book that still defines the genre—is *In Cold Blood* by Truman Capote, the original "nonfiction novel." The book was the first to extensively use fictional techniques to tell a true story. Usually, the experts who write true crime successfully are, or have been, lawyers, cops, investigators, journalists, forensic specialists, and so forth.

In *Editors on Editing*, St. Martin's Press senior editor Charles Spicer explains there are two basic types of true crime book: the gut story, that is, one that affects us on a primal level, such as Anne Rule's *Small Sacrifices*, about a mother murdering her children; and the glamour story, set in the world of the rich and famous, such as William Wright's *The Von Bulow Affair*, about the murder trial of Claus Von Bulow, who was accused of killing his socialite wife, Sunny.

Beyond powerful and, of course, accurate characterization with identifiable villains, and, if possible, also heroes, the narrative nonfiction true crime book should present some sort of unraveling investigation. It is the writer's job to learn the art of the newspaper reporter, capturing not only the spirit of what was said and done, but doing it accurately without boring readers with unnecessary detail or speech in the process. It is a fine tightrope to walk.

True crime books allow us to peer into the fascinating minds of the demented, though we are also very much influenced by the production of a gripping story, by the peripheral characters, by the story's setting, and so on. True crime books are usually psycho-sexual in nature. One of the elements of narrative nonfiction that many writers do not consider carefully enough is that it takes the techniques and skills of a journalist and a novelist to write a compelling story. How the story is told is as important as what happened.

Dramatic License?

*We all know that Art is not truth. Art is a lie that makes
us realize truth, at least the truth that is given us to
understand. The artist must know the manner whereby
to convince others of the truthfulness of his lies.*
— Pablo Picasso

If you're going to write a piece of narrative nonfiction you need
to make clear to the potential publisher in your proposal, as well
as the reader in your book, what is "true" and what is embel-
lished. Randall Silvis' proposal for his book *Heart So Hungry*,
which we sold in auction to Knopf Canada, is a good example of
this, and it can be found in the appendix.

Over the last few years, as narrative nonfiction has become
increasingly popular as a storytelling vehicle, there have been
several high profile "scandals" involving books that were touted
as being "true" stories but which turned out to be complete fabrications designed to deceive the reader. And this is the ethical
line one shouldn't deliberately cross. Fictionalizing nonfiction is
fraught with all kinds of traps and obstacles, but deliberate deception clearly crosses a line that Lorenzo Carcaterra's *Sleepers*
(for example) frankly hugs. However, Carcaterra at least warns
you that the book is not exactly true, though it's up to the reader
to figure exactly how far Carcaterra went in treading the line
between truth and fiction.

Two well-known, out-and-out deceptions are James Frey's
A Million Little Pieces, his 2003 memoir of being a 23-year-old

alcoholic drug abuser in a Twelve Step-oriented rehab center, and Margaret B. Jones' (aka Margaret Seltzer) 2008 memoir *Love and Consequences,* which purports to describe her life as a foster child in gang-infested South-Central Los Angeles.

In both the aforementioned cases (and others I haven't mentioned), what's most interesting is that in our "gotcha" era of Internet and tabloid journalism, clearly talented writers brazenly tried to pass off pure fiction as nonfiction and thought they would get away with it; and, more importantly, it is interesting for those of us who care about books and publishing to know why these writers felt they had to go to such extreme lengths in the first place. It's only a book, after all, and it likely won't save anyone's life, and, furthermore, for all the hard effort that goes into the writing of a book, no one can ever guarantee a book's financial or critical success, and the innate dishonesty of passing off fiction as narrative nonfiction condemns whatever is worthwhile in its creation.

Also, the more successful a book becomes, the more scrutiny the book and its author are placed under, particularly when the story is supposedly about the author's life. Thus, the intentional use of fiction under the claim of its being "truth" suggests an utter ignorance about or disdain for the industry the author is a part of, while paradoxically it suggests a sense of insecurity or lack of self-worth in the sense that the author somehow doesn't believe anyone would pay that much attention to a given work or its writer because books just aren't that important these days. Rather incredibly, it could also suggest that an author is so conscious of his talent that he believed it should be reason enough to be given a pass "this time." Or, perhaps the publishing industry itself is somehow culpable for encouraging more and more accounts of extreme life stories without checking rigidly enough the veracity of these stories. Perhaps it's all of these things, and then again, perhaps it's just the arrogant stupidity of someone who doesn't give a damn, particularly for the gullible reader addicted to "reality TV" who is looking for a similar "authenticity" of the "real" in their literature.

In some ways, these books and others like them are the grandchildren of Clifford Irving's famous 1971 fake autobiography of Howard Hughes.

The Hughes autobiography is worth mentioning because it has many of the same characteristics as Jones' *Love and Consequences* in the depth and extent to which the writer went to convince people that what was said and done in the book was really true rather than fantasy.

To set the scene: By the 1960s, the millionaire filmmaker, engineer and inventor, and all around brilliant eccentric businessman Howard Hughes had become a hermit, living in self-imposed seclusion. He had not been seen or heard from publicly in years. It was commonly thought, and often discussed in the popular media, that Hughes was either deranged, dying, or dead—his persona kept alive by an impersonator so the executors could continue to gain access to Hughes' considerable fortune.

In 1970, Clifford Irving, a mildly successful American novelist living in Spain, got together with his friend and children's book author Richard Suskind and hatched a scheme to fake Hughes' "autobiography." The writers naively figured that hermit Hughes, who it was conjectured was both agoraphobic and mysophobic (afraid of open spaces and germs), would never emerge from his secret, luxury cave long enough to denounce the book. Suskind set about doing the research, and Irving forged letters from Hughes, imitating his handwriting.

Once all was in place, Irving contacted his publisher, McGraw-Hill, and showed the editors three forged letters purportedly from Hughes, one of which claimed that Hughes wished to have his "autobiography" written by Irving.

McGraw-Hill agreed to the deal, Irving forged Hughes's signature on the contract, and McGraw-Hill paid an advance of $765,000, a remarkable amount of money for the time. Irving then faked a series of interviews with Hughes in remote locations all over the world, although in reality Irving was instead meeting with various of his mistresses. Through networking contacts, Irving and Suskind got their hands on *Time-Life*'s private files about Hughes, as well as an unpublished ghostwritten manuscript by Noah Dietrich, Hughes' former business manager.

When Irving delivered the manuscript, he also included "notes" in Hughes's forged handwriting that several handwriting experts declared genuine. However, the moment McGraw-Hill announced the book's pub date in March 1972, a number of people who knew Hughes and/or worked for him came forward to say they thought the book was a fake. Irving replied that Hughes had simply not told them about the collaboration. Frank McCulloch, the last journalist to interview Hughes, said he had received an angry call from someone claiming to be Hughes, but when McCulloch read the Irving manuscript he declared it appeared to be accurate. TV journalist Mike Wallace did an interview with Irving and he too found Irving utterly convincing. Not so with Wallace's camera crew. According to Wikipedia, Wallace is quoted as saying that his camera crew told him Irving was a phony. "They understood. I didn't. He got me," Wallace said.

In early 1972, Hughes arranged a televised telephone conference with seven journalists who knew him, during which he denounced Irving and the book as frauds. Irving countered the voice recorded in the Hughes interview was probably a fake, and Hughes was not actually speaking. Nevertheless, Hughes' attorney Chester Davis sued McGraw-Hill, *Time-Life*, Clifford Irving, and several others on behalf of his client. Irving was soon hinting that perhaps he might have been dealing with an impostor. Then James Phelan read an excerpt of the book he had ghost written for Noah Dietrich and realized that Irving had taken information from his unpublished manuscript. Irving's scheme was starting to unravel.

Eventually, Irving confessed, and along with Suskind, he was indicted for fraud and quickly found guilty. Irving spent 17 months in prison; he returned the three-quarter million dollar advance to his publishers. Suskind served five months.

Once released, Irving continued his writing career, having a success in 1981 with his account of what happened in 1971, entitled *The Hoax*. The book was eventually turned into a movie in 2006, starring Richard Gere. Ironically, on his website Irving wrote about the film, saying, "After reading the final script I asked that my name be removed from the movie credits. I didn't want anyone to believe that I had contributed to such a histori-cally cockeyed story where the main character, almost by coinci-dence, happens to bear my name."

This entire episode strikes me as being a bit like the kid who kills his parents and then appeals to the court for mercy on the grounds that he's an orphan.

The bottom line is that even today, publishing is still at heart a cottage industry uncomfortably wearing the clothes of a corporate entity. We believe in the integrity of the writer; we believe that verbal contracts have meaning and are binding. We still aspire to the genteel aspirations of earlier book-making and book-loving generations despite the pressures of twenty-first-century global business practices. When someone says he's writing a nonfiction book about something extreme or extraor-dinary, we may make reasonable attempts to verify the story's veracity (because who wants to look like a doofus to one's peers and the general public if it's discovered you were tricked, besides the ethical considerations involved), but it's not really our job to give a writer the third-degree about his book. We expect the writer to provide some substantiation for his claims, but if this is done, why should we disbelieve the writer? What's more, given the modest size of the book-reading public, and given its general inclination towards intellectualism compared to the audiences for other forms of entertainment these days, it rather boggles the mind that anyone would feel the need to go to such lengths to perpetuate such a literary fraud in the first place.

Contrary to popular belief, we editors and agents don't spend our time finding reasons to reject material sent to us; in fact, we actively long to find well-written material that is inter-esting. And there's the rub: In the case of the examples above, and in a number of others I could cite besides, all the writers were talented. And, finding writers with genuine talent who are not already represented or with extant book contracts is not that common. So when one comes along with an intriguing or exotic story to tell, there is a natural tendency for the agent or editor to not exactly turn a blind eye, but to sometimes ignore that nagging little voice inside that raises questions about the narrative, questions that we might have paid more attention to if the writer wasn't so damnably good.

Why, for instance, didn't anyone with an ounce of awareness think to seriously question James Frey's claim that he had root canal surgery without anesthetic, when anyone who knows anything about drug addicts in particular knows that they have an infamously *low* tolerance for pain.

In *Love and Consequences*, a critically acclaimed memoir published by Riverhead books in 2008, Margaret B. Jones wrote about her life as a half-white, half-Native American girl growing up in South-Central Los Angeles as a foster child among gang-bangers running drugs for the Bloods. The problem was, none of it was true. In fact, Margaret B. Jones was the pen name or, more accurately, the alter ego of Margaret Seltzer, who is white and grew up in the well-to-do Sherman Oaks section of Los Angeles, in the San Fernando Valley, with her biological family. She has never lived with a foster family, nor did she ever run drugs for any gang members.

The warning bells, admittedly somewhat recognizable only after the fact, could be heard faintly in the reviews. Michiko Kakutani's review in the *New York Times* (one of the aggrieved parties in this sad story) stated, in part:

> Although some of the scenes she has recreated from her youth (which are told in colorful, streetwise argot) can feel self-consciously novelistic at times, Ms. Jones has done an amazing job of conjuring up her old neighborhood. She captures both the brutal realities of a place where children learn to sleep on the floor to avoid the random bullets that might come smashing through the windows and walls at night, and the succor offered by family and friends. She conveys the extraordinary stoicism of women like Big Mom, her foster mother,

who raised four grandchildren while working a day job and a night job. And she draws indelible portraits of these four kids who became her siblings: two young girls she would help raise, and two older boys, whom she emulated and followed into the Bloods.

Vanessa Juarez, in *Entertainment Weekly*, commented that "Readers of *Love and Consequences* may wonder if Jones embellishes the dialogue—much of which she remembers from childhood. But what shines through is a powerful story of resilience and unconditional love, in a country that can too easily forget the people it fails."

If only Seltzer had treated her book as a novel, or framed it as a piece of realistic meta-fiction not unlike *Sleepers*, Lorenzo Carcaterra's controversial 1995 memoir of growing up in Manhattan's Hell's Kitchen and as an inmate at a sadistic detention center, it would have garnered the legitimacy and respect it truly deserved.

In her original *Home* section interview with *New York Times* reporter Mimi Read, Seltzer explained, rather tellingly I think, "The reason I wanted to write the book is that all the time, people would say to me, you're not what I imagine someone from South L.A. would be like."

Ms. Read's article continued, "I guess people get their ideas from TV, which is so one-dimensional and gives you no back story." Long stretches of unrelieved violence shut a viewer's brain down, Ms. Seltzer added, "but one of the beautiful things about a book is you get to put in all the little things that touch people. If you can find a way to combine ordinary moments like being at a birthday party or making dinner with the kind of violent things that people can't even wrap their brains around, then people can relate."

Once Seltzer's sister "turned her in" by calling the *New York Times* and letting them know the facts of her sister's true identity, the *Times* ran a piece by reporter Motoko Rich that said, in part, "In a sometimes tearful, often contrite telephone interview from her home..., Ms. Seltzer, 33, who is known as Peggy, admitted that the personal story she told in the book was entirely fabricated. She insisted, though, that many of the details in the book were based on the experiences of close friends she had met over the years while working to reduce gang violence in Los Angeles."

The next day, the *Times* ran a Motoko Rich story about how everyone had been taken in – including, of course, the paper itself. Riverhead books recalled 19,000 copies of the book and offered everyone their money back.

Sarah McGrath, the editor at Riverhead who worked with Ms. Seltzer for three years on the book, told the *Times* she was "stunned" to discover that the author had lied. "There's a huge personal betrayal here as well as a professional one," she said.

It began in April 2005, when agent Faye Bender submitted about 100 pages to four publishers. Ms. McGrath was then an editor at Scribner, an imprint of Simon & Schuster, and she made an offer for what was reported to be "less than $100,000." When Ms. McGrath moved to Riverhead in 2006, Ms. Seltzer moved with her, an unusual occurrence in the publishing industry.

"I've been talking to her on the phone and getting e-mails from her for three years and her story never has changed," Ms. McGrath later told the *Times*. "All the details have been the same. There never have been any cracks."

Meanwhile, Ms. Seltzer's older sister, Cyndi Hoffman, 47, told a reporter: "It could have and should have been stopped before now." Referring to Riverhead, she added: "I don't know how they do business, but I would think that protocol would have them doing fact-checking."

But this is a little disingenuous and unfair. Geoffrey Kloske, publisher of Riverhead Books, said, "The fact is that the author went to extraordinary lengths: She provided people who acted as her foster siblings. There was a professor who vouched for her work, and a writer who had written about her that seemed to corroborate her story." He might have added that she also signed a contract with a warranties clause agreeing to tell the truth.

"The one thing we wish," Mr. Kloske said, "is that the author had told us the truth."

"There was no reason to doubt her, ever," said Faye Bender, her agent. And the editors at Riverhead and Seltzer's own agent were not alone. Reporters who interviewed Ms. Seltzer were also taken in by her story. Tom Ashbrook, the host of "On Point," a program aired on public radio, ran an interview with Ms. Seltzer (as Margaret B. Jones) in which she recounted her fake life. Mimi Read, the freelance reporter who wrote the profile of Ms. Seltzer that brought down the house of cards, made perhaps the most insightful comment: "The way I look at it is that it's just like when you get in a car and drive to the store—you assume that the other drivers on the road aren't psychopaths on a suicide mission. . . . She seemed to be who she said she was. Nothing in her home or conversation or happenstance led me to believe otherwise."

In his daily industry newsletter "Publishers Lunch," Michael Cader wrote, "Why is this story so much bigger than coverage of Misha Defonseca's decade-long fraud [about her holocaust "memoir"] (where her French publisher has announced they will continue to publish her book and just call it fiction)? Or stories in the past about Nasdijj, or Norma, Khouri? And when will the *NYT* [*New York Times*] and others report more substantially on the unresolved questions about elements of Ishmael Beah's book.... Lots of questions, most not answered by today's newspapers (many of which would like publishers to engage "fact checkers," even as the papers do not)."

The short answer to why everyone is so upset is not just that it was a consciously executed fraud, but that we wanted to believe someone could escape her chains as "Ms. Jones" seemed to have and then write about it so powerfully. We all feel so betrayed because Ms. Seltzer has somehow cheapened and diminished the achievements of those people, so far unwritten about, who have overcome against great odds, by pretending to be one of them rather than just standing up and writing about them with no pretense, as Upton Sinclair, John Dos Passos, John Steinbeck, and Barbara Ehrenreich have all done.

She is also, unfortunately and ironically, to some extent a victim of modern reverse racism. It's pretty clear that Ms Seltzer genuinely felt a passion about the lives of the people she created and felt they are under-represented honestly in contemporary literature. Her agent and publisher felt the same way. But many critics, in the black and Latino communities especially, roundly denounce anyone who is not a minority as inauthentic and patronizing if they write about the miserable, violent world of the ghetto. With "Ms Jones," those who know the ghetto but have managed to rise above it believed they had found someone who could finally voice their distress with eloquence, only to discover it was just a *fiction* masquerading as "reality." This speaks more eloquently to how most people currently view novels, than to the betrayal and dishonesty of the writer. Now, combine all this sociological and psychological turmoil with an author's passion to use his talent to say something about a topic that many partisan critics feel he should be disqualified from writing about, and toss in an opportunity to actually get one's message out, and the temptation becomes strong enough that most compassionate people should feel a little sympathy for the wrong choices Ms. Seltzer made in order to *do* something definitive with her life.

Of course, underscoring all this for the publishing company is the lure of money that flows from a successful book of narrative nonfiction, such as *Seabiscuit*, or my own client, Chip St. Clair's memoir *The Butterfly Garden* (whose proposal is also in the appendix), combined with a perceived general ennui by publishing folk, as well as the reading public, that the same story if told as outright fiction just won't sell as well. So the pressures on editor, agent, and writer are mounting to find "product" that will not only capture the attention of the Oprah crowd, but make money for the publishing company.

In the case of agents who earn their living through commissions on an author's successes, this money pays the bills; in the case of editors, it can earn profit for their corporate masters and establish an editor's value within the house and his or her reputation within the industry. For an author it is the Holy Grail of what they are trying to do, that is, make a living writing in a society where the writer is considered either a hack, an ivory tower elitist, or a disposable amateur, because, well, "we all write," so how hard can it really be to write, particularly about yourself?

What these stories reveal, I think, more than anything else, is an unfair and unconscious cultural cynicism about the relevance of books in our society and the role of fiction in particular. It's a kind of "loss of nerve" on the part of the nonfiction authors who commit these frauds and those responsible for getting them into print, a kind of fear that their work will only garner the kind of respect and reward that it should if it is done as nonfiction rather than as fiction. I'm as guilty as anyone else for pointing this out to potential authors who approach me with exotic stories based on their lives that they want to write as a novel.

But as the success of a novel like *The Lovely Bones* shows, while the cynics may be closer to the truth at times than we in the publishing industry comfortably want to admit, they aren't right.

Powerful writing published well, still wins out—even when it's fiction. So if you choose to tell your story as narrative nonfiction, make sure it is verifiable—or the Chinese curse of "Don't ask for what you want or you might get it"—will almost inevitably visit you.

So, the question for the writer considering tackling a book of narrative nonfiction is: how far can you—and should you—go in recreating a fictionalized version of your true story?

As much as you try to make your story real and "true," you must always be aware that your story and the events that constitute it have been deliberately chosen and linked by placing them in a linear or circular sequence, and they have been shaped and refracted through the lens of your intellect and prejudices. What began in *real life* as a series of random acts of mostly cause and effect has now led, in hindsight, to an emotionally gripping story with a beginning, middle, and end, something that does not naturally occur in real life for the most part.

To understand the "why" and "what" of things, we are forced to give them a coherence they usually lack in the anarchy of everyday reality, and thus we begin to create art through interpretation and insight. Truth is, even the traditional reporting of a news story is an artificial concoction. (Read two different journalists' accounts of the same event and you'll quickly see what I mean.) The question becomes, how artificial should one make it? Where is the boundary between insightful interpretation and fraudulently misleading the reader?

New Journalism and Real Life

In his 1973 book *New Journalism*, Tom Wolfe wrote that the goal of "new journalism" (what we now called narrative nonfiction) was to intellectually and emotionally *involve* the reader—to show the reader *real life*. In other words, to find a way to help the reader understand the "why" and "what" of subjects that seemed to lack any. I think it no accident that "new journalism" sprang up during the turbulent 1960s and 1970s.

Gonzo reporters looked for a way to explain to mainstream America the growing revolutionary subcultures of the 1960s and beyond. They wrote about the hippie drug scene and the importance and meaning of radical political movements such as the anti-Vietnam movement, the women's movement, the burgeoning environmental movement, and the Black Panthers. To do this effectively, they looked for a writing technique that would somehow convey the "truth" of these subjects in a way that conventional reporting did not. The experimental search for the technique that would best capture in print the spirit of their subject and that subject's intent led these reporters, consciously or otherwise, to rediscover the work of an earlier generation of writers, particularly Jack London, Stephen Crane, John Dos Passos, Upton Sinclair, Edith Wharton, George Orwell, and even Charles Dickens, all of whom used their skills as novelists (mostly, but not entirely, in the form of novels) to report true stories of journalistic merit, usually involving social injustice and inequality.

Thus, the "new journalists" of the 1960s experimented with recreated dialogue, points of view, and even interior monologue, all in an attempt to "get into" a subject's head, and give us the "why" of a person or situation in the news that to many middle American readers was bewildering and was, in some cases, viewed as being threatening to the mainstream way of American life.

The Inverted Pyramid

The traditional newspaper story structure is the "inverted pyramid." That is, you state the essence of the story at the top, and then expound on it as you progress, thus allowing an editor to cut from the bottom of the story without losing anything vital if the story has to be shortened. The "revolution" of narrative news reporting has led to what is generally considered a more engaging read. Unlike the inverted pyramid structure, which really just conveys information objectively, although employing hooks and élan at its best, the narrative story form gives readers a reward—an emotional denouement—for making it through a story. It's familiar and comforting. Culturally, we use the narrative form to understand, to remember, and to find meaning in our everyday lives.

The problem with using fictional techniques to make a story of facts "sexy," however, is that it can seductively lead an inexperienced or lazy writer into believing it's okay to either embellish or shoehorn the "facts" into a convenient storyline that may grossly distort not only what really happened, but also undercut the spirit of the event—the very reason for using the technique in the first place. Turning "real life" into a narrative carries with it the inherent temptation to sacrifice "truth" for the sake of "effect"—usually sentimentalized drama.

In 1981, for example, *Washington Post* reporter Janet Cooke was fired and had her Pulitzer Prize for feature writing repudiated after it was revealed that the eight-year-old drug addict depicted in her column was not a real person, but a composite. Mike Barnicle and Patricia Smith both resigned from the *Boston*

Globe after admitting they had "fictionalized" their columns, as also did *New Republic* associate editor Stephen Glass. All fell afoul of the seductive sirens of narrative nonfiction that lure unsuspecting or ambitious reporters onto the rocks of professional ruin. All made the mistake of believing it's more important and "sexy" to use sentiment and metaphor in their stories than to research and use verifiable facts.

In general, the narrative nonfiction story is usually told from the perspectives of one or more characters. We get to know the innermost thoughts of these characters, but we're not always told how these thoughts were determined or selected by the author, and this can be a problem.

The Wrong Subject

"Sad things can happen when an author chooses the wrong subject: First the author suffers, then the reader, and finally the publisher, all together in a tiny whirlpool of pain," observed the novelist and critic Wilfrid Sheed. This is especially true when, like a lover questioning the faithfulness of a spouse, the reader begins to doubt that an author is treating them honestly, even if the writer appears to be putting all his cards on the table.

Take Joe McGinniss' *The Last Brother*, a "biography" of Senator Ted Kennedy (brother of John and Robert, both of whom were assassinated in office), in which he speculates on what Ted Kennedy thought or felt about his career, but admits his attempts to interview Kennedy were rebuffed. In a note at the end of the book, McGinniss' response to criticism about this wholesale "supposition" (let us not call it an "invention," please) was that the book was an author's highly personal and interpretive view of his subject. At times, McGinniss said, "a writer must attempt an approach that transcends that of traditional journalism or even, perhaps, of conventional biography."

An interesting example of this was Edmund Morris' biography of President Ronald Reagan, *Dutch: A Memoir*. Edmund Morris had been designated as Reagan's official biographer. After years of trying to figure out how to write the book, he resorted to creating a fictionalized version of himself in Reagan's past. The result was a highly questionable "memoir" rather than a biography, narrated by an "Edmund Morris" several decades older than the real author, who purported to have known "Dutch" Reagan since the 1920s, and who, among other things, had a son who joined the Weather Underground in the 1960s. The problem was, that in a supposedly nonfiction biography where one assumes the facts, above all else are true, none of these "facts" were true. Alas, the fictive Edmund Morris bore little resemblance to the "real" Edmund Morris, the writer.

This overt mixing of fact and fiction caused a great deal of discussion amongst critics and readers, most of it unfavorable, and did not do a great deal for Morris' reputation as a writer. In the end, the fictional parts were not that convincing and interfered with the nonfiction parts, forcing the reader to keep track of what was true and what wasn't. Why Morris, clearly frustrated by his subject, didn't simply write a conventional biography is a mystery, and although the book he actually wrote may be explained as a type of biographical experiment, it failed on nearly all counts as a result. For a man who in the past had been praised as a graceful and scholarly writer, it was a particularly disappointing experiment that in hindsight seemed to have been doomed to failure from the first.

McGinniss' 1993 "biography" of Massachusetts Senator Edward Kennedy, *The Last Brother*, makes up for its lack of verifiable fact through the application of shear, unadulterated hubris. In some ways, it can be considered "the missing link" between the traditional biography and Morris' *Dutch*.

McGinniss had made a name for himself with several outstanding books earlier in his career, including *Fatal Vision*. However, in a note at the end of *The Last Brother*, he boldly acknowledges using articles and books as a "verifiable source" from which he "distilled an essence." He says quotations in the book "represent in substance what I believe to have been spoken."

Commenting in general on the problems of fictionalizing fact into a story, Farrar Straus & Giroux publisher and editor-in-chief Jonathan Gallassi advised that a "writer (of any-thing) always has to be aware of how his/her method of narration is affecting the treatment of the subject."

Observing Distorts Reality?

Perhaps the increasing popularity of nonfiction narratives is a re-flection of our taste for more "reality-based" entertainment. This new form of entertainment is not "real" of course. Although we can't see them, there's a camera crew present affecting the behavior of the people we're watching. It's almost a visible example of Werner Heisenberg's theory that watching a scientific experiment somehow effects the thing observed, distorting the result.

In *Dutch,* Edmund Morris invented pages of fictitious dialogue and, indeed, even fictitious characters, but at least he admitted up front he was doing so.

Bob Woodward's book about the Clinton administration, *The Agenda*, while listing sources, is still problematic, I believe. While we're told in the book that the sources of reconstructed dialogue and quotes come from a participant in the reported events, from memos, or from notes or diaries of the participant, we're never told who the participant is. We are forced to take on trust that everything is kosher, as it probably is, the experiences of Cooke, Glass, Smith, Barnicle, Joe McGinniss and Edmund Morris notwithstanding.

On the other hand, in *Black Hawk Down,* Mark Bowden went to great lengths to detail the sources for his book, and it shows in the writing. Charlie Spicer, a senior editor at St. Martin's Press, once told my friend Gary Provost, "I worry sometimes where the line is, but frequently I leave it to the lawyers. You can invent a little bit with physical description, but you have to be careful to document everything factual because our lawyers query everything. They want the documentation."

True crime writer Jack Olson, whose books, in my opinion, are models for how to write the genre, was deeply critical of anyone who cheated an audience through deliberate "invention." (We shared several e-mail discussions about the rights and wrongs of Lorenzo Carcaterra's *Sleepers* when the book was first published.) In another interview, Olson told Gary Provost, "My books take two years to write because I don't invent any details. But I'm not saying it's wrong. If a woman always sits on the floor or the ground with her legs crossed, then I don't think a writer is going very far afield to write something like that in a scene.... In your research you develop certain characteristics and physical attributes of people and I suppose you would be justified in slipping one in now and then without knowing for sure that it happened. I probably should do it. I'm not a fanatic. You can't be a fanatic about every single letter of every single word."

Upping the Ethical Ante

In a *New York Times* Sunday book review of Bob Woodward's *Bush At War*, Thomas Powers commented, "What's remarkable about Woodward's book is the same thing that was remarkable about many of his others—extraordinary access to secret documents, like contemporaneous notes of National Security Council meetings, and to high officials, including President Bush...."

At one point in the narrative Woodward directly quotes national security advisor Condoleeza Rice reproaching Secretary of Defense Donald Rumsfeld in an off-the-record exchange. Powers writes,

> The earlier quotations [in the meeting] might have come from N.S.C. minutes, but what about Rice's chiding of Rumsfeld for being sulky? It would be nice to know who told Woodward that, but more important is the question whether it is true.
>
> Woodward has been writing books in roughly this way for twenty years, and during that time he has rarely been attacked by his subjects for getting things wrong.... The lack of protest [including from Rumsfeld and Rice, on this occasion] inclines me to trust his account as solid until something else comes along that says different with footnotes.

This is a tough path for Bob Woodward to tread to avoid criticism, though, and it's extremely treacherous for a "young" (meaning, inexperienced) journalist without Woodward's reputation and track record. Just ask Janet Cooke or Mike Barnicle.

When asked about the bad-boy reputation narrative writing has earned with some reporters and editors, Don Fry, an independent writing coach, made the following comments: "Bob Woodward is the problem. He doesn't bother to cite sources and he reads minds.... One of the problems with Woodward is he doesn't tell you where he got it. All the information just floats by."

Readers should be more trusting of his work, Woodward told journalist Chris Harvey in 1994: "My books are scrupulously reported," he said. For *The Agenda*, for example, he interviewed more than 250 people. "All that's missing is who said it, whose diary it's in, what memo it's in."

Jack Hart, former managing editor of *The Oregonian* newspaper, has commented that "Choosing to tell a story in narrative form ups the ethical ante. Plucking a coherent story line from an almost infinite number of possible details is highly subjective. It inevitably reflects the writer's basic beliefs about how the world operates. Narrative writers and editors therefore have extra ethical obligations. As one of our editors put it: 'Your ethical antenna needs to go up a couple of feet higher if you choose narrative.'" In an interview with me in late 2002, Hart added, "The big ethical issue these days revolves around attribution. I'm still struggling with ways to attribute in a nonfiction narrative in a way that doesn't interrupt story flow. And if...recent discussion on WriterL [an Internet forum] is any indication, so are a lot of my colleagues."

How to fictionalize a true story with no firsthand sources and still keep it honest was interestingly tackled in *A Perfect Storm*. Sebastian Junger was faced with dealing with the demise of the crew of a commercial sword fishing boat, the *Andrea Gail*, while not having any possible firsthand evidence of what happened to them, although it is presumed the ship sank with all hands. The author was thus forced to admit he was going to hypothesize parts of his story by using accounts from others who had found themselves in similar (but obviously less fatal) circumstances. He continually draws a picture of supposition based on these sources, and at the end of his book, he gives us a detailed description of what it is like, generically speaking, to drown. It's an adventurous and experimental way to tell a story of fishing and fishermen while recreating for the reader on the printed page what it means to undergo the rare experience of the terrifying, but exquisite, "perfect storm," as weather people described it.

Jack Hart commented on Junger's book: "*A Perfect Storm* was honest in that it clearly differentiated between fact and speculation. *Sleepers, Midnight in the Garden of Good and Evil* and much memoir are not. And the opposite of honesty in this business [i.e. journalism] is fraud, pure and simple."

Random House executive editor Peter Gethers has a similar, but more forgiving attitude: "There are obvious dangers in Junger's technique (although he pulled it off beautifully). There are different types of accuracy, I suppose; one would be technical accuracy—what exactly did this person say and do; another would be capturing an accurate emotion. This is where technique really comes into play. The best example of this is Junger's description of what it's like to drown. By writing that the way he did, he didn't have to go into the minds of his characters at the moment of their deaths. By showing us the physicality of drowning, he made us know and feel the terror his characters had to have felt."

His take on *Sleepers*, however, is quite different. "I was the editor of *Sleepers*, so I know much about it. The controversy was a fake one," he explained.

Many critics were concerned that too many facts had been changed, so that nothing in the story could really be trusted. Carcaterra's narrative is a sort of memoir of growing up in the tough New York City neighborhood of Hell's Kitchen in the 1960s. Four young men (of whom Carcaterra was one) wound up in a correctional home for boys. There, they were abused, beaten, and raped by the guards. A decade or so later, one of the boys had become a lawyer, and two of the boys had turned into cold-blooded murderers. One night they walk into a bar and run into one of the brutal guards who had forever changed their lives. What happens after sighting the guard sets a brilliant plan for revenge into motion, with the four boys (now men) together once again, but now in a scheme to get back at their persecutors in a very public way and expose the horrible wrongs they suffered.

The trouble was, Carcaterra admitted to changing many of the facts in *Sleepers,* so once again, we have no touchstone, other than Carcaterra's word, about what is true and what is fancy.

Gethers is insistent that "almost all nonfiction books that are about contemporary matters and people have facts changed—to avoid lawsuits. Names are changed and descriptions of people are often changed so they're unrecognizable. In other words, people who do bad things get 'saved'—so they don't sue. All Lorenzo did was change certain things so several good people—the priest and the young lawyer in the book—would be unrecognizable and thus not suffer by being recognizable. The media went crazy because they couldn't find the real people (although they were quite lazy and probably could have if they were more competent). Along with the Random House lawyers, I oversaw the changes Lorenzo made—they were nothing out of the ordinary."

Objective vs. Subjective Reporting

I guess I should declare my probably obvious bias at this point: I was trained in the older traditions of Belgrano and Fleet Street newspapers of the late 1960s and 1970s before they fell into the thrall of the tabloid mentality that is rampant in British journalism today. It was important, my editors in print journalism and radio insisted, to tell both sides of a story equally, maintaining as best one could an unbiased objective reporting of the story. If you have an opinion, get an interview subject to say it for you, retaining at least the appearance of impartiality. Let readers make up their own minds about what the events meant, after being given all the relevant facts.

Of course, "objective" reporting is a near impossibility, because the "art" of the print journalist is to pick and choose "relevant information" from the thousand shards of it either lying around or prized free through incisive interviewing. After gleaning that "relevant information," the reporter then explains to her audience what is happening and what it means.

In other words, even "objective" reporting is dependent on the character, general knowledge, and intellect of the journalist doing the reporting. At least, there is an "attempt" to be objective using this technique, an attempt which is abandoned when writing in the narrative form. So the pressure to be accurate in narrative re-creation is stronger because the temptations to "get away" with invention that "captures the spirit of the event" (in the reporter's mind) without substantiating facts are equally greater. *"She wore a red dress."* How do you know? *"She winced as she sat down, unsteadily easing her aching back."* Who said so? Again, how do you know? Perhaps she flounced. Or did she flop down? Description is not just a visual aid, it is also an indicator of character. Someone flouncing into a seat is very different than someone sitting down carefully so as not to exacerbate a bad backache. You don't have to put the sources into the text of the narrative and break up the flow, but you should have a note at the end of the book detailing information for each chapter where such claims are made.

There is an undeclared, inherent bias on the part of the reporter that is built into her understanding of an event that she has observed or reconstructed and then reported. Only by actively and honestly trying to present both sides of an issue can the reporter hope to balance her natural bias on an issue and present enough information for readers to make up their own minds independent of the reporter's personal conclusions. Writing a book about an idea or an incident allows the author the luxury—or pitfall, depending on your point of view—to choose a particular viewpoint and write a story through that prism. Yet the best nonfiction writers, such as Mark Bowden, Tracy Kidder, and John McPhee do not abandon journalistic integrity in order to contrive a good yarn on the page.

Thus, in the best of circumstances, one finds eyewitnesses and experts and people intimately involved with an event who say, in their own words, what it is the reporter feels should be said about an event.

"Doctoring" the Truth

There's an idea that some teachers put forward that a novelist, or an inexperienced writer of nonfiction can give themselves "permission to lie" in order to write a narrative account. As far as it goes, that's okay, given the exceptions I've noted. It's best, if you're unsure, to have the interviewees verify their quotes, even though as a journalist that goes against the grain a little to me, allowing the subjects the chance to veto or edit what they said. (Think what might have happened if Trent Lott in early 2003 had been given the chance to edit his remarks made at Strom Thurmond's birthday party. Instead of supporting Thurmond, and implicitly his 1948 racist politics, in hindsight Lott might have been able to remain the majority leader in the Senate.)

It's also okay to "tidy" up quotes, in effect to "doctor" the truth, in order to make them more readable. People are usually somewhat inarticulate and yet what they are saying may be profound when divested of a myriad of "um's" and "ah's." Some people can also be quite profane in their speech and, as an author, you certainly won't always want to quote them verbatim with every curse word intact. It is fine to reconfirm with the source, if you need to, and as long as you don't change the meaning or sense of what they say when you quote them, they probably won't even notice that you have tidied up their speech.

Many young reporters use subjective narrative nonfiction techniques as a subterfuge for laziness or willful ignorance of events and their context and history. Emotion (which is often confused with sentimentality) is more important than fact, they argue. Commenting on this, Peter Gethers said that "As with all trends, [I agree that] this one goes too far. The best writing is one that does it all—gets the facts right, tells us what happens, *and* achieves the right level of emotional impact (which I'm all in favor of; I'm not in favor of sentimentality)." He added, "The ultimate value of [narrative nonfiction] . . . is that it lets the author explore the depth and scope of a given situation—and it allows for much more depth than a tabloid piece of journalism, a movie or a piece of television reporting."

The case of Janet Malcolm and psychoanalyst Jeffrey Masson is instructive of what can happen if the reporter is not careful. Masson was a rising analyst who had been placed in charge of the Freud archives in the Freud house in London. Within a relatively short time he had antagonized his boss, Kurt Eissler, who had been described by journalist Craig Seligman in a Salon.com essay as "the high priest of Freudian analysts." Masson was fired from his job and was in the process of suing his former employers when he met Malcolm.

Janet Malcolm was a journalist with a reputation for edgy, uncompromising writing. Still, Masson spent hours talking to her. She encouraged his trust, even putting him and his girlfriend up in her New York home. And then, as Craig Seligman described it, she "unearthed a frightening talent. [Her book] *In the Freud Archives* is a masterwork of character assassination." And, the book led to ten years of litigation between Masson and Malcolm, whose major crime was to compress and conjoin quotes made at different times to form several long monologues, purportedly by Masson.

Seligman went on: "It's all but impossible to read Masson's long monologues (many of them, it came out in testimony, cobbled together from more than one interview) without thinking, 'What an asshole!' When the articles appeared, their flabbergasted victim howled in shock at the betrayal, and his howl took the form of a libel suit.

"The case hinged on five quotations that Masson claimed were fabrications and that Malcolm, embarrassingly, couldn't produce on tape—although, as David Gates pointed out in *Newsweek*, 'what Malcolm *does* have on tape—only a few lines are in dispute—is more than enough to make Masson look silly.'" The suit became a byzantine affair that threaded its way through the courts for years like some unending Dickensian civil action until a jury finally found against Masson in 1994.

"But for Malcolm the victory was a Pyrrhic one," wrote David Halberstam. "The public spectacle had been huge and humiliating, her reporting widely criticized and mocked. The lawsuit gained her more notoriety than any of her books ever had; thenceforward, everything she wrote would be a target."

Nevertheless, many writers of narrative nonfiction find a way to compress quotes without experiencing the same problems Janet Malcolm suffered. It's advantageous to be forewarned, however. Masson did not accuse Malcolm of tidying up his quotes, but of *fabricating* quotes. The first jury found for Masson against Malcolm and the *New Yorker* magazine, where the long articles had first appeared. A second jury, however, while finding that two of the passages were fabricated, nevertheless found in Malcolm's favor because in the view of jury members neither of the offending passages was libelous.

Poisoned Tales

A serious downside to narrative nonfiction journalism is that it can create an atmosphere where emotionally charged anecdotes force the creation of public policy, driven by a political quick-fix mentality that is a knee-jerk emotional response rather than a rationally considered solution to a problem. It's much easier, for example, for a legislator to vote against a sex offender registration law that he thinks it's too draconian and challenges constitutional notions of civil liberties if the bill is called a sex offender registration law rather than say, Megan's Law. Suddenly, because of the way the story has been reported, the legislator is voting against a victimized little girl and her grieving family, not a potential threat to our constitutional freedoms.

To survive as an effective, open society we need to be continually and accurately informed about our world and about what is happening in it. Today, many seem to either dismiss or forget that journalists were once called the Fourth Estate, unelected, but nevertheless for the most part committed to keeping society honest and equitable by making those in power accountable for their actions through the conscientious reporting of what elected officials did and why they did it. If journalists abrogate their responsibilities through lazy, populist, or overtly biased reporting, it can lead eventually to the madness of endorsing government and corporate propaganda rather than questioning it, enhancing ignorance of issues among the voting population, and, at the extreme end, help destroy the very foundations of democracy by allowing politicians to steal elections through bully tactics.

There is a reason that any modern government attempting to gain control of a population first silences or muzzles the press, and writers in general, by either shutting off avenues of publication or, in extreme cases, by putting them in jail or killing them.

The reporter is faced with two choices: take a story and use it to help people understand or think about a larger issue, or take that larger issue and trivialize it by reducing it to an easily digestible though not very accurately reported story.

The art and integrity of reporters has become particularly relevant in recent times, as a debate heats up in the United States, following the 9/11 tragedy, between the government's declared need for secrecy and a free hand to protect the nation from terrorism (even using potentially unethical and brutal means) and the constitution's insistence on a free and open society. "Liberty," said John Adams in an open letter to Thomas Jefferson in 1816, "cannot be preserved without a general knowledge among the people. . . . Power must never be trusted without a check." In an important opinion concerning the government's attempt to hold hearings and trials in secret, issued in late 2002, Judge Damon J. Keith, of the United States Court of Appeals for the Sixth Circuit wrote: "Democracies die behind closed doors."

He went on to say that the people had traditionally deputized the press as "guardians of their liberty."

Quoted in the *New York Times* (Sept 2, 2002), Herschel P. Fink, a lawyer who represents the *Detroit Free Press*, commented on the ruling: "Secrecy is the evil here [not terrorism]." He went on to say that the government "absolutely" has an obligation to "vigorously" fight terrorism, but excessive secrecy was intolerable.

This principle underlines the need for journalists to pay attention not only to what they report, but also to the thoroughness with which they report it. The evolution of narrative nonfiction could be argued to be an attempt by some journalists to develop their role in detailing and exploring the important stories of our time as the pressures of tabloid journalism press writers into more and more superficial news accounts of events that flirt with being merely propagandistic or sentimental, irrelevant pap in a misguided effort to emphasize feeling over relevance because it's more "entertaining" to the general public and less threatening to the "powers that be."

You may well ask, what has all this to do with writing narrative nonfiction?

Former Grove Atlantic editor Brendan Cahill commented: "It's hard to have novels that channel into every aspect of American life. In the Age of Information, the sheer amount of fact that is...overwhelming us day by day instills in us a need for stories to make sense of all the views of our lives."

Lee Gutkind, founder and editor of the magazine *Creative Nonfiction*, an author and editor of numerous articles and books, and professor of English at the University of Pittsburgh, explained that, ". . . the world has changed so suddenly over the past few years that now there is nothing that a novel can give us that hasn't already happened in our world.... It's hard as hell to compete with our realities of today for nonfiction."

Jack Olsen, I think, summed up the issue of dramatic license pretty well. In his interview with Gary Provost, he remarked, "Truman Capote, that little, gifted, brilliant son of a bitch put such pressure on all subsequent true crime writers, especially the ones who can't write as well as he, and that's all of them. He said that all the quotes in [the book] *In Cold Blood* were verbatim, but we know he made a lot of them up. He sold the public on the idea of,'Oh, look folks, at last we have an accurate true crime book.' He put such pressure on all the poor slobs that followed him to do the same thing, even though he hadn't done it himself. To me that is the single biggest outrage ever perpetrated under the name of true crime. If there was a gloomy setting in the courthouse, Capote wouldn't think twice about making it a gloomy day. *In Cold Blood* is a brilliant book, wonderfully written, and fraudulent."

Searching, Searching: Discovering a Subject

Nothing in the world can take the place of Persistence. ...
The slogan 'Press On,' has solved and will always solve the
problems of the human race.
　　　—Calvin Coolidge
If at first you don't succeed, try again, and then try
something else.
　　　—Mason Cooley, U.S. aphorist

You would think, given the blizzard of information constantly swirling around us, that finding ideas for stories would be a pretty simple matter. Yet, despite the daily assault of oceans of uncategorized, indistinguishable data, much of it is questionable, and some of it passes itself off as information when it is really not at all informative. In fact, very few pieces of information that cross our path are potent enough seeds to take root in the fertile earth of research and development. And of the pieces of information that do take root and grow into newspaper or magazine articles, fewer still are likely to develop beyond that into successful books.

First of All—Check It Out
This doesn't mean we shouldn't pay attention to the constant barrage of information around us. Quite the reverse—it's just that we should be skeptical about the viability of any particular idea before committing too much time and resources to it.

The first thing to do if a good idea strikes is do some research. Go online and see if the idea has been pursued before and, if so, to what extent and by whom. Run a search on Google,

Yahoo, Amazon, Barnesandnoble, or Booksinprint and see what book titles turn up on the idea or topic.

For example, when I first got the idea for writing this book, I ran a search of the terms "narrative nonfiction" and "book" and "writing" and "how-to," and while I turned up many hits on Google and Amazon, even when I re-ran the query for the revised version of this book very few referred to how-to books on the subject, and most referred to writing articles and "creative nonfiction."

Some of the Google hits led me to transcriptions of interviews or roundtable discussions with authors, editors, and agents on the subject. Yet there were few entries that explicitly mentioned books covering how to write about the topic, and a number cited this book's first edition (though not enough!).

When I first got the idea to write this book in 2001, I knew of three others that might qualify, and, as I mentioned in my book proposal, two of those were old: *The Art of Creative Nonfiction* by Lee Gutkind, published in 1997, (which I knew about because Wiley, Gutkind's publisher, was also the publisher of my book *The Elements of Storytelling)*; and *Writing for Story* by Jon Franklin, published in 1986. Both of these books focus on New Journalism and writing short creative nonfiction for magazines and newspapers, rather than on the production of long pieces or books. I have been friends with agent and former editor Susan Rabiner for some years, so I knew about her book, *Thinking Like Your Editor*, although it focuses mainly on writing serious nonfiction, books like *The Physics of Star Trek,* or Stephen Hawking's *A Brief History of Time.*

In short, I was both surprised and pleased to find that even after six years in print, there were *still* no books other than mine that explicitly tackled the how-to's of writing a book like *Black Hawk Down, Longitude,* or *The Right Stuff* by Tom Wolfe (described by the publisher as a novel, even though it is a dramatization of the true events of the United States' space program of the 60s and 70s). James B. Stewart's *Follow the Story,* published in 1998, is probably the book that came closest to what I wanted to write, and thankfully his approach and mine are different enough that readers will hopefully learn equally from both books, without much overlapping.

This dearth of books on how to write narrative nonfiction amazed me in 2002 when I first wrote this book, and it continued to surprise me in 2008 as I worked on the revised edition, because narrative nonfiction is, as I've maintained throughout the previous chapters, arguably the fastest growing genre in publishing. Yet doing it right and doing it well (not exactly the same things) are barely considered by most authors who are attracted to the genre, and who may be tempted to use books such as McGinniss' *The Last Brother* or Frey's *A Million Little Pieces* as models, when in fact they are shining examples of exactly what you *shouldn't do* if you want to write something that is both engaging *and* responsible.

I definitely didn't want to write merely another turgid diatribe of "writing rules," just so I could add another book to my name, and perhaps confuse people even more about what they should and shouldn't be doing in the production of quality narrative nonfiction. Yet here was an idea that seemed to beg to be written, on a topic I specialize in as an agent, and which had received minimal coverage between 2002 and 2008.

The truth is, rather like knowing how to look for a true "soul mate," most writers don't have a clue where good ideas come from; we just seem to know them immediately when they cross our paths. A good idea will hit you in the face like a wet fish. The best thing to do is just put yourself "out there," particularly through voracious and wide reading, people study, meaningful conversations, and the thoughtful analysis of current and historic ideas, and so increase the chances of an elusive, but perfectly adaptable idea crossing your path. However, recognizing and taking advantage of a potentially good, original (and I stress *original*) idea is as much a skill as coming up with the idea through voracious reading and discussion with others.

Looking for One Thing, and Finding Something Better

Sometimes what you think you are going to write becomes something else. It is the smart writer who is flexible enough to adapt ideas. For example, when Manuela Hoelterhoff, opera critic for the *Wall Street Journal* for 20 years or so, wrote *Cinderella & Company: Backstage at the Opera With Cecilia Bartoli*, Ms. Hoelterhoff intended to draw a portrait of an operatic mezzo-soprano who had achieved an unusually loyal and popular following in the opera world before reaching her 30th birthday.

For two years, the author immersed herself in Bartoli's world: from her 1995 appearance at the Houston Grand Opera in the title role of Rossini's *Cenerentola* (*Cinderella*) to her Metropolitan Opera debut two years later in the modest role of the maid Despina in Mozart's *Cosi Fan Tutte*. Hoelterhoff had access to the singer; her mother, who doubled as Bartoli's vocal coach; Bartoli's Italian boyfriend; her manager; plus a supporting cast of recording executives, agents, public relations types, and orchestra conductors, all of whom seemed to be outlandish characters straight out of the *Commedia del'Arte*.

The intended biographical story of the meteoric rise to fame of a young singer with a beautiful voice but miniscule repertoire of roles instead became a much broader and more interesting portrait of the rarified world of professional opera at the turn of the twenty-first century. Even if opera does not particularly interest you, the book is so well written, witty, and fascinating that it easily takes its place alongside anything Tracy Kidder or John McPhee has written, in terms of quality narrative nonfiction. Ms. Hoelterhoff specializes in word pictures and a Dorothy Parker-like incisive wit.

A quick example of Ms. Hoelterhoff's wit: On witnessing the large soprano Deborah Voigt (who on occasion could appear to weigh at least 300 pounds) singing next to the elfin-looking tenor Francisco Araiza in Verdi's *A Masked Ball*, she described Voigt as "looking as if she were ventriloquizing with a hand puppet." Also, Hoelterhoff immortalizes Kathleen Battle, who was commonly disliked in the opera world because of the unpleasant way she treated people, in her account of how Battle called her agent from the back seat of a limousine to have him tell the driver to turn down the air conditioner.

What Manuela Hoelterhoff did, of course, was to recognize a good idea when it presented itself, but, more importantly, she was able to adapt it entirely, and successfully, despite its becoming something far different from what she had intended to write at the outset.

The Story Sense Workout

More than anything, coming up with a subject that works both as a book and as an engaging and relevant story is a skill that must be developed. It is a "muscle" that must be exercised and nurtured, and like hardening muscles by working out in the gym, the writer's "story sense" muscle is developed only through constant practice and conscious mental exercise. While it is not likely to be very useful the first few times you use it, that should not discourage you from continuing your efforts to develop an active and alert "story sense." You are nurturing what journalists call "news sense" or "story sense" and that is an indefinable quality born of regular practice. Like good art, most journalists "know it when they see it," even though there is (happily) no rigid, scientific-type formula that can be applied.

Journalists are intrigued by people saying "no" to them, particularly, for example, when there should be no reason to do so. Back in the 1960s, the *London Times Sunday Magazine* decided to run an A to Z series about remarkable people, events, and institutions of the twentieth century. One of the institutions to be profiled was a famous department store in London. When the store was asked to provide what was essentially a public relations piece about its history the store's officers point blank refused to cooperate. This so intrigued the reporters of the *Times* that they checked into the store and into why it was being so evasive. The reporters uncovered the fact that the name of the store, known only by its initials, took those initials from the owners, two Dutch brothers who had been major supporters of the German Nazi party prior to and during WWII. The store in London was a favorite of British Jews, and, undone by journalistic curiosity, lost a great deal of business when the truth about the store's past was reported.

In *Follow the Story*, Pulitzer Prize-winning journalist James B. Stewart says: "Curiosity is the great quality that binds writers to readers. Curiosity sends writers on their quests, and curiosity is what makes readers read the stories that result. These days, when there is increasing competition for people's time, writers cannot count on anyone to read their work out of a sense of obligation, moral duty, or abstract dedication to 'being informed.' They will not read because someone else deems a subject important. They will read because they want to, and they want to because they are curious."

Curiosity is fueled by questions: Why wouldn't the London department store supply the *Times* reporters with a simple store biography as they were asked to do?

Curiosity, however, needs to go hand in hand with a passion for a subject. Jonathan Galassi, of Farrar Straus & Giroux summed it up: "[Authors of narrative nonfiction] should try to find topics that interest them deeply on a personal level, first of all, and work on ones that they see are related [to those passions] in some way—not always surface-obvious."

Writing about how *The Perfect Storm* came about, Sebastian Junger remarked: "My own experience of the storm [of the century] was limited to standing on Gloucester's Back Shore watching thirty-foot swells advance on Cape Ann, but that was all it took. The next day I read in the paper that a Gloucester boat was feared lost at sea, and I clipped the article and stuck it in a drawer. Without even knowing it, I had begun to write *The Perfect Storm*."

For Jon Krakauer, *Into Thin Air* was even more personal. Whilst on Mt. Everest, writing an article for *Outside* magazine, he experienced a rogue storm which killed nine climbers from four separate expeditions. Three more would eventually die on

Everest before the end of the month. "The expedition left me badly shaken," Krakauer wrote. His article was published four months later in *Outside* magazine. "Upon [the article's] completion I attempted to put Everest out of my mind and get on with my life, but that turned out to be impossible. Through a fog of messy emotions, I continued trying to make sense of what had happened up there, and I obsessively mulled the circumstances of my companions' deaths." He went on, "Several authors and editors I respect counseled me not to write the book as quickly as I did.... Their advice was sound, but in the end I ignored it—mostly because what happened on the mountain was gnawing my guts out. I thought that writing the book might purge Everest from my life.

"It hasn't, of course."

If you're a professional writer who has been published in magazines and newspapers, you probably already have an idea of how to find stories. Often, an editor at a magazine or a newspaper features editor, will come up with an idea, and the editor will either commission it or ask a particular writer to write up a couple of pages "on spec"—that is, on the speculation of an eventual purchase of an article-length project.

The book world does not tend to work quite that way. It's true that if you have an agent, and/or you're published, with a good relationship with an editor at a publishing house, it may be a little easier to run ideas past your agent or your editor and come up with something that is going to work for everyone. But the odds are you're not in that position. A client of mine, for example, had a major house publish her first book, which got an 80 percent sell-through. That means over 80 percent of the books printed by the house were eventually sold to the general reading public through bookstores and other sources, which is a success for a writer. However, the total sales didn't reach 20,000 copies, so even though her editor loved the idea for her prospective new narrative nonfiction, his new boss decided that he couldn't buy my client's new proposal. I gently pointed out to the editor that with an 80 percent sell-through rate, the only reason the book had not sold 20,000 copies was because the publishing company had not printed enough copies to allow her to sell that many. This made no difference to the corporate decision, however.

Thus, my job became finding another editor for my client's new book, which in this case was not very difficult. However, the point is that the publishing industry is plagued with such situations, most of which are not within an author's control.

Former HarperCollins senior editor Dan Conaway (now an agent with Writer's House) feels that "the most important thing—virtually the only important thing, to me—is the quality of the writing, the depth and nuance and insight and drama that comes organically from great writing. I'm not called on to do "ripped-from-the-headlines" books as my bread and butter, so I don't much care whether it's a fantastic story, unless it's fantastically well told. So-so writing always comes back to bite one on the ass, especially if one does as much editorial work as I do."

Peter Gethers of Random House feels similarly: "When looking at a submission, I basically look for the same things no matter what the category: a compelling story, characters I care about (or whom I find interesting), and, if possible, some kind of emotional attachment rather than just purely an intellectual one. I suppose that's my definition of a good narrative nonfiction book—it establishes an emotional connection with the reader."

George Gibson, publisher of Walker & Co., says much the same thing. He looks for the following qualities in a book proposal: "First, can the author write; second, is there a good story here; third, will it expand the reader's knowledge and understanding of the world"

Deciding What's Worth Writing

So how do you find a good subject to write about? Mark Twain once said, "In the real world, the right thing never happens at the right place, at the right time—it is the task of journalists and historians to rectify this error."

If you are already selling consistently to magazines and so forth, at first blush finding great subject matter might not seem that difficult. But here's the problem: What may work well as a short piece may not work as a longer piece. So the problem falls into two parts: first of all, how to find a good subject to write about, and secondly, how to tell if that idea will work as a book.

Jack Hart of the *Oregonian* newspaper comments, "I'm not sure all narrative nonfiction needs to read like a good novel. It should be a pleasure to read, of course, but good narrative can do productive work even if it doesn't tap a good novel's great human truths and deep characterization. Explanatory narrative, like Rich Read's *The French Fry Connection* is a case in point, as is almost anything by John McPhee."

In a May 2001 interview in *Writer's Digest*, magazine author Colin Colm Toibin described how he came up with the idea for his book *Fingerprints*:

> Basically, my agent and I were sitting around his office one rainy day, and I was having trouble coming up with some ideas. And he said, "Well OK, I have this idea." So I left his office feeling obliged to do some research because he was my agent, and he'd kindly offered me [the] idea, but I was like, "Oh God, the history of fingerprints?" I went to the library, and it was like synchronicity because one of the first books I came across talked about this kind of unsung hero of fingerprinting who had basically had his idea stolen from him. And then all of a sudden it wasn't this ungodly dry subject to me, but a real human story about justice and giving credit where credit is due.
>
> ...In narrative nonfiction the key is to find a story. If you want to write good narrative nonfiction, what you have to realize is that, just like fiction, it's about people—all stories are about people. And just like in fiction, in narrative nonfiction—although you're more constrained by the facts—what you're looking for are stories that intrigue people and characters that are interesting.

All knowledge involves change in the recipient. If it does not involve change, it is not knowledge, but information without meaning. If I say, "You're reading this book," that's not knowledge. It's self evident and you've learned nothing. If I say, "If you continue to read this book, you'll catch a nasty social disease," you have learned something that will effect a change, probably quite rapidly. (It's not true, of course, in case you're wondering.)

So, too, topics for narrative nonfiction books should add to our understanding or reveal previously unknown things.

Peter Gethers commented, "I truly don't think there's much difference between good fiction and nonfiction storytelling. The best writers—ranging from Dostoeyevsky to Stephen King to Truman Capote to Robert Caro—are also great storytellers." He went on, "The best narrative nonfiction involves human interest stories about ordinary people who accomplish extraordinary things in extraordinary circumstances, even if [the crux of the work] is about the story of an idea."

For example, while *Longitude* is the story of the invention of the chronometer, and the discovery of how to measure longitude, it is really focused on the trials and tribulations of John Harrison, the man who eventually solved the puzzle. Similarly, while Simon Winchester's *The Professor and the Madman* is about the creation of the *Oxford English Dictionary* and the codification of the English language, the story is humanized by focusing on two figures: James A. H. Murray, the editor who faced the monumental task of compiling the initial version of the *Oxford English Dictionary*, and Dr. William Chester Minor, one of his most reliable and thorough volunteer contributors. Minor, however, had a secret: After serving as a physician in the Union Army during the Civil War, he fixed upon an obsession that Irishmen wanted to kill him. After the war he visited London, but his worsening psychosis led him to murder a complete stranger and he was tried, convicted, and institutionalized in an asylum for the criminally insane. Being in prison, as well as being well-educated, however, made him well suited to becoming a major contributor to Murray's enormous undertaking—and it contributed hugely to the reader's emotional involvement in Winchester's book.

Three Basic Ways to Find a Story

There are basically three ways to find stories:

- First, you can either directly observe an event, or be involved in one. This ranges from the experiences of, say, Fire Battalion Commander Richard Picciotto, whose first-person account of the World Trade Center catastrophe on 9/11 is presented in *Last Man Down*, to historian D. Graham Burnett's experiences as the foreman of the jury in a murder trial in New York City, recounted in *A Trial by Jury*.

- Secondly, there are stories told by third-party observers, that is witnesses or sources to something that you, as the author, haven't actually seen or experienced. Woodward and Bernstein's *All the President's Men* would fall into this category, as would Robert Conot's 1967 book *Rivers of Blood, Years of Darkness* about the brutal 1965 Los Angeles riot, an event considered by many to be a turning point in race relations in America.

- Lastly, there are purely written or published accounts taken from information totally outside of the author's personal experience. Almost any historical account, be it a biography or the re-creation of an historic event, would fall into this category. Books by A. Scott Berg, Alison Weir, or Simon Schama would fall into this category.

The truth is, outside of travel writing, it takes a sensational or bizarre personal experience to be worth considering as the basis for a book. If you have *really* been taken by aliens and experimented on, and you can convince me of the experience, this is subject matter for which it is clearly worth putting together a proposal. It worked for Whitley Streiber, for instance, when he wrote *Communion* and then its sequel *Confirmation*. (But because Streiber has already done this story, your story will need to be more than just a repetition of the experience. *Just* because it's true, doesn't make something innately interesting to others.)

This kind of personal experience writing is a form of memoir. Jon Krakauer's book *Into Thin Air* is really a memoir of a disaster he was involved with, as too was Picciotto's *Last Man Down*. When weighing the prospects of writing a memoir, one of the major questions you should consider as objectively as possible is: Why would someone else really be interested in my experience. James B. Stewart poses interesting questions in *Follow the Story*: "What about my [own] experience do I find puzzling [or incomplete], and what might I better understand given additional reflection and research." The most obvious answer is the overcoming of adversity, as was the subject of Frank McCourt's memoir *Angela's Ashes*. As moving and popular as that book was, it is interesting to note that many felt the sequel *'Tis* was disappointing.

George Plimpton blazed the trail for a style of story that involves the reporter as observant participator. In the mid-1960s he wrote one of the seminal narrative nonfiction books, *Paper Lion: Confessions of a Last-String Quarterback*, which details his adventures as a 36-year-old rookie quarterback wannabe with the Detroit Lions from their preseason training camp through to an intra-squad game a month later. It's a funny and perceptive book, and it is still a model of what has been called "immersion reporting." The question that comes to mind with this kind of writing, of course, is why not just interview a professional and tell his story? In following this "immersion reporting" path, there is a danger of the writer's ego getting in the way, and the writer bringing little real perception or value to such a project. Another concern is that anything you, as a regular Joe or Jane, can actually talk your way into doing may not be that interesting to the rest of us. An exception to this particular concern might be an undercover or expose sort of story.

For example, Barbara Ehrenreich went "undercover" to write *Nickel and Dimed: On (Not) Getting By In America*, a close-up look at the working poor, which demonstrated that even at the height of the economic boom of the late 1990s, many unskilled workers couldn't earn enough to meet basic human needs. Ehrenreich decided that the best way to understand the plight of the working poor was to become one. She left her comfortable home and steady income as a writer and tried to live on the income from a series of jobs in restaurants, hotels, stores, and nursing homes, where she earned an average of $7 an hour. That was well above the minimum wage in 1998, the year of her experiment, yet even so, she discovered that it was nearly impossible to live on such wages

Narrative nonfiction is often the "story behind a story." As in the *Wizard of Oz,* narrative nonfiction often affords the drawing back of the veil from the appearance of a thing, to expose the machinery beneath. Narrative nonfiction often answers the chronic questions: What really happened and why did it happen that way.

Mark Bowden worked as a reporter at the *Philadelphia Inquirer* for 20 years before he wrote *Black Hawk Down.* "When I began working on [*Black Hawk Down*] in 1996," he wrote, "my goal was simply to write a dramatic account of the battle. I had been struck by the intensity of the fight, and by the notion of 99 American soldiers surrounded and trapped in an ancient African city [and] fighting for their lives. My contribution would be to capture in words the experience of combat through the eyes and emotions of the soldiers involved, blending their urgent, human perspective with a military and political overview of their predicament. . . . I wanted to combine the authority of a historical narrative with the emotion of the memoir, and write a story that read like fiction but was true."

Why They Did What They Did

All successful stories involve some sort of relationship between a person, what the person does, and why he or she does what is done. If you can't develop and satisfactorily interrelate these elements, your book will fall flat. It may take a while, but once you develop what journalists call "news sense," you'll start to see potential book ideas everywhere.

There is a danger in searching for a larger narrative, however, when you only have the part of the picture that originally grabbed your interest. Narrative is seductive, and the temptation is to use it for its own sake. The danger is that we will distort reality by forcing it into a narrative template. We may find a protagonist where none really exists. We may create a climax to a story that has never been resolved. When looking for a narrative nonfiction book that appeals to him, book publisher Jonathan Galassi explained, "[Farrar Straus & Giroux is] interested in the significance of the subject and its relation to the approach of the author—style, research, point of view, attitude."

The larger question to consider is: Who is the audience for this book? What other books in this field can be used as models for your proposed book? Were they successful? Is the audience (that is, the market) easily definable, reachable, and large enough?

It should go without saying—and yet, here I am saying it— that it is a seriously bad idea to try to second guess the commercial viability of an idea. Trying to write something because you are sure it is going to be a bestseller, and yet it is a topic that you do not particularly care for, is a bad idea for many reasons, not the least of which is that you will have a miserable time writing a book you'll likely have to live with for perhaps a year or more. You are also not likely to inject much passion into it, and passion is the one thing editors and agents, and readers, look for in successful books.

At a panel discussion at the Washington Press Club, award-winning journalist Paul Dickson (author of forty-plus books, including *Sputnik: The Shock of the Century*) commented that, "Every day when you wake up, you've got to think of the reader."

To make his point, he told the story of writing what he now calls a "snake-bite book": "One time—I had [already] won three awards [for investigative journalism]—I wrote a book that was tough, it was investigative, [it] used every tool I had as a journalist but no commercial publisher was interested, so I did it with a university press. And I remember going to the zoo, and there was a sign in the zoo over a poisonous snake that said that 'Every year in America, 1,906 people are bitten by poisonous snakes,' and I realized that fewer people had bought my book [that year than had been bitten by a poisonous snake]....You've got to think of the reader."

Sources

Anything that someone else witnesses or knows about and tells you falls under the rubric of "source" material. The person telling you is your source. Be warned that while you should cultivate conversation with everyone you meet (in a work sense), and listen nonjudgmentally to them, most people have stories they are busting a gut to tell you and most of these stories are hopelessly useless in book publishing terms. The most useful sources are usually people you have to cultivate: a cop, or fireman, or emergency worker, or doctor, or scientist, or nurse, or secretary or . . . almost anyone *except* someone who does public relations for a living. Public relations people desperately want to give you stories that are stripped of any real interest except what works for them and their clients, and they also want to control you and the way the story is presented. Taking someone out for a drink, schmoozing on the phone, or just listening to something someone wants to tell is a perfectly acceptable and time-honored way of getting an idea for a story from a source.

Sources can be named or unnamed, depending on the circumstances, but we'll talk more about that in the research chapter (see Chapter 4).

Networking and Using Local Resources

Become familiar with your local colleges and universities. Know who teaches there and what they teach. Read the campus newsletter, and start trying to find out what seems to be the hot topics of the day, either in a particular discipline, whether it's animal husbandry (remember Dolly, the cloned sheep?), or perhaps architecture and engineering (do we need to rethink how we build tall buildings now that terrorists crash airplanes into them?). Consider unique subjects, such as spectacular failures that have occurred in the past. Do you recall the stories about physicists who claimed to have produced cold nuclear fusion a few years ago? What happened to their claim; why is cold nuclear fusion not an applicable science today? Colleges are filled with athletes, scientists, artists, and others who often have intriguing stories about themselves, or know stories about others, or have thoughts and opinions on a wide variety of subjects, any one of which may spur your interest to pursue as a topic for a work of narrative nonfiction.

Put the word out—mention to friends and colleagues that you're looking for a new idea for a book. They'll probably inundate you with stuff you can't use, but there's always that one intriguing tidbit!

Make sure that you read not just national magazines, including even the tabloids, but also read regional magazines and magazines that cover specific areas of interest, magazines like *Outside, Pacific Golf, Texas Highways*, etc. These days there are magazines that cover almost any topic you can think of, and if there isn't a magazine for something, you've got to wonder whether that's because there might not be a large enough audience for that particular subject. Bear in mind, though, that if a magazine article catches your eye, you should consider (and investigate) whether the author of that piece is working on his own book for which the piece was either an excerpt or a teaser. Do not overlook the Web, and stay current with webzines, such as *Salon*, etc.

Tabloid TV can be an idea source, even shows like *Oprah* and *Dr. Phil*. Cable TV channels, such as the History Channel, or Discovery, and programs, such as PBS's *Nova* or *Frontline*, can start the old grey matter ticking with short pieces that may intrigue and have more expansive histories that bear investigation. Also, there are the classic idea-related programs, like *Dateline* and *60 Minutes*. It's alway worthwhile talking with scientists, doctors, policemen, firemen, and lawyers, people who often have stories that could form the basis of at least an article, and possibly a book.

The truth is that we rarely see a story as a whole, at least at the outset. Something about a story will speak to us, will catch our eye in the same way that a potential girlfriend or boyfriend might. Often, we don't know or can't recall exactly what it is that caught our attention but somehow it was something that lit a spark and we realized we could make our own. Sometimes, it is the basic situation that speaks to us. How did the character (person involved) get into that situation, we think. And how on Earth did he get himself out of it? And, the process begins...!

Browsing Sources, Old and New

Try to avoid old stories, unless there is something new they can tell us or you find some new aspect about them. A client of mine, for example, discovered that despite the many books on the subject of spying during World War II, no one had ever told the remarkable story of Virginia Hall, an attractive Baltimore socialite with a wooden leg who was first a British undercover operative and eventually an OSS operative in France during the Nazi occupation.

Jim Srodes is a Washington D.C. journalist who also writes biographies. He is the author of a number of books, including *Allen Dulles: Master of Spies* and *Franklin: The Essential Founding Father*. He commented that he reads endlessly, often going over ground that others have seemingly covered thoroughly, searching for things that they may have overlooked. "I love to prove other people wrong," he said. "I'm a journalist, so I guess I'm something of a professional smart-ass. I look for overlooked stories, to see where someone else has screwed up, to find a new angle on something that could be otherwise considered familiar. I read all the time, looking for the 'aha' factor. . . When I was researching my biography of Benjamin Franklin, for example, I noticed that many previous biographers . . . came away unsatisfied as to who Franklin was. Aha, I thought, I can do this [write a biography of Franklin], and my interest quickly turned into a passion."

One of the simplest things to do is keep abreast of current events. When you pore over magazines and newspapers, always consider whether there is an interesting story that has a human interest angle. In the true crime category, for example, a brutal local murder might really catch the local headlines. But what is there about the crime that would interest someone in a state several thousand miles away? If you live in Phoenix, Arizona, for example, and something happens there, why would a book about that subject sell in Alaska or Vermont?

Looking for stories in magazines and newspapers is not about trying to steal someone else's efforts—or at least it shouldn't be. Newspapers and magazines, by their very nature, only introduce you to a topic and maybe raise some questions about the why and wherefore of the subject in question. What really makes a potential book are the answers (or search for the answers) to the unanswered questions the story has raised. A good example of a book that came from the seed of a small newspaper article is John Berendt's *Midnight in the Garden of Good and Evil.*

Look around you. What are the trends and social forces that you see at work? In early 2002, for example, everyone was chasing Enron stories—the biggest financial story of the decade, it was claimed. The books centered around tales told by some of the people involved in the financial scandal. But what about the larger ramifications of the story? What did the story tell us about who we are and why we do the things we do? What could a book tell us that a magazine article could not? If you can find answers to these types of questions, then maybe you have a potential book on your hands.

The truth is, though, that the Enron story was so big, and attracted such immediate attention, that unless you possessed some personal experience that you wanted to confess or reveal, other, more experienced, writers would undoubtedly have beaten you to the punch on such a story and it's probably not the story worth your time pursuing.

A Topic Is Not a Subject

A client of mine is a leading immigration lawyer. He writes a column for the *New York Daily News*,as well as for the Spanish-language *El Diario*. Yet a dry policy book about immigration would need to overcome the huge obstacle of audience indiffer-ence—not to say hostility, following the events of 9/11. The aver-age American citizen doesn't care about immigration, except in terms of how it is impacting his or her immediate environment. It may make a good basis for an article in a magazine, but it does not appear to be a "grabber" subject for a book.

During a conversation we had, my client and I decided that one of the key aspects of immigration in the early days of the first decade of the twenty-first century was civil rights. In effect, as part of the fallout of the events of 9/11, there is a continuing assault on individual civil liberties, particularly for non-U.S. citizens.

The argument could be framed that if the government can take someone away and put them in jail indefinitely without trial, without access to a lawyer, and without an explicit charge—all in the name of homeland security—most Americans would say it is a necessary price to be paid for safety—that is, they would say it until the day the government did the same to them, to someone they loved, or to a respected and beloved neighbor. But still there was no book in the conversation and conjectures between my cli-ent and myself; there was only a topic. And topics do not make great book subjects.

However, in further conversations, my client and I discussed the fact that the Immigration and Naturalization Services is able to not only imprison noncitizens on a whim and a suspicion, it can deny asylum to those who face certain disaster in their own homelands. A book could use fictional techniques to introduce us to, say, a family of three from Iraq who sought asylum because they had fallen victim to death threats from Saddam Hussein's secret police. After many dangerous adventures they arrive on American shores, pleading for their lives, only to be rebuffed. They are sent back to Iraq, where the father of the family is summarily executed. Not knowing where else to go, the mother and son return to the United States and once again plead for asylum—this time they are successful in their attempt. A dry, intellectual idea that might work for an academic press would thusly be clothed in passion and human interest, and it would be far more likely to successfully catch a reading audience's attention and make its point far more vividly—to powerfully suggest that what happens to others if we let it happen, will eventually happen to us as well if we are not careful. A potential book proposal for this type of book would now argue for universal appeal, even though it focused upon telling a specific and localized story.

This touches on a major obstacle writers don't grasp well enough: Passion may be a prerequisite to writing, but a topic, however passionately one feels about it (you know them—health care, gun control, abortion, immigration, welfare cheats, and so on) will make a lousy book, unless and until it is humanized.

The way America treats its working poor is a national shame, and Barbara Ehrenreich found a powerful and emotionally grabbing way of taking this topic and making it a relevant book subject: "When someone works for less pay than she can live on—when, for example, she goes hungry so that you can eat more cheaply and conveniently—then she has made a great sacrifice for you, she has made you a gift of some part of her abilities, her health, and her life."

The trick is to write a book that is compelling enough that people will read it. In an interview she gave to *Publishers Weekly,* Barbara Ehrenreich said, "You don't start out thinking about who the audience is—or at least I don't. It's too constraining. I've written about economic issues a lot since the 80s, trying to show through statistics that people couldn't live on the minimum wage. I wrote expository books, I interviewed women, I approached it basically from an economic point of view. But nothing

I did seemed to make much difference. I mean, abolishing welfare was not what I had in mind. . . . I realized the next step was
to get out there and try to draw some attention to these issues
by personalizing them. . . . [Writing the book] really changed
the way I saw the world. I began to see all the invisible people—
I know this sounds like [the movie] *The Sixth Sense*—but I became aware of a world of discomfort and pain all around me: in
the grocery store, at restaurants. I also found that writing in the
very immediate first-person was a lot of fun."

Good Idea—Great Article, Weak Book?

Another difficult truth is that a good idea might make an excellent article but a weak book. You need to be able to look for
and find the universal in the details and the specifics in order to
transmute an article into a book. You need to determine whether
anyone will want to read an entire book (as opposed to an article), or whether it will even be relevant to readers three years
after you sell the idea to a publisher?

So how do you know if your idea has stronger possibility as
a magazine idea or as a book idea? It's true that many nonfiction
books start out life as articles. *Longitude, Into Thin Air, Black
Hawk Down, The Hot Zone,* and *No One Left Behind* all began
life as articles or as a series of articles. However, in general, if
a story is particularly timely, it will probably work better as a
magazine or newspaper piece than a book. If a story appears to
have a relevance two years from the time you start working on it,
and hopefully a continued relevance beyond that (to create backlist life), then maybe it's a book. The magazine article may tell
us what happened superficially, or it may present the portrait
of a character, for example. But what is the deeper story? What
will cause us to look back on an event or issue or character and
see our current world afresh? It took years, for example, for the
British government to admit the truth about the sinking of the
Argentinian cruiser *Belgrano* during the Falklands War.

In early 1982, the Royal Navy nuclear submarine HMS
Conqueror torpedoed and sank the Argentinian cruiser the

General Belgrano. The ship sank within an hour, leaving approximately 290 crew members dead and a further 30 dying of burns and exposure in the icy waters of the south Atlantic.

It took over a decade and the exposure of a great deal of stonewalling and blatant misinformation on behalf of the British government before the full story came out: The *Belgrano* was sunk when it was outside the 200-mile total exclusion zone that Britain had declared around the Falkland Islands after an Argentine force seized the colony. The revelation came despite then-Prime Minister Margaret Thatcher's claim that the ship was inside the exclusion zone and steaming to engage British ships; the truth as it was later determined was that the *Belgrano* was in fact heading for home and traveling *away* from the exclusion zone. By all reasonable accounts, it was sunk to make a political point. The best way to tell this story in book form would be to zero in on several characters who were on both ships, characters who were privy to the decision making processes made in London and Caracas, and to show what happened to each of them, and how the decisions they made affected the lives of others, both known and unknown to them.

The 12-Point Book Idea Checklist

The following are 12 points to consider when taking into account whether or not a story is worth pursuing as a book:

1. Play to your strengths. Write something you can be considered an expert about, and if that's not possible, make sure you have experts intimately involved in the telling of your story.

2. Play to your passions. Look for ideas and stories that genuinely interest and move you. If you're really a good writer—and as Peter Gethers comments "part of being a good writer is to have good instincts about things that are interesting and moving"—then readers will be attracted to your idea because of that passion.

3. Who is the audience for this book? What other books in this field can be used as models for your proposed book? Were they successful? Is the audience, that is, the market, easily definable, reachable, and large enough?

4. Will the book be relevant approximately three years after you manage to sell it to a publisher? Does it have "backlist" life, as well, of course, as "frontlist" appeal?

5. Is the protagonist a consistently interesting person? There is nothing more boring for an audience, or more challenging for a writer to capture on paper, than a character whose one claim to fame is a fleeting, dubious moment of glory in an otherwise humdrum, very ordinary existence. The central characters of *The Professor and the Madman,* for example, made the book stand out, because author Simon Winchester was able to contrast a character who had no formal education, the editor Murray, with a psychotic but highly intelligent character, the murderer Minor.

6. Is the antagonist interesting? If the story is true crime, for example, is the victim interesting? Those who are picked at random by killers are of less interest than those who were chosen by the killers for a specific reason.

7. Find an interesting setting, particularly in terms of geography. Jon Krakauer's *Into Thin Air*, for example, takes us to the summit of Mount Everest. Flying in a Thai Air jetliner, the author stared out the window at the peak of Everest, 29,028 feet above sea level and level with the airplane window. "... it occurred to me that the top of Everest was precisely the same height as the pressurized jet bearing me through the heavens. That I proposed to climb to the cruising altitude

of an Airbus 300 jetliner struck me, at that moment, as preposterous, or worse. My palms felt clammy."

8. Find and portray an interesting, different world. For example, in the late 1980s, ebola fever, an African virus with a 90 percent kill rate, broke out in a research facility in the suburbs of Washington D.C. A biohazard SWAT team from the U.S. Army was called in to work with scientists from the Centers for Disease Control to secretly contain and decontaminate the place. In Richard Preston's *The Hot Zone*, we are introduced to the fascinating, frightening world of lethal viruses and the secret world of the men and women who try to defeat them by rendering them harmless.

9. Find a story that has complications, or at least, twists and turns. John Harrison, for example, the protagonist of *Longitude,* had no formal education nor any apprenticeship to a watchmaker. Yet he managed to solve the foremost puzzle of his time, how to accurately and effectively determine longitude at sea. It should have been a simple matter for him to claim the prize set out by the British parliament for the first person to achieve this goal. However, for many years Harrison's every success was deflected by members of the scientific community of the time who deeply distrusted the simple answer of two clocks set to differing times. The commissioners responsible for awarding the prize changed the rules several times in order to favor scientists who they felt were more deserving of the award, despite the fact they had not solved the problem. It took the intervention of King George III, when Harrison was an old man and 40 years after he initially solved the problem, to settle the matter in Harrison's favor. The complication, needless to say, must be a basic one: an injustice (as in Harrison's case), a theft, a setback, or something

that relates to the human condition involving jealousy, hate, love, pain, etc.

10. If possible, find a story that has a resolution. Stories whose resolutions are still hanging at their end may make good magazine articles, and although this is the most flexible of all these twelve points, for someone just starting out, it is one that is worth paying attention to if you hope for success.

11. Find a story that ideally has a "local" or regional focus, but will at the same time appeal to a national or global audience. *The Professor and the Madman*, for example, is essentially centered around the Oxford region of England, with occasional forays to London, where the character Murray was based, and some 30 miles or so from Broadmoor, where the character Minor was imprisoned. Yet, the universal range of the entire book and its ramifications clearly have global relevance.

12. Is yours a major national or international story? If it is either, the large national and global context will almost certainly suggest that a number of seasoned and previously published writers will be already working on it, and unless you have an inside track, or you can shine a unique and illuminating light on the subject, it probably won't be worth your while in pursuing it. Publishers hate to "crash" books—i.e., bring them out quickly. It usually takes a minimum of nine months from delivery and acceptance of the original manuscript at the publisher's offices to landing the printed copies of the book on the shelves of the nation's bookstores. Shorter time frames make everyone's life miserable and don't allow the book an opportunity to build the "buzz" that may help distinguish it from an

otherwise crowded marketplace. Only experienced professional writers are usually contracted to write books that have a particularly timely aspect to them.

· 4 ·

Researching Your Subject

Research is formalized curiosity. It is poking and prying with a purpose. It is a seeking that he who wishes may know the cosmic secrets of the world and that they dwell therein.
— Zora Neale Hurston, novelist, folklorist,
and authority on black culture

I learned several valuable lessons about researching and reporting stories during my early years as a journalist in England in the 1970s: Don't believe anything you read or are told until it is confirmed by at least one other objective source; always CYA—cover your ass: Get time, date, place, confirm correct spellings, get contact telephone numbers, city addresses, etc., in case you have to revisit the document or person you interviewed; and keep careful notes and hang on to them for at least five years after you've used them.

My first job as a journalist was on a weekly newspaper—the *Slough Observer*—in England. It was the nearest thing to perpetual studentship I could find at the time, and besides, I loved the idea of writing for a living. It had taken me a few months to decide what I wanted to do (not economics, that was for sure, which is what I had been studying at university) and when I finally got a job as an apprentice reporter it was late in the year. A typical British winter, cold and damp, was starting to settle in.

My second day on the job, after I had been bawled out for bad spelling in front of the assembled news room staff by the editor-in-chief, the news editor, Bob, took me aside and told me about my predecessor, who had been as inexperienced as I was, who had been asked by the editor-in-chief to confirm the spelling of someone's name in a story the reporter had written. The reporter was not sure, and he did not have a contact telephone number. So the editor had ordered the reporter to get on his bicycle and cycle five miles in the cold rain—he was on deadline, of course, so he had to cycle the five miles back immediately, rather than stopping off at the pub for a quick one—to confirm the spelling with the man in question in order for the newspaper to go to press that week with accurate information.

First Stop: The Library

Like a treasure hunt, research first starts with small steps, often at the library and on the Internet. However, online research can be a quagmire. I'm lucky though, because of a connection to New York University, to have access to the NYU library facilities. I can search for published articles on Lexus-Nexus, Proquest, and other databases, an access capability that has proved extremely useful.

Go to your local library and use its Internet services, in addition to its permanent collection; it's a great first step. Many libraries provide access to these huge Internet databases. (A little trick here: Don't print out the articles and pay for the printed piece. Instead, e-mail each article to yourself for free.) There are many sources and places to find various indexes of information, and most of these are now available on the Web. One of the best websites to visit for leads in researching just about anything is the Library of Congress.

Once I've discovered some source material, I start reading and making notes of questions that occur to me and of thoughts that flitter across my consciousness. To write effective narrative nonfiction you will need to immerse yourself in the world of your subject and in the lives of the characters who live in that world. In this sense, like with all good fiction, narrative nonfiction takes us to strange new worlds, and it introduces us to people we haven't met before. Consider, for example, the world of

Berendt's *Midnight in the Garden of Good and Evil*, set in steamy Savannah and filled with a fascinating assortment of colorful eccentrics that the city seems to nurture; or consider the world of Richard Preston's *The Hot Zone*, a chilling story of an ebola virus outbreak in a suburban Washington, D.C. laboratory.

How to Research: Reading and Talking

Research takes two forms: sifting through documents, and talking to people. It is not an easy thing to learn to do well. It takes practice and diligence, a great deal of thought, and frankly, a certain ethical mindset. Don't just trust the Internet, which is famous for having a great deal of poor source material plastered all over it. Don't accept one version of something as gospel just because it appeals to you. Always make the supreme effort to confirm any piece of information with several independent sources.

Commenting on the elusiveness of research he did on his book, *Into Thin Air,* Jon Krakauer wrote: "At one point during my research I asked three other people to recount an incident all four of us had witnessed high on the mountain, and none of us could agree on such crucial facts as the time, what had been said, or even who had been present."

Journalist Iris Chang, who wrote the bestselling *The Rape of Nanking*, a gripping account of the Japanese atrocities in the Chinese city of Nanking in the 1930s, grew up in the academic community of Champaign-Urbana, Illinois. She explained that she had first heard the story of the Nanking atrocities from her parents:

> "Neither of my parents witnessed it," she said, "but as young children they had heard the stories, and these were passed down to me.... Throughout my childhood Nanjing Datusha remained buried in the back of my mind as a metaphor of unspeakable evil. But the event lacked human detail and human dimensions. It was also difficult to find the line between myth and history. While still in grade school I searched the local public

libraries to see what I could learn about the massacre, but nothing turned up. That struck me as odd.... It did not occur to me, as a child, to pursue my research using the mammoth University of Illinois library system, and my curiosity about the matter soon slipped away."

It took another twenty years before Chang again became caught up in the story, realizing from a new line of research that the story was not just myth, but there existed a thoroughly documented, accurate oral history of the Nanking atrocities, despite Japanese insistence that the holocaust in Nanking never happened. She became determined to bring the truth of the incident to light and her research was remarkable, involving the review of both thousands of pages of documents and many interviews.

Random House executive editor Peter Gethers (who is a published writer as well as an editor) had an interesting point to make about research. "The key to research," he commented, "ultimately, is not what you use but what you don't use." He added that even though "one has to be thorough and accurate... it's necessary to walk the fine line between accuracy and over-detailing."

In *How to Write*, the Pulitzer Prize-winning writer Richard Rhodes makes an interesting point about researching facts.

On the first day of my college course in...the methodology of writing history...Louis P. Curtis, the historian who taught the course, proposed that we prove what every English schoolchild knows, that Charles I, king of England from 1625–1649 was beheaded....

The class reconvened. Everyone had discovered a fact that proved that the English people had beheaded their Scottish king. Mr. Curtis listened patiently to our reports. Then he summarily demolished them. An order for paint doesn't prove a beheading. A conviction of treason and a death sentence doesn't prove a beheading. Not even an eyewitness account proves a beheading. All might be misinformed or mistaken or fraudulent. History, Mr. Curtis shocked us by saying, is past, gone, unrecoverable in its authentic facticity [sic], and the writing of history is necessarily provisional, a matter of sifting the limited evidence and deducing what is probable and plausible and what is not. No accumulation of documents proves anything in and of itself.

Standards of Evidence vs. Proof

In other words, history provides standards of evidence on which responsible people can agree, but there is no final proof. As a trained and experienced journalist, my first reaction on reading Rhodes' account was to dismiss it out of hand. After all, some things are self evident and pretty much scientifically proven: The world is round, the earth travels around the sun, the holocaust happened, and so forth. And yet even now, I reminded myself, in the early twenty-first century there are people busy trying to prove the reverse of all these things. Rhodes' caution (via the instruction of Dr. Curtis, his professor) is well taken when we shift from day-to-day congress to the realm of creating or (more accurately) re-creating on the page events that by their nature are interesting (and commercially viable), because as readers we don't know much about them or the characters involved in them. The truth is, however, whatever the facts do—or do not—prove, one can't write a piece of narrative nonfiction without thoroughly collecting and assembling them. Even in writing convincing historical fiction, for example, it is the veracity of a key fact or two in the narrative, an observation that really nails the scene into its time and place, that leads us to believe in the authenticity of the story, and thus its credibility.

In his essay "Rewriting the Rules of Nonfiction," *New York Times* award-winning reporter and book author Kurt Eichenwald talked about researching his book *The Informant: A True Story*:

When writing such books, every fact—from the weather conditions, to the color of the wallpaper, to the types of meals eaten by the characters—has to come from somewhere. Oftentimes, it requires the reporter to be as dogged in pursuing minutiae as in trying to crack the big secrets of a criminal investigation. In many ways, the reporting of such books is like working on the world's largest jigsaw puzzle. Everything provides a piece—an interview here, a receipt there, a document, a video—and all of these pieces must be brought together into a cohesive narrative, one that doesn't show any of the seams. What that means, of course, is an enormous amount of rewriting. Each new discovery of information must be run through the narrative and accounted for.

Connections?

Scientist Stephen Jay Gould once commented that his chief talent was the ability to see connections between things that to most people seem unrelated. Along the same lines, I wonder if you remember the British science reporter and writer James Burke? He had a successful series of TV shows and several books published called *Connections I, Connections II,* and *Connections III.* You can still catch them in reruns.

Burke always looks for the story in his material, and he focuses not just on one aspect, but on the thread of events and their potential meaning. Using a kind of Six Degrees of Separation game with science and history, he tells a story that is not so much "cause and effect" as it is "change and serendipity," which leads to inventions and discoveries. Burke attempts to demonstrate three phenomena: Seemingly inconsequential events can lead to major innovations, inventions lead to new discoveries, and the technological advancements resulting from these discoveries can have profound effects throughout history on people and society. He created stories, in other words, like Stephen Jay Gould, from material that at first blush did not seem to go together but was based on his expert knowledge and his ability to research strange and unusual things and connect them.

Here's a thumbnail example of how he tells the story of how the search for a navigation device led to the invention of the toilet roll: In 1707, off the southern coast of England, a British Admiral, Sir Cloudisley Shovell, decided to turn right when he should have turned left (the ability to accurately determine longitude was not yet a part of the sailor's toolkit.) As a result, his fleet foundered on the rocks and 2,000 men were lost at sea, including the unfortunate admiral.

The British government decided this longitude thing needed to be taken in hand, and it offered a prize (in today's money, worth several million dollars) for the person who solved the problem. It became a competition between journeymen clockmakers and astronomy scientists.

The problem with using the stars and the heavens to determine longitude is that if the weather if crappy, you can't see them, and it takes years to accumulate data which is then published in an almanac and requires complex math in order to translate the data into an identifiable geographic position. However, using two watches, one showing the time in London and the other showing the local time where the ship is, it's possible to figure out longitude [east to west] relatively easily, and thus determine where you are. The longitude problem was actually solved (and the prize eventually won) by a clockmaker called Harrison. (Harrison is the subject of Dava Sobel's book *Longitude*.) This competition, however, inspired a clockmaker called Huntsman to find a better kind of steel for a spring to put in his watches in order to make the watches keep better time.

The steel Huntsman discovered was also very good at cutting other metal, so an Englishman called Wilkinson used it to bore out very thin cannon barrels. Despite the fact that the British were fighting the Napoleonic and Revolutionary wars at the time, Wilkinson, good capitalist that he was, nevertheless decided to sell the new cannon to both the French and the Americans!

Napoleon, now equipped with the latest high-tech weaponry (a light accurate cannon) invented a new army division called horse artillery, which allowed his troops to maneuver these new lightweight armor pieces to great advantage by carting them around the battlefield on the backs of horses. This allowed his armies the freedom to move further, faster. Both horses and men needed to be provisioned, however.

Thus, in 1810, Napoleon set up a prize which was won by a French winemaker called Nicolas Appert, who discovered that you can pack and preserve food by boiling it and putting it in a corked champagne bottle. This discovery allowed the emperor's well-fed army to travel longer and farther afield. Napoleon used his technological advantage to win lots of battles and conquer Europe until he lost his last and most important battle at Waterloo in 1815.

Several years later, a British company was preserving food in cans because they had bought Appert's patent, which they obtained, serendipitously, because they were actually in France to buy something completely different—the patent to the first continuous paper making process, which in turn brought about the invention of the first toilet roll.

So, applying the reasoning of Gould and Burke, one could say that the invention of the toilet roll was the direct result of having to solve a complex (and bowel loosening) navigation problem.

Who Knew? Who Cares?

A good researcher combines the skills of a reference librarian and a police detective. The first step in conducting any kind of research is to think through the project and try to plan some general lines of approach. In researching history or biography or a current event, for example, it's a good idea to ask two questions:

- Who would know about this?

- Who would care enough about this to help put it in print?

When my client Judy Pearson started research on a biography of Virginia Hall, America's most famous female undercover agent of World War II in France, she was amazed to discover no one had ever written a book about Hall. Judy uncovered a fascinating story that, in brief, took a Baltimore socialite with a wooden leg, who worked in Europe for the U.S. State Department during the 1930s, to London, from where she was air-dropped into France as an operative of the SOE (the British equivalent of the OSS), and then escaped back to London after she became the number one target of the Nazi Gestapo who had orders to kill her on sight, before finally returning to France as a disguised undercover operative for the OSS (later to become the CIA) to help prepare for the D Day landings behind the German lines.

Judy first got in touch with Hall's niece, who was prepared to help with the book and who possessed previously unpublished material she would give Judy. The author also got an unprecedented commitment from the head librarian of the CIA museum to become the first civilian allowed access to recently declassified wartime OSS papers. She also planned to go to London, France, and Germany in order to find documentation about Hall from the SOE, the French Resistance which Hall helped set up, and Gestapo files. With this kind of travel involved in researching the book it was imperative, not to say financially very important, to think through where she was going, why, and what she hoped to look for when she got there.

The Five Basic Resources for Research

There are five basic resources for research:

- Published books ;

- Unpublished manuscripts and letters, etc.;

- Limited edition documents, such as reports by organizations, newsletters, restricted memos, court documents, and so forth;

- Magazines and newspapers, etc.;

- Interviews.

The Four Basic Ways to Carry Out Research

There are four basic ways to conduct research:

- Reading and viewing source material (e.g., books, papers, films, pictures, etc.). Biographers, historians, and investigative journalists do it all the time;

- Interviewing people face to face, or by letter or e-mail. I did it for this book, Richard Preston did it for *The Hot Zone,* Mark Bowden did it for *Black Hawk Down,* and Sebastian Junger did it for *The Perfect Storm*, to mention but a handful;

- First-hand observation. A great example of this is D. Graham Burnett's "memoir" of jury duty on a murder trial in Manhattan, *A Trial By Jury*;

- Deductive reasoning, which connects the dots drawn by the other three methods. This last is the method most fraught with danger because it does not involve something empirically tangible, but instead involves supposition, which can land an unsuspecting writer in a lot of trouble if he or she isn't careful.

One of the most interesting examples of this last kind of research informing a book is Sebastian Junger's *The Perfect Storm.* This is how he describes tackling the problem:

> Recreating the last days of six men who disappeared at sea presented some obvious problems for me. On the one hand, I wanted to write a completely factual book that would stand on its own as a piece of

journalism. On the other hand, I didn't want the narrative to asphyxiate under a mass of technical detail and conjecture....

In the end I wound up sticking strictly to the facts, but in as wide-ranging a way as possible. If I didn't know exactly what happened aboard the doomed boat, for example, I would interview people who had been through similar situations, and survived. Their experiences, I felt, would provide a fairly good description of what the six men in the *Andrea Gail* had gone through, and said, and perhaps even felt.

A classic example of Junger's use of this technique is a chapter toward the end of the book titled "The Zero-Moment Point." It is the point where the boat sinks and the crew drowns. The whole chapter is based on the experiences of people who almost drowned, and the science of what happens to a boat when it sinks and to a human being's body when it drowns. Given that it is pure conjecture, it is conjecture rooted in hard fact, and it does not pretend to be anything other than a way of trying to understand what happened to the crew of the *Andrea Gail* at the moment of its demise. I'm a little uncomfortable holding up this kind of "substitute" research and writing style as a paragon of "how to" deal with such narrative problems, but there is no doubt that Junger's experience and integrity as a reporter make all the difference in carrying off this kind of storytelling in the book.

At a panel discussion on writing nonfiction at the National Press Club in Washington in May 2002, journalist and author Jim Srodes talked about writing and researching biographies: "My message is context, context, context. You have to build a time line, and you have to be able to...say with some authority who these people are, and what they knew, and more importantly what they didn't know. What other people knew and what they didn't know, and what was going on [at the time]....

"You [also] have to discipline yourself to grab context where you can and make it work for you while you're following the time line of your subject's life...."

As an example, he mentioned writing the biography of Allen Dulles, one of the founders of the CIA: "Writing [the Allen Dulles biography] was largely the story of how we came to get the intelligence services we have today, [presented] against the life of this rather extraordinary man."

What is important to be wary of are those blind alleys of information that beckon seductively away from the main trail of the story you are trying to tell. If you're not careful, before you know it, you have stopped writing about the life of say, Thomas Jefferson, and instead you are writing about the War of Jenkins' Ear.

How to Take Notes

A skill worth developing when plumbing the depths of material is a good note taking technique. Most reporters are never taught this skill: they just learn through trial and error and through the fear of screwing up on deadline. When I worked on a daily newspaper with a midday deadline for stories for first edition, I often had to jot down an opening paragraph in my notebook, phone in the story and dictate it to a typist by reading the written lead paragraph from my notebook, and then creating the rest of the story extemporaneously from my notes. You shouldn't have to write a book that way, but writing newspaper articles on the fly certainly taught me the value of keeping good notes.

The following are some tips on note taking:

- When you tape record an interview, always obtain the permission of the person you're interviewing before you begin to tape. Some people don't mind, but others can be intimidated by the idea. In some states it's actually illegal to tape someone, even over the phone, without their express permission. ("Do you mind if I record this so I get what you say accurate?" is always a good approach.) Always carry a fresh supply of batteries with you, and from time to time actually check to see if the machine is recording. If you're using a tape recorder, for example, look carefully to see if the tape wheels are turning.

- Think about converting your interviews from tape (or mini discman) into wave files on your computer. Then, using a wave editing program, you can cut and splice the interview and bookmark and move to any point in the recording pretty rapidly. It may take a couple of days to get comfortable with the program but it's worth it if you have extensive, taped interviews. And, they won't deteriorate with time and are easily stored by burning them onto CDs.

- If at all possible, get photocopies of original material you may need to refer to when writing your story. If not, then at least be thorough and record enough information so that you can make sense of what you wrote when you return to your notes in a few months' time. Don't make your notes so cryptic you have no clue what the note is exactly about, or where it came from.

- If possible, take notes in spiral-bound notepads no larger than the size and thickness of the average mass market paperback (approximately, 5" x 7"). According to journalist and author Richard Rhodes, this is what author Tracy Kidder told him was his preferred method. "Don't try to tape record," Kidder said, "People freeze up, and besides it'd take years to transcribe all that tape. I just buy a stack of pocket-size spiral notebooks and make notes whenever I can."

- If you do use paper, make sure you use only one side. There's nothing worse than forgetting to turn over the page (we've all done it, trust me) and inadvertently throwing away something you need because it's on the back of something you don't need.

- Write down full notes on the sources of your information, partly so you can find those sources again and check their accuracy if you need to, and partly so that you can establish its veracity if challenged.

- Use a laptop computer if you can, so that you don't have to worry about not being able to read your handwriting.

- Work to a system. I recommend using a system that relates to the project you're researching rather than say the sources of the information you've found. (Don't categorize all information from the Baltimore Public Library as "Baltimore" and all information from the CIA Museum as "Museum," but instead by "Hall's life prior to 1939," and "Hall's work for the OSS," for example.)

- Truman Capote claimed that he had trained himself to remember as much as a four-hour interview verbatim. Personally, without aids I can't remember 10 minutes these days, and I suspect most people are nearer to my side of the spectrum than Capote's. However, the acclaimed journalist David Halberstam (*The Best and the Brightest*) was reported to have said that when interviewing people who don't want to be recorded in any way, he often used his memory, and then transcribed notes soon after the interview.

Interviewing

As a young reporter, I used to hate to interview the relatives of people who had died traumatic deaths, particularly immediately after the event. It made me feel like a vulture. The kid was hit by a truck; she drowned while swimming in the local swimming pool; his airplane crashed; her car was smashed in a 10-car pile up on a highway in the fog; he was mugged and killed for $5 on the mean streets of Bedford Stuyvesant in New York City . . . . What could the survivors, in the midst of their grief and mourning, add to the facts of the story? Why would they even want to talk with me in the first place?

The funny thing is, nearly all the relatives of these recently deceased people wanted to talk to me, and the stories and details they gave me always enriched and humanized the story. What's more, it showed me that my initial fear (or panic when on a deadline, because of my somewhat tyrannical editor-in-chief) that sources would not talk to me was wrong. In fact, for the most part, people *want* to talk about their deceased loved ones, about themselves, and about their own experiences. It's a natural human instinct, and when someone believes that what they have to say is not being judged or treated with scorn or contempt, it's sometimes hard to shut them up. What turns out to be much harder than getting someone to start talking is keeping them focused on topic.

The fear that people don't want to be interviewed by a reporter and will spurn the reporter entirely is an understandable qualm from the reporter's perspective, but it's an indulgence that most professional journalists can't afford because they have to answer to editors who need the story. If someone says "Go away," so what? If they hang up on you, call again, just persist in getting the information some other way.

Bob, my first news editor, told me a story about his experience with what used to be called in England the "foot-in-the-door" technique of journalism, a technique that helped keep much of my later career as a writer in perspective. Bob was a short, thin man in his 40s at the time I knew him, a man who sometimes liked to smoke a pipe while he edited. He had an easy laugh and great sense of humor and was one of the most mild-mannered people I ever worked for. He was a terrific journalist who could smell a good story the moment he saw it, and he also knew when he was being bullshitted. He went out of his way to make life comfortable for those who worked for him, while not compromising on standards in any way.

Early in Bob's career, working for a British Sunday tabloid newspaper not unlike the *National Enquirer*, he was given the job of interviewing a woman who was one of the wives of a convicted bigamist awaiting court sentence. He spent all day camped out in his cramped Volkswagon Beetle, parked on a suburban street of semi-detached houses and small postage-stamp gardens guarded in a number of instances by plastic garden gnomes, some few doors away from the woman's house. Many of the people in the street regularly read Bob's newspaper on Sundays.

Bob saw the subject arrive home late in the morning, carrying shopping bags, and he immediately went to her front door and rang the bell. When she answered the door, he said, "Hi, I'm Bob from So-and-So newspaper and I'd like to interview you about . . ." This was as far as he got. She said, "I don't want to talk to you, and my old man works nights and is upstairs trying to sleep. If you wake him up he'll come down here and beat the shit out of you. You've been warned." With that she slammed the door closed—almost.

Taking the concept of "foot-in-the-door" journalism a little too literally, Bob put his foot between the door and the door jamb, thinking that when the door bounced off his foot he would get a few more precious moments to press his case as to why she should talk to him. Unfortunately, the door latched shut with his foot still caught in it. Now he was stuck, and his foot was starting to hurt.

He rang the bell. She ignored him. He rang the bell again, and again, and again. Eventually, a large and very unhappy truck driver jerked open the door and said, "Oi! She told you to piss off." As Bob limped quickly away, he was chased by the truck driver. In fact, Bob did not have time to get out his car keys and had to run—or rather quickly hobble—down the street for some ways before he was able to hide behind a bush for what seemed like ages while the truck driver stood in the doorway of his house, hands on hips, glowering and surveying the street, keeping an eye out for Bob's return. Eventually, he went inside and Bob was able to sneak over to his car and make his getaway.

What happens to you if your persistence to obtain an interview is turned down by a potential interviewee is not likely to be worse than what happened to Bob, and take relief in the fact that Bob survived and went on to have a good career as a journalist after that incident.

Don't assume that people won't talk to you, or don't want to. A musician acquaintance of mine regularly toured with Miles Davis many years ago when Miles worked a lot in Europe. One night he sat in with me and some friends as we played a jazz gig and we all had a ball, of course. Afterwards, Gordon explained that he played very little in England because everyone assumed he worked all the time as a result of his connection to Miles and thus no one ever bothered to call him and ask him to do gigs, which he would have been perfectly happy to do if he were available.

One of the remarkable things about the previously mentioned book, *Cinderella and Company,* is that all the people interviewed for the book already knew Hoelterhoff's reputation for being an acerbic writer, but they were nevertheless happy to talk freely with her. Of course, she was well aware of the plethora of arrogance that is rampant in opera and used it to her advantage. The truth was, her subjects didn't care what she thought or said about them as long as they were portrayed as major players in the book. This is particularly true of the powerful agent Herbert Breslin, whom Hoelterhoff admits that she so hated that she used to go through the *New York Times* obituary pages looking for his, "a little squib tucked under the fold, somewhere beneath retired postmasters and minor-league ballplayers from the 1950s." She describes Breslin as a "motor-mouthed, bullet-headed, forever tan egomaniac," and his monologue (obtained in an interview with Hoelterhoff) on how he got his main client, Luciano Pavarotti, to show everyone how real money could be made in opera is breathtaking in its overt shamelessness.

Two things are important when interviewing someone: Be as prepared as possible before you start the interview, even to the extent of writing down some questions if you need to; and try to be a sort of fly on the wall while you're conducting the interview. The notion of going into an interview to get someone to confess, or otherwise "spill the beans," is frankly foolish for the most part. People are far more likely to "confess" in an attempt to explain themselves. The truth is, most people want others to like them and will provide all sorts of information to someone they don't find threatening or judgmental.

But you have to be willing to listen without comment or contradiction or argument, at least at first. Let people hang themselves with their own words. Encourage them to speak, and don't insert yourself into the interview if you can help it, just prod the interview along. Towards the end of the interview, you can always say something like, "I'm a bit confused." Then, referring to your notes (I recommend that you take notes even if you are recording your interview using a tape recorder or mini discman for the sake of accuracy) ask: "I thought you said earlier 'blah-blah.' That seems to contradict 'yada-yada.' Help me out here." Then sit back and record the response.

Robert Conot, the author of *Rivers of Blood, Years of Darkness,* a book about the 1965 Los Angeles riot, decided he was going to compile "a complete historical account" of the event. To that end he spent from August 1965 to May 1966 gathering material that filled "an entire filing cabinet."

Conot remarked, "This represented, in addition to information culled from documents compiled by various agencies, interviews and discussions of varying length with nearly 1,000 persons, and the written accounts of occurrences, as well as personal opinions, of some 500 more."

Conot added, "[I] became familiar with the south-central area a considerable period of time before the riot, and, by exercising prudence, was able to move about the area even while the riot was still in progress, thus observing some of the happenings firsthand."

Conot's vast array of sources included the Los Angeles County District Attorney's office, the California National Guard, the California Attorney General's office, the Los Angeles Fire Department, the Los Angeles Police Department, the Los Angeles County Probation Department, the Bureau of Public Assistance, the California Fair Employment Practices Commission, the complete transcript of the McCone Commission hearings on the riot, the records of some 200 felony trials, the Los Angeles County Human Relations Commission, the Bureau of Public Assistance, plus hundreds of interviews.

How Accurate Is the Recollection?

The passage of time is an important element of storytelling, although it needs to be true to its period. When interviewed, people tend to "edit" themselves, aligning their memories more with the tenor of the time they are being interviewed in, rather than trying to re-create exactly what they thought at the time they are now recollecting. This can lead to anachronistic storytelling that seems to read well now, but is untrue for the period actually being reconstructed. We are more enlightened now, it can be argued, but that is no reason that "good guys" of yesteryear can't be portrayed as displaying opinions and traits we would find objectionable now. At its extreme, biographers of historical figures, such as Jefferson and Lincoln, struggle with this issue a lot.

One of the most potent tools at your disposal as an interviewer is silence. Don't rush to fill in a silence in the interview (unless it's a radio or TV interview you're conducting, of course). Just wait without talking. The strain of the silence almost always prompts the interview subject to fill it in some way.

For some people, the aggressive approach works, but it has a limited success in my experience, and most of the journalists who use it regularly are, frankly, assholes. In a Craig Seligman there may be room for such an interview technique, but an aggressive approach is not usually effective in many other places. Still, if aggression is your style, I guess you must go with it, particularly if it affords results. I would also avoid overt flattery unless you really mean it. Most people can smell insincerity a mile off and that's likely to shut down any meaningful interview early on because your subject will feel contempt for you.

I've found that if you treat people with respect they will respond much better to you and give you what you want or help you get it most of the time. Most interviews are done "on the record," that is, the source is willing to be identified and quoted directly.

When dealing with institutions, you sometimes have to resort to "attribution." That is, you may have to use expressions like, "a White House spokeswoman said," or "an executive from Enron, who refused to be named, explained that," and so forth.

Lastly, there is "off the record," which is essentially someone who will give you leads and background information, but who cannot be quoted directly in the construction of your story. However, that doesn't mean you can't use that nameless person's information to pry a response or confirmation out of someone else who will be on the record.

What do you do when someone refuses to talk? Here's an interesting phenomena: when telemarketers call on the phone or solicitors knock on the door, even when we don't want to do business with them, most of us take time to explain that we are not interested. The telemarketer argues back, "But just give me a minute . . ." and before we know it, because we have maintained the relationship in some manner, we have provided the opportunity for the salesman to hook us. The only way to avoid the situation is to politely but firmly say, "No, thank you, I'm not interested" and then close the door or hang up the phone, severing any further connection.

If your interviewee stays with you, even if they have so far refused to answer a question or cooperate, then the door is still open. Threats rarely work and are unnecessarily antagonistic, as I've discussed. Outright lying is not something worth attempting because you usually get caught, and it will make interviewing others harder as your reputation for dishonesty proceeds you. Shading the truth is acceptable, however. Woody

Allen once gave a wonderful description of how he won a fight by using his chin to smash his opponent's fist, quickly following that with a crushing blow from his groin to his opponent's knee. It's all in the perspective.

What my editor, Bob, taught me to say was something like this: "Look, we're going to write this story about you whether or not you give me an interview. I've already got two people [or however many there are] who claim such-and-such, but frankly that doesn't quite make sense to me. It's really in your interest to talk with me because we really want to do a fair and accurate piece, and we need to hear your side of what happened."

Listen Quietly, but Be Tenacious

John McPhee is possibly today's most successful and well respected writer of narrative nonfiction. He has been doing it since 1964 and has garnered a multitude of awards and nominations, including two National Book Award nominations. In the *John McPhee Reader*, editor William Howarth describes why McPhee is so successful at his job. McPhee, he explains, is a person who "inspires confidence, since people rarely find someone who listens that carefully to them. . . He cultivates a certain transparency in social relations, a habit derived from practicing his craft. To see and hear clearly, he keeps his eyes open and mouth shut."

In writing *Black Hawk Down,* Mark Bowden explained that he had been fascinated by the battle in Mogadishu, but as he had "no military background or sources, [I] assumed that someone with both would tell the story far better than I could."

Sometime later Bowden read that at a Medal of Honor ceremony for two of the Delta Force soldiers killed at Mogadishu, the father of one of the men had insulted President Clinton, telling him he was not fit to be commander in chief. After a meeting with the father of another dead soldier who knew little of what had happened, Bowden made up his mind to learn more.

Some three years after the actual event, Bowden made requests to the Pentagon media office which were ignored. He then filed a Freedom of Information request for documents which still hadn't arrived two years later. "I was told that the men I wanted to interview were in units off-limits to the press. My only hope of finding the foot soldiers I wanted [to interview] was to ask for them by name, and I knew only a handful of names. I combed through what little had been written about the battle and submitted the names I found there, but I did not receive a response."

At such a dead-end point what was a good reporter to do? As in all good stories about reporters, persistence paid off in an unexpected way. Bowden received an invitation from the father of one of the dead soldiers to the dedication of a building at the Pixatinny Arsenal that was to be made in memory of his son. The trip would take Bowden a day of traveling, and given his lack of success up to that point, the story had become less important. "Still," he said, "I had been moved by my conversation with Jim. I have sons just a few years younger than his Jamie. I couldn't imagine losing one of them, much less in a gunfight at someplace like Mogadishu. I made the drive.

"And there, at this dedication ceremony, were about a dozen Rangers who had fought with Jamie in Mogadishu. Jim's introduction helped break down the normal suspicion soldiers have for reporters. The men gave me their names and told me how to arrange interviews with them. During three days at Fort Benning that fall, I conducted my first twelve interviews. Each of the men I talked to had names and phone numbers for others who had fought there that day, many of them no longer in the Army. My network grew from there."

Bowden visited Somalia and obtained the Somali side of the battle. He discovered the battle had been videotaped and he was able listen to radio traffic from which he transcribed actual dialogue, and he was eventually able to watch the 15 hours of Army video of the battle. Along with documentary material he recovered, the material "gave me, I believe, the best chance any writer has ever had to tell the story of a battle completely, accurately, and well."

One of the best descriptions of a self-effacing interview technique can be found in the *John McPhee Reader*: "When McPhee conducts an interview," editor William Howarth says, "he tries to be as blank as his notebook pages, totally devoid of preconceptions, equipped with only the most elementary knowledge. He has found that imagining he knows a subject is a disadvantage, for that prejudice will limit his freedom to ask, to learn, to be surprised by unfolding evidence. Since most stories are full of unsuspected complexity, an interviewer hardly needs to feign ignorance; the stronger temptation is to bluff with a show of knowledge or to trick the informant into providing simple, easily digestible answers. . . [McPhee] would rather risk seeming ignorant to get a solid, knotty answer."

As a result, some of his interviewees have mistakenly believed he is thick-witted. At times his speech slows, his brow knits, he asks the same question over and over. When repeating answers, he so garbles them that a new answer must be provided. Some informants find his manner relaxing, others are exasperated; in either case, they talk more freely and fully to him than they normally would to a reporter. While McPhee insists that his air of density is not a deliberate ruse, he does not deny its useful results. Informants may be timid or hostile, unless they feel superior or equal to their interviewer. By repeating and even fumbling their answers, McPhee encourages people to embroider a topic until he has it entire. In an ideal interview he listens without interrupting, at liberty to take notes without framing repartee or otherwise entering the conversation.

What better example of the art of research than that?

Order Out of Chaos: Building the Skeleton of the Book

Obviously, where art has it over life is in the matter of editing.
Life can be seen to suffer from a drastic lack of editing.
It stops too quick, or else it goes on too long. Worse, its pacing
is erratic. Some chapters are little more than a few sentences
in length, while others stretch into volumes. Life, for all its
raw talent, has little sense of structure. It creates amazing
textures, but it can't be counted on for snappy beginnings or
good endings either. Indeed, in many cases no ending is
provided at all....Even in a literary age like the nineteenth
century it never occurred to anyone to posit God as Editor,
useful as the metaphor might have been.
　　—Larry McMurtry

Originally, this chapter was going to be about writing a book proposal, so it may seem a little out of sequence, if not premature, to start discussing the structure of your narrative nonfiction book before covering how to create a proposal for it. After all, nearly all nonfiction is sold in proposal form first and then written from the outline included with the book proposal. Except, of course, that as more research is done, and the writer gains more knowledge of his subject, the book often begins to deviate from the proposal in detail, if not in broad outline.

And that's the point here: A proposal is a separate entity from the finished manuscript and explaining how to create one doesn't really fit into a sequence of chapters concerned with the techniques of writing a book. Placing a chapter on proposal writing here could be seen as interrupting a logical structural flow.

Aha! A comment about the structure of this book, as an example of structuring books in general. How cunning. The chapter on writing a proposal could fit anywhere, theoretically, but my editor and I agreed that actually it should be at the end of the book so as not to interrupt the flow of chapters dealing with how to write a book of narrative nonfiction, rather than how to *sell and market* one.

Art Must Have Its Own Logic

"Let's get the rules straight first," Butch Cassidy says to the gang member who challenges him to a knife fight in William Goldman's movie *Butch Cassidy and the Sundance Kid*. "Huh?" says the gang member. "There are no rules to a knife fight." "OK," says Butch, and delivers what Goldman describes in his screenplay as "the biggest kick in the balls ever seen in the history of motion pictures."

Similarly, there are no "rules" in writing. Do what works for you—and your readers. Here's a clue to whether or not you're right: Are you getting published? If you're not getting published in some form, then you're not the best judge of your own material. I'd go further and venture to say that if you're reading this, clearly you lack at least the confidence, if not the expertise, to carry off extravagant storytelling and you are looking for some guidance about this book writing business. Don't confuse what follows as "rules"; they're not. What follows are analytical tools that will help shape and tame your creative endeavors if you're having trouble getting them down on the page.

It's a universal law, like gravity, that all art must abide by its own internal logic—a natural structure inherent to the piece of art you're creating, be it overtly pastoral, or be it *avant garde* in the extreme. Without a coherent internal structure that creates and follows its own rules—which may not be at all obvious sometimes—there is no creativity, only random chaos.

Second Thoughts?

So, having come up with a book idea and having completed some initial research around it, you should pause for a moment and consider if you want to live with your subject for a year or more.

If you have the right book idea, the problem of living with your project for an extended period of time won't really be an issue, because you'll be excited by each revelation you uncover. However, it's worth remembering that the historian David McCullough (author of the bestselling biography *John Adams*) once contracted with Simon & Schuster to write a biography of the artist Pablo Picasso. The more he researched Picasso, however, the more McCullough decided he didn't want to spend time with the artist. Luckily, he had a better idea: a biography of Harry S. Truman, and he managed to convince his publisher to let him write that book instead. (Thus, are the origins of some great books.)

Another bad reason to write a narrative book is to capitalize on its timely "news" value. With a potential eighteen-month lag between signing up a book with an editor to seeing it arrive on a bookstore's shelves, the "breaking" news value of any book is going to be dubious at best.

And, of course, you want to tell the story, but don't leave it there. What does this story mean to the rest of us? How does the story somehow become *more?* How does it take on a symbolic or universal quality, despite cleaving to the specifics of its details?

Although the book *Into Thin Air* is certainly "about" the disaster on Mt. Everest, it is actually "about" much more; for instance, it is also about the challenges of mountaineering and why people are attracted to the sport. In 1953, Sir Edmund Hillary became the first man to reach the summit of Mt. Everest, following nearly 100 or more years of people dying in the attempt. Then, by 1996, there were "traffic jams" of people paying upwards of $70,000 each to be "tour-guided" to the top. Krakauer set out to explore the "why" of this phenomenon. "The notion that climbers are mere adrenalin junkies chasing a righteous fix is a fallacy, at least in the case of Everest," he wrote. "What I was doing up there had almost nothing in common with bungee jumping or skydiving or riding a motorcycle at 120 miles per hour. . . . I quickly came to understand that climbing Everest was primarily about enduring pain. And in subjecting ourselves to week after week of toil, tedium, and suffering, it struck me that most of us were probably seeking, above all else, something like a state of grace."

The best reason to write about a given subject in story form is so that the reader can reflect on the true meaning of the event, and/or so that the reader can reflect on how the event was perceived at the time, particularly by those who were involved in it.

The Man in the Bar...

One of the most convenient ways to start ordering your thoughts and material is to practice what can be called the "man in the bar" technique. In other words, tell the story as if you were telling it to an involved audience over a drink. This is an interesting experience that happens to me at dinner parties with friends, who make the foolish mistake of asking me what I'm working on at the moment. To a writer absorbed in a new project that's an invitation to bore people to death, so I always hesitate in order to judge whether the questioner is serious in his or her interest. Many writers might disagree with this, but I figure if I can't hold this audience's interest when recounting the essence of what fascinates me about this subject, that's a definite clue there's something adrift somewhere.

Many writers don't like to talk about works in progress, and the reasons are myriad. Certainly, if I get into too much detail, I'm always terrified I'm going to bore people to death with the crude fumblings of my effort-of-the-moment, and I fear I may actually manage to convince myself at the same time that I must be mad in continuing to work on something that no one wants to hear about.

However, I have learned that telling the heart of the story becomes an interesting and valuable task when someone genuinely wants to know what I'm working on. Obviously working from memory, and with a determination to make the story as "sexy" as possible, I lay out the bare outline of the story and explain why it fascinates me. If you can't do that, if you don't have a grasp of the elemental story you're trying to tell, you're going to have real problems writing it. As I tell the story, I find a natural structure starts to emerge. This is an extension of the first piece of advice I was ever given on how to write a news story (by Bob, my wonderful news editor mentor on the *Slough Observer*): "Write the piece as if you were writing a letter home to your mother. Start with the most interesting aspect: 'Dear, Mum, guess what happened to me today? I met a man who blah blah blah.'"

Find Your Audience

A writer is no less a performer than a singer or actor, and like an actor or singer, a writer should try to take into consideration how his audience is going to react to his work. This is not pandering or compromising your "art," but honing your material so it actually says what you *mean* it to say and will appeal to harried but interested recipients. As you assemble your material and start to construct the book, ask yourself: Who's going to read this book? Why? How can I make the book compelling to this audience?

Narrative nonfiction should do more than just tell a story that has probably been recounted already in a newspaper or magazine. People are much more likely to read short pieces in magazines about things that they might not want to buy books about. For example, why pay $25 for a book that basically says you're screwed, unless it also suggests ways you can get un-screwed? You can frighten people (consider *Silent Spring,* Rachel Carson's classic, or Richard Preston's *The Hot Zone*), but it's hard to sell a book that tells a story that leaves the reader no hope, no optimism, nor anything profound to think about. Regardless of any publicity you get from your name, it should be obvious that the content of your book is the major factor in its commercial viability.

Take the case of *Creating a Life: Professional Women and the Quest for Children* by Sylvia Ann Hewlett. The book discussed the growing fear among middle-class and professional women (and provided statistics to prove its point) that women who sacrifice families for careers may well wake up childless at the age of forty-five. Great things were expected of the book and its author. The publisher, Miramax Books, paid the author a six-figure advance and printed 30,000 hardcover copies. In its first two months, the book generated the kind of publicity authors dream about. It was featured on the TV show *60 Minutes* and on the covers of *Time* and *New York* magazines. It was promoted on *Oprah*, *Today*, *Good Morning America* and NBC *Nightly News*. It was debated on the editorial and op-ed pages of the *Los Angeles Times*, the *San Francisco Chronicle* and the *New York Times*. But after two months, in the spring of 2002, the most talked-about book in America (and in the United Kingdom, as well) had sold somewhere in the region of 8,000 copies—a poor performance under the circumstances. Why did things go so wrong?

The explanation seems simple: Women were just not interested in shelling out $22 for a book that front-loaded depressing news about their biological clocks and that offered only a couple of cursory final chapters (which they probably never got to) on what they could do about the situation.

Jonathan Burnham, the editor in chief of Miramax books was quoted in the *New York Times* as saying, "What people [came] away with [was] the frightening data. They [were] taking in the bad news and not paying attention to the prescriptive elements."

Ironically, many experts also felt the tsunami of media coverage actually dampened readers' interest. "The woman who feels devastated that her life didn't work out doesn't want to read about it," Roxanne Coady, the owner of R. J. Julia Booksellers in Madison, Conn., was quoted as saying in the *Times,* "The woman who gets it as a cautionary tale [can] get what they need from the press." And there's the rub. Who needed to read a book that made them feel bad when, instead, they could get what they needed to know from the press coverage of the book itself or the subject, in general?

A Good Title

A title and subtitle are important elements of a book. A good title and subtitle will help focus your book, and without such a lens attached to your creativity you will struggle to decide what should be in the book and what ultimately does not fit. Each time you're unsure of how to apply information, or interpret it, it's useful to think to yourself: What's the title of what I'm writing?

Your Spine—The Table of Contents

A couple of tricks that may help involve using colored 3" x 5" or 5" x 7" index cards. Each group of colored cards represents a chapter (e.g., pink for chapter 1, blue for chapter 2, green for chapter 3, etc. You can reuse colors after a while.) Once you've constructed this colored card system, you can shuffle the chapters around and find the best structure for the material.

Gather your index cards and your notes, and lay them out on the floor before you. Start moving them into some sort of order, both chronological and in terms of sequences of action. Have you conducted all the research you need to do? Are there holes in the time line? Are there parts of the action you can't re-create or track? Can you show the events of your story in enough detail? What have you uncovered that no longer seems to be relevant to the story you're telling? Can this material be discarded?

Assemble the information into a rough table of contents (or TOC). This is essentially your "spine," and it should be comprise of chapter headings, with perhaps a line or two about what will be in the chapter in question. Allow yourself the luxury of writing pretty freely, jotting down anecdotes, stories, facts, etc. that you can gather under each of these chapter headings. If you can't fit new material into the existing TOC, either create a new heading, or put the new material under a miscellaneous heading to be inserted later (maybe). Start accepting that some of the information, even the more interesting or entertaining aspects of what you've discovered thus far, may have to be left out of the book because it simply doesn't fit.

Structure Is Organic—Trust Your Instincts

Do you remember that scene in the very first *Star Wars* movie when Luke has to make a nearly impossible shot as he battles the Death Star? He hears Obi Wan's voice tell him to "Use the force," and he calms himself and listens to his instincts, which guide him in delivering the *coup de grace* to the Death Star. The point? Sometimes, it's best not to force things, to just relax and, like Luke, gather your material around you, reorder and reshuffle it as you would a bunch of Scrabble tiles as you look to form words, and let the natural structure of a story emerge in an organic way from the way the material all fits together naturally. This, leads to that, and that leads to the other.

How will you know if your structure is solid? It will be the structure that comfortably lets most of the facts and information you've gathered neatly slot itself into place. This may sound simple, but it shouldn't automatically be assumed that it's easy. If the structure of the narrative (that is, the story) isn't right, then people won't understand the importance of what you're writing or grasp the importance of the facts you've assembled.

The structure of the narrative is what's going to get people to the facts, and a reader isn't going to get to the facts without the story. For many writers the story seems to come naturally as they gather their material and try to mentally synthesize it for themselves. It all depends on what it is you're writing about, who the characters are, and what they've done.

At a roundtable discussion on narrative nonfiction, sponsored by the English Department of the University of Pittsburgh, Brendan Cahill, at the time a senior editor at Grove Atlantic Press, commented that "there's definitely a concern that the story and the truth is what's being served...I think what creative [i.e., narrative] nonfiction allows you to do is to create an arc of storytelling to allow the facts and people's thoughts and emotions to all have a coherence to the interpretive framework that the writer uses to recap and then tell or relate it to the reader."

Structure is a reassuring thing. It's what helps the reader trust the narrative voice, but most of the time readers are not, and probably should not be, aware of the artifice of a structured story. A book that obviously plays with this convention is Dave Eggers' *A Heartbreaking Work of Staggering Genius,* as well as some of the books of Tom Wolfe and Hunter S. Thompson. In such cases, style is as important as content but the writer has to establish somehow (through published articles mainly) that he or she is a recognized stylist. This kind of writing became known as gonzo reporting (i.e., idiosyncratically subjective) and it slowly morphed into memoir. It's a tough choice to emulate as a role model. Like Henry Miller, one of the original gonzo writers of the twentieth century, such authors write the only way they know how to because it's an extension of who they are and not merely self-conscious artifice designed to attract attention, but not illuminate.

The Two Kinds of Structure in a Narrative

A narrative has two distinct kinds of structure: *what* it is and *how* it's put together. *What* your narrative is begins with your outline. It includes what sets your story in motion, i.e., the instigating event; the goal your protagonist is ultimately striving for; the conflict he or she faces, and the opposition the protagonist must overcome to achieve that goal; how the protagonist overcomes this obstacle to achieve his or her goal; and what it costs the protagonist to succeed, the stakes, in other words.

How a narrative is put together is concerned with the kinds of drama you create for your scenes, the action that you put in them, the kind of language you choose to use, the tone of the piece, and so on. Without these two structural elements—the what and the how—working together in deliberate harmony, your narrative will not have an enabling structure.

You need to figure out the "bookends" of your story—when it starts and ends—so that you get a sense of the time frame you're writing about: a week, 24 hours, two years, etc. *The Perfect Storm*, for example, is ostensibly about three days or so in late October 1991, yet it ranges far and wide from those days, reaching back as far as 1850 at one point. The passage of time is hazy in the book. *Black Hawk Down,* on the other hand, tracks from midday Oct 3, 1993 to 5:45 A.M. October 4, although the major action of the story is followed with epilogues about people in the States, and the release of the captured pilot Durant, which took a few days longer. The passage of time is generally very explicit and helps the storytelling immensely.

Robert Conot described organizing *Rivers of Blood, Years of Darkness,* his book on the 1965 L.A. riots:

> In order to coordinate and cross-reference material from the many diverse sources with the actions that occurred during the riot—in some cases [I] discovered . . . files [that] contained a half dozen or more descriptions of what proved to be a single incident—[and I] began an hour-by-hour plotting of the riot. This graph, [originally] two feet long, ultimately grew to twenty-five feet in length. Among other things, it enabled [me] to discover an apparent witness to one of the riot deaths recorded by the district attorney's office as a homicide by person or persons unknown....
>
> With one or two exceptions, all of the agencies who had personnel involved in the riot displayed a commendable frankness and honesty. As Deputy Chief Richard Simon of the LAPD told the McCone Commission: "We feel it's better to tell the truth. Even if the truth is not good, it's better than rumors, which are generally horrible."

Having worked out a strict chronology for your own edification, you will undoubtedly also find there are more questions that need to be asked and answered in order to verify what happened when. Almost certainly, just as in fiction, what makes a story compelling is not just *what* happened and *why* it happened, but *who* it happened to. And it is in the ordering of the best way to tell the stories of the characters who animate your narrative that the best structure will likely emerge.

In his essay "Rewriting the Rules of Nonfiction," Kurt Eichenwald talked about how he structured his book *The Informant*:

> [*The Informant*] was a story about a criminal investigation that was replete with lies. In this case, the FBI secured the assistance of the highest-ranking corporate executive ever to serve as a cooperating witness. For more than two years, that man, Mark Whitacre, provided the government with an unprecedented array of evidence about corruption at the nation's most politically powerful corporation, the Archer Daniels Midland Company (ADM).
>
> But, unknown to the FBI and ADM, the entire time that Whitacre was working for the two organizations, he was simultaneously losing his mind. Eventually, the case spun out of control, as Whitacre became trapped by his own lies, and the government struggled to find out where the truth began.
>
> Wrapping lies within truth was complex for narrative nonfiction, but, fortunately, many others had shown the way to soar while using this narrative technique. Indeed, in attempting this project, I was standing on the shoulders of giants—great authors who had blazed the trail for writing powerful narrative nonfiction.
>
> For me, one of the most influential was undoubtedly Ken Auletta's 1986 masterpiece, *Greed and Glory on Wall Street*....
>
> Before I decided to commit myself to writing books using this technique, I educated myself; I read every narrative nonfiction book I could find....
>
> I began with the true trailblazer, Truman Capote, who certainly boasted of being the first to use the technique for [his book] *In Cold Blood*. But over and over, the best seemed to be either in the worlds of

politics or business: *The Final Days* by Bob Woodward and Carl Bernstein [and] *Indecent Exposure* by David McClintock. There was [also] J. Anthony Lukas' masterpiece, *Common Ground*. Back in the business world, there was *Barbarians at the Gate* by Bryan Burrough and John Helyar, the brilliant *Den of Thieves* by James B. Stewart and . . . Jonathan Harr's triumph, *A Civil Action*.

With *The Informant*, I wanted the format to reflect the substance: What better way to tell a story where truth and lies meld together than by using a narrative technique that closely followed those used by novelists? And so, after my review of nonfiction works, I pored through dozens of novels....

As I began writing my book, the most complex choice involved the decision of where to begin the story. Using the dictates of most nonfiction, the answer would have been easy: I start where the action begins. Instead, I drew charts of the storyline, attempting to find the starting point that would allow me to hide the truth for as long as possible. Once I started down this path, the setup became easy. The story evolved into five plots, with each new one redefining the facts of the last. In essence, I was putting the readers in the position of the characters in the book who were deceived. With that plan in mind, I set off on my reporting extravaganza, seeking out the details that would allow me to write what is essentially a nonfiction novel.

The Architecture of a Narrative

Before he died, my friend Gary Provost, a terrific writing teacher and author, used to talk with his students about structure in very simple terms. Think about the house or apartment you're living in, he would say. It will almost certainly still be standing after you're gone despite sometimes punishing weather. It's made up of bricks and concrete, and steel truss rods and wooden framing all dependent on one another. The difference between the building you live in, and a chaotic pile of wood, brick, and the concrete that make it up is forethought and organization—a coherent sense of orderliness.

What's more, that orderliness is not only functional, it can be molded into a shape that is pleasing, graceful, perhaps even beautiful, to boot. Someone thought about how to put together your building ahead of time. Where to put a foundation, the best place to put beams so that they take the right amount of weight and stress, the best way to construct a frame that would hold everything together, where to cut holes for windows and doors, etc.

Every part of the building supports every other part, and your building was carefully put together to achieve that effect. That's structure, and it applies to your book just as much as it applies to the building you live in.

The building blocks of writing narrative—the beams, bricks and mortar, walls, etc.—of your book are scenes, exposition, half scenes, bridging passages, sequences, chapters, sections, actions and so forth.

Something that may have occurred to you about structures, if I may prolong the architecture analogy a bit longer, is that they are made up of small things (e.g. scenes) that make up larger structures (e.g. sequences), which in turn make up even larger structures (e.g. chapters and book sections), so that by cementing one brick on top of another in a certain way we can amazingly create self supporting arches and hollow buildings as well as just walls.

The Four Basic Elements of a Narrative

There are broadly four basic elements to creating a narrative:

- The first, obviously, is the recognition that you are taking the reader on a journey, using storytelling (i.e., fiction) techniques.

- The second is a good eye for visual detail. The telling detail or two or three will give us just the right sense of place, of time, of character (if possible) to set the scene and give it meaning. Don't just dump a bucketload of researched details over the reader as if drowning them in facts and hope that will suffice.

- The third is a good ear for aural detail. Obtain and accurately use quotes and dialogue that conveys to us the characters you're portraying in your narrative. Don't make up these quotes, or use stiff, generic or artificial dialog just because "it's true." The spirit of how something is said is as important as what was said. (There's an old Yiddish joke about a Russian immigrant in a citizenship class at Ellis Island in the 1950s. When asked to write a sentence in English, from Trotsky to Stalin, he writes: "You're right, I was wrong, I should apologize." When the teacher reads it out in class the old man says, "no, no you got it wrong." Then he puts the following inflection on the sentence: "*You're* right? *I* was wrong? *I* should apologize?")

- Lastly, use your heart to help your intellect. Have some compassion for your subjects and their situation and you will ultimately get much closer to the truth of the story you are writing, and certainly make it a lot more emotionally involving to a reader.

Organizing Principles

It's not necessarily the best idea to tell the story chronologically, or in the same sequence you discovered the information when you began your research. As I mentioned earlier, you need to decide for yourself first what the story is, and then how best to tell it.

One of the ways to make that decision is to consider why you're telling the story in the first place. What's the story's significance? And thereby hangs an organizing principle that may guide you as to how to tell the story.

In *The Perfect Storm,* for example, Junger starts by introducing us to the poor, blue collar fishing town of Gloucester, Mass., and through that the crew of the *Andrea Gail.* It becomes the point of a triangle, in a sense, where the human elements of the story—the crew of the lost ship—personify the town, the town in turn becomes the personification of the East Coast fishing industry, and the dangerous and difficult conditions they often work in sets the scene for the story, in this case experiencing a terrifying "storm of the century." As the book progresses in chapters, we switch from the worsening deterioration of the weather to a history of how tough it is to earn a living as fisherman because of the arduous and dangerous conditions of the job, to the specific though intuited story of the doomed crew who sail, quite literally, into the heart of the storm.

In a similar vein, though less obviously, *Into Thin Air* is a memoir principally structured around Krakauer's decision to write about climbing Mt. Everest as a reporter for a magazine. It is infused with glimpses of mountaineering, particularly man's attempt to defeat Everest, and becomes in some ways an involuntary meditation on why people not only climb mountains in general, but this one in particular.

Richard Preston's *The Hot Zone* covers the period from 1967 to 1993, though not chronologically. He outlines the presumed origins and history of the ebola virus in Africa, and its effects, almost as a living predator, much like the shark in *Jaws.* But he intersperses that chronology with more contemporary events involving Lt. Col. Nancy Jaax, a U.S. Army biohazard specialist who works alongside her husband, Col. Jerry Jaax, the SWAT mission team leader during a near catastrophe involving the virus at a lab just outside Washington D.C.

We move further along the scale to *Black Hawk Down,* which is structurally something of a model of complex but linear chronological narrative. Here the author's task was to recreate the battle of Mogadishu, and he humanizes the story by focusing on various individuals who were at various places during the battle, piecing the narrative together in a sort of mosaic like fashion. This is not a million miles away from the structure of various movies, such as the 1962 D-Day landing epic, *The Longest Day*, or the 1993 *Short Cuts,* inspired by characters in the short stories of Raymond Carver. It may seem strange mentioning movies, but if there is one unarguable point it is that films are all structure, and a study of them can really inform the structural possibilities open to a narrative writer, be she journalist or novelist. Robert Altman's movie crosscuts between two dozen or so principal characters, most of whom cross each others paths. Quentin Tarantino used a similar structure in *Pulp Fiction*, as did John Herzfeld in *Two Days In The Valley*. Each movie didn't just follow an assortment of characters, though; the filmmakers also manipulated time sequences, going back and forth in chronologically to track how their various characters' lives intersected.

The most obvious structure is a chronological structure: start at the beginning, progress to the middle, detail the denouement. However, sometimes the story's chronology works most effectively when told backwards, as in Martin Amis' novel *Time's Arrow,* and Harold Pinter's play (and then film) *Betrayal.*

There is also what could be called the circular structure. *Sunset Boulevard* follows this shape. We begin with a body face down in a swimming pool, and a voiceover of the drowned man announcing that this movie is essentially going to tell us the story of how he came to die. It goes back in time, and gradually progresses us to the point where we rejoin the scene that began it all, but now we able to see it in a completely different light with the hindsight of what has gone before.

Forest Gump does something a little similar, starting with him sitting as an adult on a bus stop bench and then telling his story.

In *The Rape of Nanking*, Iris Chang wrote that "the book describes two related but discreet atrocities. One is the Rape of Nanking itself, the story of how the Japanese wiped out hundreds of thousands of innocent civilians in its enemy's capitol.

"Another is the cover-up, the story of how the Japanese, emboldened by the silence of the Chinese and the Americans, tried to erase the entire massacre from public consciousness, thereby depriving its victims of their proper place in history.

"The structure of the first part of my book—the history of the massacre—is largely influenced by *Rashomon*," a famous movie by Akira Kurosawa.

In the movie, a rape and murder is recounted from the perspectives of the various people who were involved in the crime. Each tells the story slightly differently.

Susan Rabiner, Chang's editor at Basic books, recalls (in *Thinking Like Your Editor*) that, "[Iris's] main problem lay in how to present Part One, the events of the rape itself. Would dividing the categories of violence by time...prove to be a viable organizing principle?"

This plan made for effective storytelling. But it didn't sit well with Chang...

> Should she choose a fixed number of representative moments of inhumane treatment...? That was a possibility. The rape occurred over a period of six weeks. Could she tell the story chronologically...? Again, not a bad plan, but one that screened her from getting at what she really wanted to say....
>
> The book's structure emerged when she re-examined the material she had. The Nanking massacre survived as an historical military event because it was witnessed by so many neutral noncombatants—Americans and Europeans living in the city who refused to leave despite the invasion by the Japanese. Further, while conversing with a relative of a high-ranking German diplomat in Nanking at the time, she discovered he had a diary, kept through the early stages of the atrocity. This diary later became front page news, and it seemed appropriate that she choose an organizational plan that made full use of her own contributions.

In essence she told the story of what occurred three times, from three different perspectives, in what she referred to as the Rashomon style....

Why did this organizational style work so well for Chang? Because it got to the core of the problem as she saw it—that even today reactions to the atrocity vary, depending on the perspective and politics of the commentator.

In a somewhat similar fashion, D. Graham Burnett, in *A Trial by Jury,* explains that his book was really two stories interwoven: "that of the case—a trial story, a courtroom story, a drama focused around a violent death; and that of the deliberations—the story of what happened behind the closed door of the jury room. Each of these stories [was] complex, and they [were] of course entangled. I set out to write this book in order to tell the latter, but to do so I [had to] rehearse elements of the former."

The Basic Unit of a Book's Structure

I used earlier the analogy of book structure as architecture. If words are bricks, while they may seem to be the basic units of a structure, in truth, a basic unit only takes shape once you combine various bricks together. In literary terms, it's how words are utilized, the *thought* they combine to express and capture on paper that is really the basic building block of a literary structure.

There's a tendency for some writers of nonfiction to write in what can best be described as an ever present tense. This is used mostly for analytical writing, but it deliberately ignores the passage of time and makes any kind of narrative turgid reading because it seems to lack movement. A sense of time adds pace to the story. And how chapters break is important in pacing a story. James Clavell's novel *Shogun* is a wonderful example of "cliffhanging" writing—he heightens the suspense at the end of the chapter, and you finish it wanting to plunge ahead to the next so that you find out what happens next.

Ideas and Images

A narrative is really a combination of two things: ideas and images. A documentary filmmaker uses something similar. When learning to write fiction, you'll often hear the adage: "Show, don't tell." In other words, if you're writing a narrative, find ways to show in verbal pictures rather than didactic explanation what it is you want to convey. Of course, when writing nonfiction it's not always possible to write this way, but the instinct to try to use an image to humanize your fact or piece of information is laudable.

For example, in 1971, in an article in *The New Republic,* Senator Walter Mondale wanted to convey the fact that the U.S. had six percent of the world's population and about half the world's resources, but an income distribution that awarded 77 percent of total income to the top half of the population and only 23 percent to the lower half.

This is how he set up those facts: "I went to a small elementary area school in our small ghetto in St. Paul. They had a splendid cafeteria and a very balanced meal, a warm meal, salad, and about every fifth child could not afford it. One child, whom I will never forget as long as I live, was about six or seven years old. She had a filthy dress on, and she sat at this table amidst the other children eating their good meal, eating a chocolate cookie. She had a little dirty bag that she had brought, that her mother had sent, and two other chocolate cookies. And I asked the principal, how can this happen? And he said, 'We still don't have the money to pay for lunches when the families can't afford it.' I assume there are millions like her in the country, that sit amidst their friends at lunch who have a decent meal, and they don't. It's a disgrace."

Whether or not you agree with his politics, there can be no denying that the imagery greatly enhanced the emotional power of the factual argument Mondale was making.

In *Thinking In Pictures: The Making of the Movie Matewan,* screenwriter and film director John Sayles said: "When thinking in pictures it's important to consider whether a certain image will have the same meaning to someone else as it does to you.

No matter what your experience of the Vietnam War, *Platoon* [by Oliver Stone] is a rugged movie to enter into, a meaningful assault on the senses. But the images in it are bound to have a different resonance for people who have been in combat than for people who haven't. The trick is not to ignore one group and concentrate on the other, to become either a caterer to the elite or a panderer to the masses, but to pick and build your images so that *anybody* can get into the story on some level, so that maybe people are drawn in deeper than they thought they could or would want to go. And you have to do all this without lying to them."

A narrative has this crude structure: Start with the problem to be overcome; in the course of developing a solution to this problem, show how the situation becomes more complicated; end by showing how ultimately the solution (or a solution) is applied and the problem resolved. When outlining your story you are searching for a protagonist and antagonist who have conflicting goals and problems and whose stories will humanize the narrative, provide emotional nourishment for the reader, and broadly follow the structure of narrative as I've outlined it above.

Ideas and Images, Scenes and Chapters

Ideas and images, then, are the rhetoric of narrative storytelling, its meaning and emotion. The choice of image is very important because image is often used as a metaphor for a psychological state—in other words the emotion of the moment. So a boring, static image, will produce—yes, you guessed it—a bored disinterested reader. Any old image obviously won't do, then. What you need is not adjectives and adverbs (I recommend hunting them down mercilessly in your prose and killing them seriously dead), but action words, or verbs. For example, instead of saying "the thug was kicking the dog," it's more powerful to say, "the thug kicked the dog."

By interweaving image and idea, we create a scene, which has a natural beginning and end. A series of related scenes is called a sequence. Very often, two or three sequences make up a chapter.

All writing, of course, is what you want it to be, but some things just seem to work on the page while other don't. That's because the things that work conform to internal rules of logic such as: good drama is rooted in conflict. Things that don't work ignore these rules. E.g. no conflict, little drama.

Talking about writing *Sputnik: The Shock of the Century*, author Paul Dickson said, "When I started working on the book, the conflict was [the Cold War enmity] between the United States and the Soviet Union. But the further I got into [the book], I realized that the conflict was [really] between [President] Eisenhower and the people who wanted Space for peace . . . and Werner Von Braun and the Army. The conflict was really in America. There was this huge invisible tug-of-war that was going on in the country...which in many ways was our destiny."

Chapters—the Rogue Element of Structure

Chapters, however, don't use the same kind of internal logic rules about what is dramatically successful as do scenes, action, exposition, and so forth. Chapters can be just about anything.

A writer friend once submitted a proposal for a book and the interested editor asked him for not just one but the first two chapters as a sample of the book. My friend had already written a thirty page chapter and didn't want to do any more work, so he somewhat cynically broke the chapter into two fifteen-page sections.

This actually worked much better for the reader, and while prompted by a feeling of sloth on my friend's part, it all worked out for him, because in our fast moving, thirty-second sound bite influenced world, readers like to know there are places to take a breather before plunging back into the book, even if they don't use them all. The fifteen to twenty page chapter length is the equivalent of potential rest stops along a parkway.

A chapter consists of a series of interlinking scenes or sequences, each following on as a direct result of what happened previously. In brief, a scene moves the story forward while at the same time giving the reader information about the characters.

If it doesn't do either of these things, and hopefully both at the same time, it shouldn't be there and is ill chosen.

In its simplest form, the best way to tackle writing scenes is to start the scene when the action starts, and end it when the action ends. Don't lead up, explain, or editorialize if you can avoid it.

In *A Trial by Jury*, for example, we are taken fairly chronologically through the story, though with the first person narrator's explanations for what is happening. In a sense, the book is a memoir of an event. Chapter 2, "How it Began," is comprised of a series of interconnected sequences.

First we have the sequence that depicts the author arriving first thing in the morning at the jury selection room in the Centre Street court building. The second sequence involves seeing the defendant for the first time as Burnett is called in to be considered a potential juror in the trial, being part of the *voir dire* process. The third sequence is being chosen as a juror on the case.

As you build your narrative it's useful to ask yourself, "Do these scenes relate to each other, or does this particular scene actually relate to a sequence I've put earlier or later in the book?"

You'll discover that you may well have written some scenes that are either out of place and should be moved around, or can be discarded.

Half Scenes

As you might expect, a half scene is something that's midway between a scene and exposition, that is, authorial editorializing of some form or another. The half scene often bridges two scenes and is exposition that is flavored with description. It's commonly used when you have something that's important for the reader to know but not important enough to devote a whole scene to. Here's a fictional example, but the technique is the same for narrative nonfiction:

That evening, Rachel remembered, she meet with the police officer who was investigating the accident. The

Starbucks was thinning out by now, and they found a small table in a corner where they sat huddled together with their backs to the rest of the customers. The cop was a dour old timer who looked close to retirement and had the jowls of a bloodhound, shot through with the thready veins and the red nose of an habitual heavy drinker. He sighed as he told Rachel what she had already guessed—the skid marks of the car showed that the "accident" looked like a deliberate hit and run.

"We just don't have a lot of manpower to spend on these kinds of cases. But I want to assure you I am going to track down every lead I get. It's going to take time though. We think she could have been mistaken for someone else."

And there it was, the fact that would haunt Rachel for years to come. Someone in suburban New Jersey had deliberately tried to kill her sister, an ordinary housewife, because she looked like a stranger she didn't know and had never met. But who? And why?

We could just have said, *That evening Rachel discovered that someone had tried to kill her sister, mistaking her for someone else.* But by giving us a brief picture of the cop, the setting, and hearing him tell Rachel the information as dialog rather than as exposition, this becomes a half-scene because it's made to come alive through a brief taste of dramatization.

Action in Structure

Action is simply the movement that occurs in a sentence. *She opened the front door,* is an action. *She bought a cup of coffee at Starbucks*, is an action. *She adjusted the seat and turned on the ignition*, is an action. *"Screw you Freddy," she whispered,* is an action. In a strong narrative we look for a new action in every sentence. This is what defines pacing. Lots of actions, fast pace, fewer actions, slower pace. If we write a sentence that adds no new information or movement to the story, such as: *She started up her car, it was silver with a dent in the trunk, and had red upholstery,* unless those details are going to have meaning in the narrative later on you've belabored the point. All we needed to know was that she started up her car.

The antithesis of this is pushing the pace too fast, and leaving out something. Such as: *She started up her car. The sandwich left a bitter taste in her mouth.* Excuse me? Hello? Where did that come from? The writer forgot to have her go into a store and buy a sandwich. *While she waited for her coffee, Ginny bought a sandwich. I'll eat that on the way home, she thought.* One action after another. Baby steps leading us logically forward.

Another thing you want to think about in terms of pace and sentence action is the order in which you place the sentences. Focus on cause and effect. Every sentence should be a stimulus for another action. So make sure you write sentences and actions in their logical order. For example, *She ducked. Rafe threw the plate at her*, has her reacting to something that hasn't happened yet. The sentences should be reversed.

Building Conflict

Drama is made up of conflict—no conflict, no drama, boring narrative. It's important to think about the way conflict drives a narrative. How you create conflict, and where you place it in your narrative is important to a narrative's structural success. Stories are about characters trying to go in a direction, and some force, some opposition, saying "no, you can't do that."

Here are a couple of tips about creating conflict:

- Conflict will occur naturally when two people (particularly with clashing goals) are forced together into a small space. For example, astronauts face certain disaster because their orbiting space station has a fire and loses precious oxygen among other potential life threatening events. (E.g., *The Unmaking of Mir*, by Thomas Mallon.)

- Put pressure on the narrative by imposing a time limit, like a ticking clock on a bomb. You only have so much time before disaster strikes. Force the protagonists to act in a way that could get them into trouble, make them make mistakes because of haste and worry, increase the inherent drama and conflict of their situation. *Black Hawk Down* has a ticking clock. First one bird goes down, then a second, then the rescuers need to be rescued, meanwhile men are dying and taking horrendous wounds in a bitter firefight that seems endless.

A book that managed to combine both was *Our Story: 77 Hours That Tested Our Friendship and Our Faith* by The Quecreek Miners as told to Jeff Goodell. This is the book that told the story of nine Pennsylvania coal miners who were trapped underground for more than three days. Told using the miners' own words, it is an unsentimental and accurate account of a horrifying situation and a triumphant escape.

Equal but Opposite

Conflict is best conceived as two equal forces in opposition striving to achieve what appear to be mutually exclusive goals. In fact, a protagonist is pretty much defined by the strength of the opposition (or antagonist) he or she faces. The greater the conflict, the higher the stakes for all involved and the more potent the emotional content of the narrative. Ideally, whatever is trying to stop your protagonist from reaching her goal is so formidable that all the way through the book we worry who's going to win the battle. *Take It From Me: Life's a Struggle But You Can Win* by Erin Brockovich and Marc Eliot is an interesting example of a narrative nonfiction self-help book that is also part memoir in the *Angela's Ashes* vein.

Three Basic Types of Conflict

From a structural perspective we can divide up conflict into three basic types:

- *Human vs. Human.* This is the most common conflict. Two people in a scene may not be fighting, but they have conflicting goals and mounting pressures to attain those goals. Any true crime such as *Small Sacrifices* or *Black Hawk Down* would qualify.

- *Human vs. Nature.* Guys trying to conquer Mt. Everest, or beat a storm at sea, or survive a devastating flood would qualify here. The obvious examples are *Into Thin Air* and *The Perfect Storm.*

- *Human against Himself (or Herself).* These stories are principally about internal conflict, and are very hard to write well. The danger is that the writer's fascination with the character won't translate onto the page and the story becomes wordy, self-involved, and boring.

The "trick" here, so to speak, is to find ways of dramatizing in an external fashion what is going on in the internal story. Such narratives are about regret and guilt, about people who don't have the strength to do what they have to do, such as quit drinking, stop taking drugs, etc. Internal stories, and internal monologues, in particular, are minefields and can undermine a reporter's validity if he or she isn't careful. It's a good idea to somehow telegraph to the reader that the internal monologue is the result of careful research. *"As she later recalled, Debbie was thinking that..."* kind of thing.

In general, this type of story often works better as an article than a book, but there are powerful exceptions. Some biographies and memoirs, particularly of experiencing personal suffering would fit neatly into this category. *The Diving Bell and the Butterfly: A Memoir of Life in Death* by Jean-Dominique Bauby, or even *Angela's Ashes* by Frank McCourt might be good examples.

Writing the Book:
Flesh and Blood on the Bones

But suppose, asks the student of the professor, we follow
all your structural rules for writing, what about that
"something else" that brings the book alive? What is
the formula for that?
The formula for that is not included in the curriculum.
                    —Fannie Hurst, novelist

Creativity might best defined as bringing order out of chaos, whether it's personified in the anarchic work of a Jackson Pollock and Damien Hirst, or the bucolic nineteenth-century landscapes of Constable and Turner. Regardless of art's effect on the viewer/ reader, for art to have worth the artist must have had a purpose when creating the work, even if that purpose appears to be banal. For example, Damien Hirst shocked and polarized the London and New York art worlds in the late 1990s by presenting exhibits of a sectioned cow and a shark in formaldehyde. In creating such art, he said, his aim was to "make art that everybody could believe in."

If you immerse yourself in learning the best way to write something, you'll quickly find that there are so-called "rules" to writing. In fact, there are as many rules as there are teachers who teach them. I'm not going to bore you with reciting my own set of "writing rules" here, and they wouldn't make much sense without concrete examples illuminating the points anyway. One teacher will say, "You've got to do it this way"; another says, "Oh, ignore what all those guys are telling you and do it any way you like." You find yourself confronting a choice between creative tyranny or artistic anarchy. Rarely do these teachers mention fitting the techniques of how you tell your story to the "purpose" of the narrative you're writing. It's too hard and too sophisticated a concept for most students to grasp or employ. It requires intuitively understanding that something should be presented in a particular way in order to "bring out" its true meaning, rather like the rare photographer who is able to visualize, and then capture, the essence of a person through pose and expression.

I'm going to recommend that you consider just this: I've become more and more conscious of a single governing principle on how to choose the best narrative technique to tell your story from the many options available—and it's simply this—use what best engages the imagination while at the same time providing the highest degree of emotional intensity to the narrative. This usually means employing a limited viewpoint, which is focused on the trials and tribulations of one or, at most, a couple of main characters. Even a seemingly ensemble story like *A Perfect Storm*, in the end, is more focused on Captain Billy Tyne and Bobby Shatford than other characters.

If you're reading this book you've already figured out there has to be some logic and structure to writing, and that you shouldn't have to reinvent the wheel in order to write your book. It's a sure bet that other people have already discovered that some things work better on the page than others, and for good reasons. Does this mean you should create a narrative in a particular way every time? Of course not. But writing is a little like cooking: For example, there is a right way and a wrong way to cook using wine and cream in the same dish. Used one way, the food is tasty; used another way, the cream curdles and the completed dish looks and tastes like crap.

The so-called "rules" of writing are concerned with being able to analyze and discuss what makes a successful piece of creative writing and, more importantly, why something that should be working, isn't. What's more, these rules need to be adapted and modified for every piece of creative writing you do. Writing is not (and should never be) a one-size-fits-all process, nor would

I ever try to make that claim. What I'm trying to do in this book is present some windows into philosophical principles of drama that hopefully will help you write a stronger narrative and give you, at the least, some things to reject in favor of other solutions that occur to you. This is nowhere truer than when discussing the "tricks" of narrative writing.

The Organic Book

When a newspaper reporter writes a story, he doesn't usually have a lot of time to spend crafting the piece. He must write his article quickly, accurately, and with a minimum of description and detail. Writing a book-length piece of narrative nonfiction is a different kettle of fish. The reader often knows the broad outlines of the story you're telling ahead of time, and so you are writing not just to convey *what* happened but more to introduce the reader to entirely new worlds of the subject in question, and particularly to the people involved in the narrative. Otherwise, your real focus is to give the real the who, why, and how of your story. The reader wants color and emotion and characterizations, and the writing techniques available to the novelist help in this regard. Complete books have been written on each of the various techniques I outline below, so regard them only as essential introductions, or as reminders.

A book has an organic quality and at times it seems to have of life of its own; piece by piece, scene by scene it grows, sometimes in surprising ways despite the author's efforts to plan it out ahead of time. As we've discussed earlier, while the outline is the structural skeleton of the narrative, the "flesh and blood" that turns that skeleton into a living thing is not chapters, as you might assume, but scenes. The dramatized scene is the basic unit of creativity you need to focus on once you've determined a structure for your book. You know what is going to happen; now you need to focus on how best to present that information, in almost cinematic terms.

Writing in scenes is the antithesis of academic, analytical narrative. Analytical writing uses an authorial voice to *tell* us a fact or present a piece of information. Dramatic writing, on the other hand, uses emotionally powerful language and images to animate a *distillation* of real life; it is almost as if the reader were viewing a movie that *shows* us that information. A recent movie, *Adaptation,* starring Nicholas Cage, very much played with this idea philosophically and it is worth a look by any aspiring author of narrative nonfiction. In *A Murder*, the book upon which the movie was based, author Greg Fallis, a mystery writer and former cop, sets out to take the reader through a routine murder investigation. He alternates between an authorial voice that describes in almost textbook style the various aspects of a police murder investigation, and scenes that bring to life through dramatization certain aspects of the story he is telling, from crime to investigation, to trial and punishment, and finally to aftermath.

Unlike fiction, however, there will be occasions when an authorial narrative voice will intersperse between scenes, dispensing journalistically the information we need to follow the story. Too many beginning writers, however, resort to the journalistic voice entirely, rather than creating scenes of emotional impact and dynamism, and the result is a rather flat narrative that "tells" much and "shows" little.

Basic Needs of a Scene

In general, a scene should revolve around a primary character in the story: a sense of what she (or he) needs, both in this particular scene and in the larger terms of where she is headed at story's end; and the sense of what it is or who it is that is trying to prevent her from achieving her goal or reaching her final destination. If she encounters no antagonistic force during the scene, the scene will fall flat because she won't have "earned" the information provided to her in the scene.

"Where's Bob?" Suzie demanded.

"Oh, he's over there," Jim said.

Not much of a scene, absolutely no dramatic tension, and no antagonistic force. We quickly cease to care.

"Where's Bob?" Suzie demanded.

"Get lost," Jim said.

"But he's going to die if I don't give him his medicine."

"Look at me? Do I look like I care? Leave me alone."

A clichéd scene, it's true, but at least one showing some signs of drama, emotional involvement, and a momentum that will urge us to read on to see how Suzie deals with this setback. Why? Because she has to earn her information and Jim is saying "no" to her.

If your main character doesn't have a goal or doesn't want something badly enough, the scene won't work because there will be no point to it. If the characters don't care, where's the emotional engine? A reader's emotional involvement in your story parallels that of your protagonist to some degree. If the character isn't emotionally involved in the scene, the reader will likely feel the same way.

So how do you decide when to create an actual scene?

- *If there is no conflict and little emotion.* In this case, don't bother with a scene; merely sum up your information in a sentence or two, if you can do so.

- *When major events are about to take place.* In a memoir, for example, don't just write, "On Tuesday, I decided it was time I ended my marriage of twenty-three years, so I packed my bags, got in the car, and drove away." Instead, create a scene that will emotionally involve the reader in your decision. Or, in a true crime narrative, at the moment the body is about to be discovered, don't just "tell" what happens. Instead, re-create the scene for the reader's benefit.

- *When characters are in conflict with each other.* Writers sometimes shy away from showing an argument/fight scene. They'll lead us up to it, and lead us away from it, but avoid the fight scene itself. The trouble is, the fight is what we really want to read about, not the other stuff.

- *When great emotion is being evoked.* Don't just state: "Billy woke up finally from the coma, and the next week left hospital for home." Make the reader "feel" Billy's struggle to find his way free from the haze of the coma to full consciousness.

Small Sacrifices

The opening chapter of Anne Rules' *Small Sacrifices* includes the following short scene, which I've condensed further for the sake of brevity:

> At about 11 P.M., on May 19, 1983, a distraught blonde woman brought her three children to the McKenzie-Willamette ER suffering from severe gunshot wounds. By the time the trauma staff were through, one child was dead, and two others lay near death.

This is how Anne Rule wrote it, clearly setting the scene, supplying description, and displaying action:

> The bad call came into the Springfield Police Department at 10:40 P.M.: "Employee of McKenzie-Willamette Hospital advises of gunshot victim at that location. Officers dispatched. Arrived 10:48 P.M."
>
> Rosie Martin, R.N.; Shelby Day L.P.N.; Judy Patterson, the night receptionist; and Dr. John Mackey, physician in charge, comprised the evening shift in the emergency room at the McKenzie-Willamette ER in Springfield.
>
> McKenzie-Willamette as it existed in the late spring of 1983 was a little cramped, a little out of date. Paint on walls and baseboards had been scrubbed dull and drab; and the waiting room furniture was chrome and peeling vinyl.
>
> Facing the two sets of doors that led to the circular driveway off Mohawk Boulevard, the three

treatment rooms were to the right. Day Surgery nearest the street, Minor Treatment in the middle and the
Trauma Room at the back. On the left, Judy Patterson's
desk was just behind a small waiting area near her
[and] near the street doors. Five feet or so behind her
desk there was a small bathroom and beyond that a
larger waiting room....

That velvet black spring night Dr. Mackey and
his staff, working in an almost obsolete ER, would
be the first to encounter what was unthinkable for
Springfield, what would be unthinkable for even a big
city. None of them would have much time to think during the hours they fought to save the injured, their
white shoes sliding on floors slick with fresh blood.
Only later would terrible musings rush in to destroy
all hope of sleep.

Shelby Day is a slender, soft-spoken woman near
forty, with six years' experience in the McKenzie-
Willamette ER. She wears white slacks and pastel,
patterned smocks. When she remembers the night of
May 19, 1983, tears well unbidden in her eyes.

A car arrived at the ambulance emergency en-
trance, honking its horn. When Shelby Day and Rosie
Martin, another nurse, ran out to see what the com-
motion was about they were confronted by a slender
blonde woman in jeans and a plaid shirt beside her
car. She was pale but she was in control.

"What's going on here?" Rosie Martin asked.

"Somebody just shot my kids!"

...The two nurses and the young woman gazed
at each other for a fraction of a second, and then the
emergency personnel went into action.

The Power of the Scene

A scene can be one page or twenty pages long. There is no definitive length. As a general rule of thumb, the scene should start

when the action in the scene starts, and end when that action ends. Add as little setup, explanation, or editorializing as possible. In the above example, the scene starts: "The bad call came in ..." We don't get a set of cops whiling away the time waiting for the call and eating donuts or chatting to their buddies. It's just straight in to the action.

When you think your story through in terms of individual scenes rather than overall or general "explanation" (i.e., exposition), you are beginning to focus on creating the emotional "bricks" of your drama, which eventually become cemented one to another. Through the depiction of conflict (people saying "no" to each other, in effect) and character development, you are infusing your story with emotional power. A scene, which can be considered a "brick" in the construction of the "building" you are creating, translates the emotional life of your characters into visually powerful, engaging, and dramatic material. In other words, into "visual" scenes that work the same way in your book as they would in a film.

Before starting to write any given scene, ask yourself four questions:

· Whose viewpoint is this scene going to use?

· How does this scene advance the story?

· What problem must the main character in the scene overcome?

· What is this scene about (i.e., what is its purpose)?

Your choice of what to dramatize should be guided by the answers to these questions, which in turn should almost always take into account how your protagonist, antagonist, or both advance the story. Does the scene inform us of, or move us closer to learning, something important about these characters? Does the scene move one or the other toward his or her long-term goal?

Try to dramatize facts and events that make your characters confront opposition and the obstacles that create moral and/or ethical dilemmas. In other words, dramatize how they approach and handle questions of right and wrong.

Basic Elements of a Scene

A key aspect of a scene is that it takes place at a set time in a set place. If events don't happen at a specific time and in a definite place, you're not writing a scene, you're writing an abstract narrative.

The following are some examples of scenes (containing both a time and a place):

- Last month in the desert near Las Vegas.

- May 19, 1983 in the local hospital emergency room.

- Saturday afternoon backstage at the Majestic theatre in Manhattan.

Each example contains a distinct time and a recognizable geographic setting. If you change either of these characteristics, you create a different scene. For example, if you move the action from May 19, 1983, in the ER to May 21, 1983, in the ER, even though the geography is the same, the changed time frame sets up an entirely different scene. And, moving the action from 11:00 P.M. on May 19 in the ER to 11:00 P.M. in the station wagon outside, also creates a different scene.

Everyone and everything is in the scene for a reason, and everyone in the scene has his own agenda. For example, in the scene above from *Small Sacrifices*, nurse Shelby Day is our eyes and ears—and feelings—as the scene in the hospital emergency room develops. We're in the hands of a professional doing her job, but her job involves critical emergency care of small children bleeding to death from gunshot wounds. Seeing the scene through the eyes of the nurse is a clever choice, and it is important, because she can not only show us calmly what is going on, she can also assess the mother and question her behavior. (The mother will eventually end up on trial for the murder and attempted murder of her children.)

Three Aspects of Scene Writing

The following are three aspects of scene writing that you should focus on:

- What has caused the event in the scene? If the incident that provokes your scene has no real connection to something that happened in a previous scene, or if the scenes could be extracted from the narrative and not effect what happens next, then the narrative is going to be episodic. The scenes may share some thematic consistency, but that's not enough to ensure a flowing narrative. Cause and effect is the key here.

- When you write a scene, the reason your character is in that place at that time should be because of something that happened in a previous scene. It can be one scene ago, or several scenes ago, but the action in that earlier scene should act as a spur to future action in the story, even if you don't know it at the time you first read it. (The technical term for this is foreshadowing.)

- A test of whether or not you're writing episodically is to consider whether the reason (or impetus) for the scene happens *within* the scene, rather than before it. If so, the scene is likely not really linked in any emotional way to any other scene in the narrative.

On the other hand, a strong scene in a narrative will broadly have these elements in common with other scenes:

- It will cause a subsequent scene to occur, creating cause and effect.

- It will be driven by the main character's needs and wants. There's a reason he's at that place on that particular day. What is it?

- It will explore various ploys by the character to get his own way. We'll understand these ploys, not by having the author tell us what the ploy is, but by seeing the actions and hearing the words of the character, which creates an effect not unlike movie imagery, and allows us to judge the character ploys for ourselves. The character may try a few strategies to get what he wants before succeeding—or failing.

- The character must have changed his position, relative to the end of the story, for the scene to be worthwhile writing. By the end of the scene, we must be moved forward in some way.

Even though a scene is a self-contained unit, it's important to remember that each scene links to the next. Scenes don't just dramatize specific events in a story, they lead us to what happens next. If the scene doesn't, in some way, have an element of "... and then" in it as a response to what happened in the previous scene, you should wonder whether one or the other of those scenes ought to even be in the narrative, despite the brilliance of the writing.

Goals—the Meat of Drama

When there's no conflict on the page, there's no reader interest in what happens. The reader also has no emotional involvement in the story. In other words, readers won't much care what your characters do, why they're doing it, or what happens to them. Nothing compels the reader to stay with a story that lacks conflict and creates no interest. Conversely: The more extreme the conflict, the more emotionally involved in your narrative your reader becomes. One way to affect this is to make sure your characters have individual goals that will clash and conflict. The playwright Harold Pinter once described a theatrical drama as the fight for dominance among a group of characters. With some modification, this description works admirably for narrative non-fiction as well as for theatrical drama.

It's important your characters have goals that clash. The resulting conflicts create the highest degrees of reader interest in your book. Character conflicts create the emotional payoff, and to shortchange the reader by limiting this type of conflict is to leave him frustrated and annoyed. In narrative storytelling, you can't be afraid of conflict. It's the meat of drama.

A narrative can be thought of as a series of connected conflicts (with bridging passages in between), conflicts that are eventually resolved by one, final, cathartic conflict. As you move through your narrative, you are constantly figuring out the details of what you should write next, and how best to write it. Character goals should be the guiding principle here. In a true crime book, for example, the cop's *overarching* goal is to catch the crook. The crook's goal is to get away with his or her crime. Each may have *intermediate* goals, such as planning the crime and then executing it; or making sure all the forensic evidence has been gathered and all the wit-nesses interviewed and accounted for. And, each will have *minor* goals, such as the cop's need to appear as a witness in another case so that he can wrap up that case and get on with investigating this one, or the crook's need to steal a car so that he can get to where he is going to commit his crime.

The *depth* or severity of the conflicts each character has to cope with in the attempt to accomplish his or her goal(s) will pro-vide a parallel emotional depth for your reader.

In general, consider three questions:

- *Is there opposition?* That is, opposition in each scene and in your narrative in general. Forward momentum is the gradual overcoming of opposition. Consider the Indiana Jones movies: solving one problem moves the story forward, but only to immediately land Indiana (and the movie viewer who emotionally shares Indiana's problems) in a worse situation, from which he must extricate himself: the classic out-of-the-frying-pan and into-the-fire sort of thing.

- *Is what you're writing interesting?* As you research your book, you'll come across interesting material all the time. Sometimes there may be limited conflict in the material. If such material seduces you, be sure that even though it's interesting to you, it enhances the material you're writing in some way and has earned a right to be included.

- *Is the information essential to understand the scene or the narrative at that point?* If you can leave out certain information and you know the reader will understand what's going on, you should reconsider including that particular material. Should any given information be presented in a fully dramatized scene? Perhaps it's only worth a sentence or two of exposition.

Exposition

As a rule of thumb, it's a good idea to try to limit exposition in your narrative. However, unlike fiction, in narrative nonfiction you need to put things into a particular context because you are re-creating real life, and real life is often complex and scenes that approximate it sometimes need a context.

Because exposition a) explains, or b) editorializes, exposition works in the narrative the same way that adjectives and adverbs do in sentences; it enhances and clarifies. The right piece of exposition, like the correctly chosen adjective, can be powerful and effective. Used poorly, exposition becomes a crutch to the writer, preventing him from developing an otherwise imagina-

tive way of delivering viable information—if it's needed at all—
or becoming an anchor, retarding the forward momentum of the
narrative and diluting the emotional power of the story.

The following are some aspects to consider about exposition:

- Don't introduce expository material unless you need it
  to create an understanding of what's about to happen
  in the narrative.

- If possible, figure out a way of dramatizing the expository information the reader needs, using a scene or a
  half scene.

- Try to begin the scene before giving us the exposition.
  Put your character in a time and place, and frame the
  setting before introducing what amounts to a cinematic "voiceover."

Viewpoint

Your narrative also needs a viewpoint, what in fiction is called
a point of view. This does not mean an attitude or opinion, but a
camera-lens position, for want of a better explanation, through
which we watch the story unfold. Point of view (PoV) can make a
great deal of difference on how a story is told. It can impact pro-
foundly on a story's emotional power, so choose wisely.

Imagine, for example, if reporters Bob Woodward and Carl
Bernstein had not told the story presented in *All the President's
Men*, their account of the Watergate break-in and its aftermath,
through their own eyes, but had chosen instead President
Nixon's PoV, or the viewpoint of their famous White House
source—Deep Throat (the pseudonym given to FBI Deputy
Director William Mark Felt, Sr., the man who waited 30 years
to confirm and admit he was the one who had leaked the infor-
mation about the involvement of Nixon's administration in the
Watergate scandal).

By and large narrative nonfiction uses three broad PoV perspectives: the memoir voice, or first person. This is the *"Let me tell you about an experience I had the other day,"* kind of thing.

Another PoV is the subjective third person, a kind of "over the shoulder" camera-lens position that also allows limited access to a character's thoughts and feelings, as in: *"John moved carefully toward the door. His growing feelings of apprehension, as he explained later, came from a dread of discovering the gore that he was pretty certain was going to lie beyond it."*

The third type of PoV is the omniscient third person, as in: *"While George was out doing the family shopping, across town, Ricky and Billy were getting ready to rob the convenience store that George was heading to. Little did any of these people know how abruptly their lives would change when their paths crossed less than an hour later...."*

The subjective third person approach is much harder to do convincingly in a first- person voice. Why? Because in first person you can tell a reader what *you* think and feel, but you can't convincingly tell a reader what someone else is thinking or feeling, unless the reader has some way of knowing how the *"I"* narrator could accurately know this information. The question "How does she know that?" will distract a reader from enjoying the narrative and destroy the "narrative dream" you have been trying so hard to create in your reader's mind.

"I" in the Narrative

Inserting the author directly into the narrative is a challenging thing to do, and it is best avoided unless what you are writing directly involves you in some way.

You can use, "As told to the author" or "As reported to the author," or even a more generic tone, but it's best to try to leave the narrative voice in an "objective" third person. In *In Cold Blood*, for example, Capote never once inserts himself, and he takes very much the journalistic (noninvolved) novelist's approach. For instance, during the auction of the murdered Clutter family's belongings, Capote writes this:

The last thing to go was the contents of the livestock corral, mostly horses, including Nancy's horse, big, fat Babe, who was much beyond her prime. [Nancy was the sole-surviving member of the family who was on a sleep-over the night of the murder.] It was late afternoon, school was out, and several schoolmates of Nancy's were among the spectators when bidding on the horse began; Susan Kidwell was there. Sue, who had adopted another of Nancy's orphaned pets, a cat, wished she could give Babe a home, for she loved the old horse and knew how much Nancy loved her. The two girls had often gone riding together aboard Babe's wide back, jogged through the wheat fields on hot summer evenings down to the river and into the water, the mare wading against the current until, as Sue once described it, "the three of us were cool as fish." But Sue had no place to keep a horse.

"I hear fifty...sixty-five...seventy...": the bidding was laggardly, nobody seemed really to want Babe, and the man who got her, a Mennonite farmer who said he might use her for plowing, paid seventy-five dollars. As he led her out of the corral, Sue Kidwell ran forward; she raised her hand as though to wave goodbye, but instead clasped it over her mouth.

Editors usually try to curb a tendency for the author to personalize a narrative because it usurps the story, and it distracts the reader and takes away from the story. Most narrative nonfiction is about something you're researching, not about you. To insert your own persona is often to impinge the integrity of what you're trying to report. It's best to leave the voice in the third person and only reveal any part the author played in the narrative in publicity interviews when you publicize the book later.

Considering the use of the active first person, author Paul Dickson commented: "In the first chapter of *Sputnik: The Shock of the Century* I'm a character. I [wrote myself as] a kid seeing

Sputnik overhead. [Instead of being a nameless observer] I'm talking to people, and that's one way of getting your reader into the book. Once you're out of that moment, then [the author becomes merely an] observer, but you've given the reader a sense of belonging to the story. I've always done discursive footnotes, for example, this interview was done on an October night, etc., and you can use that discursive footnote in the back to insert yourself and give the reader the sense of validation that you really did talk to the person."

In the conversation concerning the use of the active first person author Jim Srodes added: "When you use 'I' you're creating a new character and I don't know that 'I' is enough of a character to be in the book. You have to ask yourself, is 'I' that important? You certainly have the opportunity to give your views and your impressions but a) 'I' gets in the way, and b) it's a tough character to create. It's easy to create a small boy looking at Sputnick [but] it would be almost impossible to carry him off [over the course of a book]."

This is clearly not the case with Krakauer's book *Into Thin Air,* however. His story and the narrative in general are intimately intertwined. Indeed, Krakauer described *Into Thin Air* as a "personal account." The opening sentence sets the narrative tone:

> Straddling the top of the world. One foot in China and the other in Nepal, I cleared the ice from my oxygen mask, hunched a shoulder against the wind, and stared absently down at the vastness of Tibet. I understood on some dim, detached level that the sweep of earth beneath my feet was a spectacular sight. I'd been fantasizing about this moment, and the release of emotion that would accompany it, for many months. But now that I was finally here, actually standing on the summit of Mount Everest, I just couldn't summon the energy to care.

At the end of *Longitude*, Dava Sobel does the reverse of what Dickson did in *Sputnik*. Having spent the whole book presenting the historical story of the life of John Harrison and the struggle to vindicate his discovery of how to measure longitude, she begins the final chapter this way:

> I am standing on the prime meridian of the world, zero degrees longitude, the center of time and space, literally the place where East meets West. It's paved right into the courtyard of the Old Royal Observatory at Greenwich [in London]. At night, buried lights shine through the glass-covered meridian line, so it glows like a man-made mid-ocean rift, splitting the globe in two equal halves with all the authority of the Equator. For a little added fanfare after dark, a green laser projects the meridian's visibility ten miles across the valley to Essex.

The purpose of Sobel inserting the first person "I" at the end of her story is to show that this historical story has ramifications far into the future and is, in some ways, a continuing story that touches our lives still.

Richard Preston's *The Hot Zone* is a little more complex in its use of "I." Because he is a science reporter, Preston is used to being the narrative voice that explains complex scientific issues to a reading public who looks to him for engaging information. *The Hot Zone* is an extended piece of detective work, with Preston serving as the detective. He has to explain what it is we are looking for, why it is so dangerous, and the clues that lead to its discovery.

In many ways, it is not dissimilar in approach to Frederick Forsythe's seminal thriller *The Day of The Jackal*. In Preston's book the "Jackal," the freelance assassin the good guys must hunt down and stop before it's too late, is a prehistoric virus named ebola. We need Preston's authorial voice to fully follow and appreciate the power and horror of the story he is telling. So he occasionally inserts himself in the narrative, but not overly obtrusively. For example: Col. Nancy Jaax is one of the army specialists we follow throughout the narrative as they track down the virus. Towards the end of the book, Preston writes:

> One day in spring, I went to visit Col. Nancy Jaax, to interview her about her work during the Reston event. We talked in her office. She wore a black military sweater with silver eagles on the shoulder boards—she had recently made full colonel. A baby parrot slept in a box in a corner. The parrot woke up and squeaked....
>
> She waved her hand as some filing cabinets. "You want to look at some ebola? Take your pick."
>
> "You show me," I said.
>
> She searched through a cabinet and removed a handful of glass slides, and carried them into another room, where a microscope sat on a table. It had two sets of eyepieces so that two people could look into it at the same time.
>
> I sat down and stared in the microscope, into white nothingness.
>
> "Okay, here's a good one," she said, and placed a slide under the lens.
>
> I saw a field of cells. Here and there, pockets of cells had burst and liquefied.
>
> "That's male reproductive tissue," she said. "It's heavily infected. This is Ebola Zaire in a monkey that was exposed through the lungs in 1986, in the study that Gene Johnson and I did."
>
> Looking at the slice of monkey testicle, I got an unpleasant sensation. "You mean, it got into the monkey's lungs and then moved to its testicles?"
>
> "Yeah, it's pretty yucky," she said. "Now I'm going to make you dizzy. I'm going to show you the lung."
>
> The scene shifted, and we were looking at rotted pink Belgian lace.

Not much denying this is a powerful way to learn information. Preston may be "I" in the narrative, but in many ways he has also put himself there as "Everyman." While we see this world through Preston's journalistic reporter's eyes—we feel the scene very powerfully, as if we were present.

Description

One way of increasing the intensity of the narrative is to think about how closely you focus the "camera" on the characters themselves and the details of the scene. As with movie making, you can have the equivalent of long shots, middle distance shots, and close ups, depending on how much detail you choose to reveal about the subject, and depending on the particular place and setting.

The relationship between the pacing of a story and narrative intensity is quite complex, and it includes such things as kind and amount of description, exposition, and awareness of the passage of time. Description, in particular, done poorly (as with an overly heavy hand) can sink a narrative quicker than heavy shoes on a drowning man: How much you use, and what you are using it for, are key.

By way of example: My wife is a professional actress, and she has performed in a Broadway play at the Majestic Theatre on West 44th Street in Manhattan for several years now. The Majestic is an imposing building, dating from the nineteenth century, with a confined narrow backstage area and a large proscenium stage, painted black, with a dizzying array of holes and trapdoors outlined all over it. From the stage you look out into the audience and see theatre seats that sweep up three tiers toward the roof.

The director regularly rehearses the cast to keep their performances sharp and sometimes to bring in new cast members. I've seen a couple of rehearsals, which are not usually open to the public, but I'm known enough now by cast and crew that I've become a kind of fly on the wall.

I was watching a rehearsal one afternoon when I had a sudden insight about descriptive writing. I was sitting quietly in the empty theatre staring at the bare stage. After a moment a couple of actors came out and begin to rehearse their lines. As ever, it was witty and fun and I quickly got caught up in the story.

Once the scene was finished, stagehands slipped onstage and positioned tables and chairs. A backdrop fell into place, wing flats moved into view, and suddenly we were in a room in an opera house in late nineteenth-century Paris. This time, the actors who came on stage wore partial costumes and carried hand props, while the guys on the floods painted the stage with various spotlights and the sound guy cued pre-recorded sounds, and I realized that as much as I had enjoyed the earlier scene, this new scene was that much more compelling because the lights, costumes, props and so forth all heightened the theatrical experience.

While the scene played out I suddenly recalled hanging out at a party with my wife and some of the actors now on stage. Over drinks, the actors had began swapping anecdotes about times the show had not gone as planned. There was the time, for example, when all the electrics failed except for one follow spotlight: No scenery rose from predetermined holes in the floor, no ankle-deep artificial fog flooded the stage, no boat came out from the wings—the actors were forced to re-create the climax of the play in what was essentially a black box without props and without the equipment to create a dungeon setting. But they carried it off.

And it brought home to me that despite all the "gubbins" I was watching the actors wear and hold, "gubbins" that set the scene on stage, an audience would surely stare at actors out of costume, enacting a scene on an entirely bare stage much longer than they would stare at a fully dressed stage devoid of actors.

The point of this story? Description in a narrative is no substitute for characters in a story. In fact, to be effective, description needs to be subject to the viewpoint of a particular character. Description is a function of who is doing the seeing and how they are feeling, thus enhancing a narrative, but existing for its own sake, just as a decorated stage is boring without actors performing their parts.

The most important thing to remember about description is to keep it short and pithy. Beginning writers seem to fall in love with description in their early drafts and forget that description, like adjectives, should be sprinkled on like salt, not smeared on like butter.

Dialogue

If description paints the picture and creates the image, dialogue creates the audio track. It's another form of "show" rather than "tell," and it helps to dramatize a scene and heighten the reader's emotional response to the story. Recreating dialogue, however, can be a minefield of ethical issues for the conscientious writer. We've already seen several examples of how dialog is handled in this chapter. Go back and look at Capote's *In Cold Blood* sequence, and Preston's *The Hot Zone* sequence.

Sebastian Junger's approach to dialogue when writing *The Perfect Storm* is fairly typical of writers of nonfiction. He wrote, "...There are varying kinds of information in [this] book. Anything in direct quotes was recorded by me in a formal interview, either in person or on the telephone, and was altered as little as possible for grammar and clarity. All dialogue is based on the recollection of people who are still alive, and appears in dialogue form without quotation marks. *No* dialogue was made up. Radio conversations are also based on people's recollections, and appear in italics in the text. Quotes from published material are in italics, and have occasionally been condensed to better fit the text."

Journalist Chris Harvey interviewed several writers about writing dialogue and he recorded some of their comments in a 1994 book, *Tom Wolfe's Revenge.* "The reconstruction of dialogue from situations the reporter didn't witness himself can be tricky," said Harvey, and he cited writer Jon Franklin's remarks as supportive of this position: "'If you've got several people from the scene who are willing to talk and a you have a working knowledge of psychology, it's possible.'" Franklin continued, "People can remember surprising amounts of detail from traumatic or emotional occasions. A person can often remember quite a lot of detail about a wedding day or a day he buried a parent. If you were in a serious accident, you can remember the bug smears on a truck."

To gauge the accuracy of their memories, Franklin asks the sources details he can check. "If it's a funeral, ask about the day and the weather, and go back and check. If they're accurate in those kinds of details, it certainly makes me feel better, and [I'm] suspicious if they're not."

In writing *The Hot Zone*, Richard Preston said the dialogue is his book came from "the recollections of the participants." It was extensively well cross-checked, he added. "At certain points in the story, I describe the stream of a person's thoughts. In such instances, I am basing any narrative on interviews with the subjects in which they have recalled their thoughts often repeatedly, followed by fact-checking sessions in which the subjects confirmed their recollections. If you ask a person, 'What were you thinking?' you may get an answer that is richer and more revealing of the human condition than any stream of thoughts a novelist could invent."

If a reporter is recreating a private scene—such as a conversation between two people in their bedroom—it's a good idea to speak to both people. The reporter must also make it clear in the story who the sources are and that this is their recollection of the conversation.

It's important to distinguish for the reader things said at the time and distinguish those from things remembered as said later, perhaps as a response to an interview. In an afterward to *Black Hawk Down,* for example, Mark Bowden explained that all dialogue in the book was either "from radio tapes or [directly] from one or more of the men actually speaking. My goal throughout [was] to recreate the experience of combat through the eyes of those involved; to attempt [to do] that without reporting dialogue would be impossible. Of course, no one's recollection of what they said is ever perfect. My standard is the best memory of those involved. Where there were discrepancies in dialogue they were usually minor, and I was able to work out the differences by going back and forth between the men involved. In several cases I … reported dialogue or statements heard by others present, even though I was unable to locate actual speakers. In these cases the words spoken were heard by more than one witness, or recorded in written accounts within days after the battle."

The following excerpt from *Black Hawk Down* uses both narrative quotes that were recollected and quotes from radio tapes that are contemporaneous to the moment. In the excerpt, the Rangers are already involved in a firefight in the back streets of Mogadishu in hostile enemy territory. The first Black Hawk helicopter has just been shot down:

Nelson watched dumbstruck as the chopper fell.

"Oh, my God, you guys, look at this," he shouted. "Look at this!"

Waddell gasped, "Oh, Jesus," and fought the urge to just stand and watch the bird go down. He turned away to keep his eyes on his corner.

Nelson shouted, "It just went down! It just crashed!"

"What happened?" called Lt. DiTomasso, who came running.

"A bird just went down!" Nelson said. "We've gotta go. We've gotta go right now!"

Word spread wildly over the radio, voices overlapping with the bad news. There was no pretense now of the deadpan military cool, that mandatory monotone that conveys everything under control. Voices rose with surprise and fear:

"—We got a Black Hawk going down! We got a Black Hawk going down!"

"—We got a Black Hawk crashed in the city! Six One!"

"—He took an RPG!"

"—Six One down!"

"—We got a bird down, northeast of the target. I need you to move on out and secure that location!"

"—Roger, bird down!"

It was more than a helicopter crash. It cracked the task force's sense of righteous invulnerability.

More About Conflict in the Narrative

A definition of drama is that it is a process whereby we watch a character resolve his or her problems and dilemmas. As I mentioned earlier, in a simplified sense, problems and dilemmas arise when someone or something says, "No, you can't do that."

It might not be a person, it might be a mountain personified, such as Mt. Everest in *Into Thin Air* saying, "You can't climb me because I'm going to put sudden storms and arctic weather in your way and try to stop you." It could be a prehistoric virus saying, "Mess with me, and I'll kill you quickly but painfully, and you won't be able to do anything about it."

Throughout a book, something or someone should be saying "No" to your characters. If you don't have a series of scenes with some sort of conflict in them, you don't have a narrative. Each time someone says "No" to your protagonist, it increases the narrative's emotional potency.

However, while a scene is made up of characters dealing with rejection and obstacles, at some point you have to have something happen within that scene that resolves a conflict, something that causes the oppositions to your protagonist's ideals and ambitions turn around, at least temporarily, and say "Yes." The mountain's weather system calms and the climbers can make it to the summit; the police officer finally manages to convince the reluctant witness to come forward and tell everyone what she saw, etc.

The Writer as Amateur Psychologist

Sigmund Freud defined the psyche as that part of ourselves that is responsible for our individual thoughts and feelings. For the writer of narratives, who is innately an amateur psychologist studying people and trying to figure them out enough to capture their individuality on paper, a point worth remembering is that despite outward appearances and our wishes to the contrary on occasion, we are not unified beings. We revel in our individuality. We say and do things that are constantly contradictory and paradoxical, and it is the writer's job to capture that factor, but still make sense of the complexity of the human condition.

The concept of political correctness at its best attempts to instill sensitivity into the thick-skinned, while at its worst imposes a tyranny of bland homogeneity that attacks the roots of individuality because it is anarchic, messy, and sometimes nasty. If it infects writing, it can easily become a form of literary cowardice, leading to limited controversy, little conflict, and a plethora of anachronisms in your narrative.

According to Freud, character *is* conflict. When we dream we discover another dimension of our self, a self that is far less shackled by convention and civilized behavior than the self we exhibit when we are awake. Murder, cruelty, and sexual urges of all sorts arise directly or in distorted forms within the dreaming theater of our minds. And these aberrations arise, Freud says, because they are reflections of our desires. From this yarn comes the warp and weft of the whole cloth that will eventually comprise the narratives we write about ourselves and our world.

Transitions

I've mentioned scenes, sequences, and exposition. Now, it's important to consider the ways in which we connect them, a connection which is called transitioning. The purpose of a transition is to keep the reader happily entangled in the narrative dream you are weaving. What I mean by this is that you need to write an engrossing narrative that does not, on occasion, awkwardly jerk the reader away from the world you have been painstakingly creating through the use of clumsy transition.

A transition can be as simple as, *"Meanwhile, back at the laboratory ..."* or *"Ten years earlier, on a rainy Wednesday morning ..."* Another way we can transition from sequence to sequence, or scene to scene, is through the use of a half-scene. Don't waste a lot of time getting us from one place to another if the point is to go from one scene to the next with little or nothing of importance happening in between. If it's not important, don't bother to write it down. One of the simplest ways to transition is to simply leave a white space between one section and the next, or a space with three asterisks centered like this:

* * *

Such a break in the text denotes a passage of time, a change of scene, and so forth, and a word or phrase is all that is then needed in order to orientate the reader to the time and place of the scene that is about to unfold.

Pacing

Pacing describes the speed at which you tell your story.

A narrative has a "current flow," just like a river, and you can adjust the speed of that current flow depending on how you pace your narrative. There are several techniques you can use to achieve this end, including the use of exposition, half-scenes, flashbacks, flash-forwards, transitions, and editing out the unnecessary stuff of your narrative. As Elmore Leonard defines it, the unnecessary part of your narrative is the stuff that everyone skips in order to get to the good stuff—what happens next, though the reader will not make skips at the expense of character development.

Each scene will have a climax, and one definition of pace is how rapidly a narrative moves from climactic point to climactic point. The overall pace of the narrative is also defined by how each scene builds toward the final dramatic narrative resolution.

Foreshadowing

Foreshadowing is something that comes through planning your story's twists and turns, and in reviewing the unfolding of your story during the rewriting process. At its simplest, foreshadowing ties one seemingly unrelated incident to another one that occurs later making us see that second event in a whole new light. The playwright and author Anton Chekov nailed the essence of foreshadowing: If you pull a gun out in Act I, you need to fire it in Act II (or III, depending.) It follows that if a character in a domestic drama suddenly pulls out a gun in Act II and shoots her husband, the reader is entitled to say, "Where did that come from?" When considering the plot twists and surprises that arose throughout your narrative, readers should always think to themselves, following the enjoyment of the surprise, "That's clever, why didn't I think of that." Certainly, they should not think "Where did *that* come from?"

Flashbacks and Flash-Forwards

These literary devices are sometimes considered a kind of transition between sections of a narrative, although I prefer to think of them as literary structural tools. Flashbacks and flash-forwards change the time frame of the story, and they must be handled subtlety, or they can cause much trouble for writers. The central question in the use of flashbacks and flash-forwards is: How do I get my reader from the present into the new time frame, then back again? The first rule should be: If you can avoid using one or the other of these devices, don't use it.

A flashback is often clumsy and annoying to readers and plays havoc with viewpoint. Despite the dangers and difficulties of using a flashback, there are times when you have no choice. It's not necessary, for example, to invariably tell your story in a chronological fashion, as sometimes an event that has occurred in the chronological past only becomes relevant later in the story telling process, and as a result, you may need to flashback to the earlier event only when it becomes necessary to refer or relate to that earlier event. You may need to structure your story synopsis chronologically, but you don't have to tell your story in the same way that you outline it in a chronological sense. For instance, consider the following:

> As Jimmy limped down the street, a squeal of car tires behind him made him instinctively cringe, and he was instantly thrown back to that time, a year earlier, when he was trapped in the cabin of his Ford Escort watching the terrifying weight of a 30-ton Mack truck, its tires locked and shrieking, slide inexorably towards him.

Obviously, at this point, the narrative would backtrack chronologically to recount the previous incident in Jimmy's life. The key to writing a good flashback is to lead the reader gracefully through the transition into the past and bring him back through the same door that you used to get into the past. In the example above, it was a sound that initiated the flashback. Any device that similarly activates a character's memory trip into a scene from the past would do the job as effectively.

One of the great strengths of using flashback in particular is the ability to hone in on just the meat of the event. The author leads the reader back to the precise moment something happened, and the moment the event ends the reader returns to present time. Thus the use of flashback can help pick up the pacing of the book and delete extraneous material, particularly expository material, from the narrative.

The danger with flash-forward is that is has a tendency to be portentous without being helpful. It may seem to enhance narrative suspense, but nine times out of ten it isn't particularly effective at doing so:

> Little did Jimmy know that in less than hour he would see a 30-ton Mack truck bearing down on him like an express train while he sat helplessly in the crushed cabin of his Ford Escort...

The problem with flash-forwards is that they don't often make a lot of sense. The best advice is use them like seasoning in cooking: a little goes a very long way.

Beginnings and Endings

Writers are often told to "start a story with a bang" and some authors think this instruction should be obeyed literally. However, the purpose of beginning a story with a dramatic moment is to engage the reader's emotions from the opening paragraph, and then hold the reader's interest by presenting the book's major character(s) with a problem or a dilemma of an extreme moral or ethical nature. The reader should be inspired to ask, "How did this character reach this traumatic point in her life?" And, "How will she solve this problem?" It is the reader's emotional commitment to what the main character is going through, and his intellectual fascination with how that character will solve her problems, that will compel the reader to keep turning the pages.

Consider this:

> Shortly after six o'clock on a rainy March evening in 1946, a slender, gray-haired man sat in his favorite bar, the Ritz, finishing the last of several martinis. Finding himself adequately fortified for the ordeal ahead, he paid the check, got up, and pulled on his coat and hat. A well-stuffed briefcase in one hand and an umbrella in the other, he left the bar and ventured into the downpour drenching mid-Manhattan. He headed west toward a small storefront on Forty-third Street, several blocks away.

Thus begins A. Scott Berg's wonderful biography, *Max Perkins: Editor of Genius.*

Or this one:

> At liftoff, Matt Eversmann said a Hail Mary. He was curled into a seat between two helicopter crew chiefs, the knees of his long legs up to his shoulders. Before him, jammed on both sides of the Black Hawk helicopter, was his "chalk," twelve young men in flak vests over tan desert camouflage fatigues.

This is, of course, the opening of Mark Bowden's *Black Hawk Down.*

Finally, what about this?

> 'Twas the darkness that did the trick, black as tar, that and the silence, though how the men contriv'd to clamber their way up the cliff with their musket and seventy rounds on their backs, I'm sure I don't know even though I saw it with my own eyes and did it myself before very long. We stood hushed on the muddy shore of the river, peering up at the volunteers. They looked like a pack of lizards unloosed on the rocks, though not so nimble, bellies hugging the cliff with their rumps wiggling with the effort. We couldn't see much of 'em for they disappeared now and then into the clumps of withered cedar and spruce that hung on the side of the hill. But we could feel the squirming, pulling labour of it all.

This is the opening to historian Simon Schama's long narrative nonfiction piece, *The Many Deaths of General Wolfe,* from his book *Dead Certainties.* It is the shorter of two "novellas" (the second of which is titled *The Death of a Harvard Man*). His "You are there" approach is interesting, adventurous, and clearly calculated to mimic fiction. The book was a "work of the imagination that chronicles historical events," he said in an afterward. "The narratives are based on primary sources. In many cases, including some of the most unlikely episodes.... I have faithfully followed accounts given in letters and journals... Two kinds of passages are purely imagination. In the first kind (as in the soldier's witness of the battle of Quebec) the narrative has been constructed from a number of contemporary documents. The more fictitious dialogues ... are worked up from my own understanding of the sources as to how such as scene might have taken place." Schama then proceeds to detail the sources he used to write his book. (Indeed, in nearly every case of narrative nonfiction, the author has gone to pains to detail his or her source material.)

The *change* of the status quo (at the beginning of the story) into a dynamic, evolving system will lead us to the story problem and, ultimately, its solution. In other words, the change in the status quo creates the ensuing plot. This change, or plot development, comes from the author's asking of the story and its characters the question, "Why?" The actual "story" begins at the moment the status quo is about to end.

Once the goal has been achieved, and the problem has been solved, then the story is finished.

The ending is as important as the opening. If the beginning has to "push" the reader off the mountain to begin the toboggan descent, the ending has to wrap things up satisfactorily so that one comes to a comfortable conclusion to the high-speed ride down the mountain. James B. Stewart, author of *Den of Thieves,* says, "I spend more time on endings than anything else but leads."

An ending has to do two things: bring a satisfactory intellectual culmination to the story and bring the emotional experience to a satisfying conclusion, as well. A good example of this is Jonathan Harr's *A Civil Action*, about a lawyer who goes up against two major corporations in order to hold them responsible for the deaths of local children. In the process, the Porsche-driving, high-living lawyer fights the good fight and loses almost everything he once valued.

Endings should be the climax of the narrative, the obvious driving force being a simple answer to the questions, "What happened?" and "Why did it happen?" However, sometimes an author uses a more complex type of ending, what might best be described as a story-within-a-story ending. With this type of ending, some sort of anecdote is used as a symbol of what the author feels the story is about, and without actually telling the reader what to think, the author tries to lead the reader there by using an anecdote as a summary. Stewart uses an ending like this in *Den of Thieves*, his book about Michael Milkin and the insider-trading scandal of the 1980s. Dava Sobel does something similar in *Longitude,* as we've discussed elsewhere.

An ending, by its nature, must provide some sort of closure; the one thing you should never do is leave your reader's dangling, even with a story that has no obvious conclusion. One should at least hint at the possible conclusions available, and leave the reader with the option of choosing one of them for herself.

Photos

Many narrative nonfiction books include photographs, and these may even help sell your book. It's worth knowing that all book contracts make getting the photos the author's responsibility. Your agent may well be able to negotiate some sort of modest photo budget for you, but if you're not careful you could end up spending thousands to obtain photo permissions.

The best way, and the cheapest, is to take the photos yourself, but that's not likely to work, for a variety of reasons, not the least of which is professional quality. Certainly, if you can, take pictures of all the people you interview. Also, ask you interviewees for copies of pictures they may have, of themselves, of others who were involved, of the setting of the story, and so forth.

You may need to try to track down photos that are in the public domain. You can do this through the Library of Congress, which charges a nominal fee (you can find its current list of charges at http://www.loc.gov/preserv/pds/order.html) for researching each picture.

Newspaper and photo journalism libraries can get pretty expensive—sometimes charging as much as hundreds of dollars per picture. Some photographers, depending on their reputation, can charge in the thousands of dollars. Usually, you and the editor will discuss the photo situation and what the house wants versus what you can get and can afford.

Interview Releases

The best source for information about interview releases is entertainment lawyer Jonathan Kirsch's book *Kirsch's Guide to Publishing Law* (Acrobat Books). It is one of the most readable and best books on publishing law I've come across. Anyone can copy and use the forms Kirsch drew up for use in his book.

Lawyers

For the most part you cannot leave the legal matters to the publisher. If you have concerns, make sure you get someone who specializes in publishing and entertainment law to read your manuscript or answer your questions. In general, publishing lawyers are reasonable people who are well versed in first amendment issues.

What they'll advise a writer, more than anything else, is to keep good, accurate records. Particularly the "who said what, where, and when" information. So keep all your notes, tapes, clippings, and the like, if for no other reason than that you will be able to produce them in court should (bad) things ever get that far, which is unlikely.

If you're accurate and careful, you should not have a problem with legal matters.

Find an Agent
or Submit Directly?

*We can't all be heroes, because somebody has to sit on the curb
and applaud when they go by.*
　　　　—Will Rogers, humorist
*Getting an agent is a profound personal validation for
a writer.*
　　　　—Donald Maass, agent, author,
　　　　　Writing the Breakout Novel

Okay, let's start with a confession: I earn a lot of my living as a literary agent (the rest comes from writing) so I have a predisposition when it comes to recommending that writers get themselves an agent. I know it works, because I'm convinced by experience as both an author and an agent (for over a decade, and as an editor before that) that there is no substitute for a good agent working on your behalf and advising you about your work and your career. Anyone who tells you differently should be instantly suspect.

Simply put, unless you're as talented and driven a personality as, say, Dave Eggers, author of *A Heartbreaking Work of Staggering Genius: Based on a True Story*, or really capable entrepreneurs like the authors of *Chicken Soup for the Soul*, the rule of thumb should be: Writers write, editors edit, and agents agent. It's not smart to mix these elements and it's rarely successful. However well you think you will do on your own, you'll do even better with a good agent.

I know, I know—good agents are hard to get and bad ones are like bad spouses. You write and you e-mail and you call, but all to no avail. What's wrong with these idiots? So what do you do to make the agent-courting experience successful?

Publishing is unquestionably one of the more idiosyncratic industries. From the perspective of someone trying to get in, the industry can seem painfully whimsical. Actually, it isn't. There are definitive and distinctive things you can do as an author to enhance your chances of being "brought into the fold" and getting your book represented and then published, things which I'll discuss in a minute.

There are a truckload of myths about publishing—even among those who should know better, such as professional journalists. These myths are in some cases driven by misinformation, and in other cases they are driven by wishful thinking—how publishing *ought* to be, not how it really is. Taken together, these ideas have about as much to do with being published in the early twenty-first century as bronze age metalwork has to do with constructing the space lab. There's a common idea, for example, that editors have the time or the inclination to critique material that is sent to them if they aren't going to buy it. This rarely happens.

These days, most of an editor's time is taken up with endless meetings and producing and moving "product" for the corporate bosses. This is one of the reasons you want to obtain an agent. Agents, today, are far more inclined than editors to encourage new writers who propose promising material, because they have more time to do so, though I should quickly point out agents don't have a lot more time to develop work with writers who are not likely to become their clients than do editors. (A fair few of us still do, though.) It's not our job to help you get published—does that shock you? This is a business and it's your job to learn your craft, not mine to teach you. What I want (and every other editor and agent I know wants) is a writer who has done the work and come up with a knockout proposal, a proposal that I can help put the finishing touches to in order to increase the prospective author's chances of getting published, and then helping to launch a career, and develop the literary career so that writer and agent both make money.

Do not lose sight of the ball: Publishing is a marketplace of ideas. We buy and sell the best and most commercial (in the form of books), which is where the art of writing comes in. It's a heady way to make a living, and all of us in the industry love what we do because of this. But the bottom line is that the business of professional writing and the business of publishing are both about making money, whether you're a publisher, a writer, or an agent. It's a business and needs to be treated as such.

Do It Yourself

If you want to catch an editor's eye, make sure you have an outstanding resume in your field of expertise. If you're a journalist, for example, with a journalistic story to tell, make sure you've been well published and that you have access to the best sources for your story, ideally, previously unpublished ones. You may have already published articles on the subject you want to write a book about. It's even better if you've lectured regularly on it, too. Develop a book that plays to your strengths as a qualified writer and appeals to the broadest audience without becoming too vague. (How do you market to "everyone"?)

Let's say you've written a published article that might well form the basis for a narrative nonfiction book. As a result of the article being published, not only do a couple of editors get in touch with you, but an agent or two contacts you, as well. But while the agent wants you to put together a proposal on spec (speculation), and the agent may not accept your first or even second attempt at the proposal, the editor is ready to give you a book contract on the basis of a phone conversation and the published article. It's not a big publishing house and the advance is pretty meager, but the editor is really enthusiastic and just loves the book idea and your writing. You'd be mad to turn that down, wouldn't you?

Maybe, and maybe not. If one editor is ready to buy something from you basically sight unseen, how do you suppose others might respond if you took the time to actually develop a really good proposal? Yes, it means extra work, but that extra work could pay off in a higher advance. Almost certainly, with more than one editor interested in your project, you'd be able to negotiate a better deal for yourself. What's more, are you sure you want to find yourself writing a book under a ticking contractual deadline that you're not sure you can finish because you haven't yet done the elementary work of fleshing out the book. That's a lot of pressure to handle on a first book. What if the editor leaves the house before the manuscript is submitted? What if the house decides to cut back on books being published that year, never mind the fact that you have a contract guaranteeing publication by a certain date? What if you realize you will miss your deadline by six months or more because you're sick, or someone near to you is sick, or you realize you simply can't organize, research, and write the book in the time you agreed to because the material is overwhelming? Disaster is looming.

Help may be relatively near at hand, however.

Agents? We Don't Need No Stinkin' Agents

Let's look at the previously mentioned scenario again. The likelihood is, even with a published article you won't be approached by an editor or agent, though certainly it happens. Nevertheless, you've written a strong article, and it can serve as a writing sample, and certainly as a calling card. You've polished your book proposal and now you're ready to start actively submitting it—somewhere.

First question: Do you really need an agent or can you successfully submit your proposal directly to an editor? Indeed, to misquote the bandit in the movie, *The Treasure of the Sierra Madre,* "Agents? We don't need no stinkin' agents." Why should you waste 15 percent of your hard-earned money on some interloper?

Among many other qualities (including a keen editorial eye), you get two really important assets with a good agent that you don't get from anyone else: a matchmaker's Rolodex of editors who want and like what you've written and a canny contract negotiator who likely has already arranged boilerplate agreements with publishers better than the one a publisher might offer you if you did business directly with the publisher's representatives.

So, ideally, you should try to approach an agent before you approach a publisher. However, as we suggested earlier, let's assume you just aren't having any luck catching an agent's eye with your particular project. There's no reason you shouldn't approach editors directly if you do it in a professional manner—and that phrase—in a professional manner—is extremely important. If you don't know what makes for a professional manner, by all means, educate yourself before you start calling and e-mailing editors.

There's a catch though: *If too many editors get to see your proposal and reject it, your chances of getting an agent to represent your project diminish exponentially with each rejection you receive.* There is only a finite number of places and people to whom either you or an agent can submit a project. Do not be in a hurry to submit any proposal until you're absolutely certain it's ready to be seen by either an editor or an agent, and if you've never been previously published, you're likely not the best judge of your own material. (Neither is your spouse, sibling, child, friend, neighbor, or parent, unless they happen to be a professional writer or publishing professional, so it won't help to try to sell an editor or agent on the project by saying, "My mother/ brother/sister/auntie/best friend thinks it's the best thing she's ever read, and she/he reads three books a week.")

Do some research on editors who buy the kind of book you're writing. There are lots of books that will help you, such as the Writer's Digest guides, or Jeff Herman's *Guide to Editors and Agents*, plus a multitude of frequently asked questions (FAQs) on a number of writers' forums on the Internet. Pick several books that most closely resemble the one you're planning to write, then research which editors (and agents) worked on those books. You can sometimes find this information in the acknowledgments section of a book, or reported in the deals information section of publishersmarketplace.com, or in *Publishers Weekly* magazine, the industry journal. Then write a dynamite, though not gimmicky, three-paragraph (one page maximum) query letter and a professional-quality book proposal.

Next make a preliminary call or send an e-mail to the editor. Using your query letter as a script, pitch your idea in a short (one or two sentence), simple, confidant manner, and hope the editor bites and asks to see the material.

Don't leave phone messages that say, "Hi. Ah'm Chuckie from Pine Bluff, Arkansas, and I've wrote a book that will make a great movie..." or "Hello. Charles Remington here, from Boston. My manuscript is just what you've been looking for; please call me at 555-1212, if you're interested ..."

And, don't send e-mails that reads "My name is Linguine Z. DePasta. I have recently completed my book and I am currently seeking an agent. I am 32 years old. I grew up in Pittsburgh, and I currently own a home in Revere, MA. I am employed as an accountant for a meat packing company in Everett, MA. I enjoy writing in my spare time. My book is about cycling around the beautiful United States ...."

Editors and agents are intrigued by professionals. Let us know up front if you're a freelance writer, or a former editor with *Playboy*, or a professional journalist with the *New York Times,* or if you have any credible literary credentials that might reassure us you won't be wasting our time.

Next, explain briefly what you're writing about: a book about, say, the inside story of what happened at Enron, or about being a female firefighter, and explain that you worked for Enron as a highly placed accountant, or you've been a firefighter for "x" years. If your project is a reconstruction of the battle for Mogadishu, for example, tell us up front you're a professional journalist working for the *Philadelphia Inquirer,* and the newspaper recently ran a series of articles by you on this previously ignored modern battle.

If you decide to e-mail an editor, *do not* assume he will automatically want to see your proposal and attach it uninvited. There are too many viruses and weird e-mail things floating around these days, and the odds are great that an e-mail-savvy editor will simply delete the material without even opening it.

However, if you intend to contact an editor or agent by actual, old-fashioned mail, it's okay to include the proposal with your query letter.

If you attempt to contact an editor by phone, and if you're lucky enough to be put through, first ask if the editor has a moment to speak with you. Editors are stunningly busy people, and not every time you are lucky enough to get an ear is necessarily a good time to pitch your book idea. If the editor says he has the time, make sure you pitch your book idea succinctly and intelligently. Be warm and winning. The editor (or her assistant) will tell you soon enough whether or not she is interested in seeing your project. If she says yes, then say thank you, confirm the correct spelling of her name, get her correct address, and politely ask how long she anticipates it will take her to read your proposal.

If you haven't heard back by the date the editor suggested, wait a few more days and then call and politely ask how things are progressing.

Some Reasons for Rejection

There are a number of reasons an editor may turn down your project, besides the obvious one of it not being written to a professional standard in the editor's opinion. The following are a few reasons for rejection:

- The editor may have recently acquired a book on this subject, or the house may have acquired or recently published something similar.

- The editor believes there is too small an audience for the book idea. For example: A book revealing the seamier side of the anti-abortion movement's fanatical supporters. Here, while the story might make a great newspaper or magazine article, the wretched truth is that the anti-abortion proponents won't want to read the book, and the pro-life proponents already know as much as they need to about their adversaries. *Could you write a good book about this subject?* Of course. It would have to be a remarkable book and remarkably well done to entice a commercially viable audience.

- The subject is too local, or too academic, for general audiences. Successful true crime stories, for example, tend to be psycho-sexual or concerned with people who have a national recognition. Why should someone in Texas necessarily care what happens to some unknown victim or perp in Idaho?

- The subject is too obscure and does not show promise to change the way we see and understand the world.

- There are publishing marketing and sales biases, such as that military stories are read by men who are not interested in books about women. (Unfair and untrue, but a bias to deal with nevertheless.)

- The editor believes the author does not have the expertise or experience to tell the story successfully.

- Nothing new is being brought to the table; the book is just a rehashing of what has been previously published.

Once upon a Time...

There may well be writers you know who may *say* they've represented themselves successfully, but excluding a handful of exceptions (and I mean under five people) I defy anyone to name one successful writer who hasn't improved his or her career by using either an agent, a literary lawyer, or some sort of business manager.

Let me tell you story: Once upon a time...my first agent was engaged in what seemed like one of the world's longest divorces, and she was not focused on her work.

I saw no reason why my career should stall, however. After all, I was also an agent, I had been an editor, and this was not my first book deal. What could go wrong? So I signed a small book deal with Ms. A, an elderly and experienced editor, with whom I had a good ongoing professional relationship. Indeed, earlier she had helped me shape my own book proposal.

Once I had handed in the manuscript, I learned to my horror that I was being edited not only by Ms. A, but also by Ms. B, a woman in her 40s, and by Ms. C, who was both opinionated and not long out of college. Someone would request a change, I'd make it, and a couple of weeks later the manuscript would come back with different handwriting, asking why I'd made the original change.

"I don't care if I'm edited by Attila the Hun," I cried. "Just pick one person for me to work with!"

I embraced Zen Buddhism and tried to fall asleep to images of sheep bleating out the phrase, "Better published than not." Things were looking bleak and the deal was falling apart. I wasn't sure what to do to save it because personalities—no, let's be honest, *egos*—were starting to get raw and bruised.

Finally, my original agent shook off her divorce-induced lethargy and stumbled back into the picture. When she realized what a nightmare the company was putting me through, she got the original publishers to let me keep the royalty advance and helped move the book to another publisher. It was worth the wait and the tribulations to finally have the problem resolved so neatly.

The new publisher, John Wiley & Sons, paid me a better royalty advance, changed barely a word of what I'd written, and *The Elements of Storytelling* was published to good reviews. You can still buy it in bookstores, and twice a year I get a royalty check. Of course, all's well that ends well, but without an agent on the job, the outcome in this case would likely have been far bleaker.

Sorry—Too Busy

A lot of writers chase agents who are too busy to respond most of the time. Successful agents have their hands full just maintaining their regular clientele. The average agent represents between fifty and seventy clients. However, most good agents are usually on the lookout for successful, experienced, money-earning writers who know how the game is played and who can exploit their own experience and capabilities to everyone's advantage. So, if you learn your craft and roll *with* the marketplace, rather than try to poke it in the eye, your chances of being published are quite high, because the truth is that finding good book projects with strong authors attached is surprisingly difficult. If you're an author in this category, like the pretty girl at a ball, all the beaus will notice you and want to take you for a twirl around the floor.

Successful writers have been published in magazines and anthologies, have written book reviews for local or national newspapers, have gotten their name in print somewhere, often more than once, and somewhere accompanying an article there is a byline that says something like, "Dobbie Elfen is currently working on a nonfiction book about domestic enslavement."

Successful writers attend writers' conferences and network discreetly with other writers and with people in the writing community. They get their writing noticed by people whose opinion counts and by people who can talk to friends or colleagues in the publishing business about an up-and-coming writer and her work. One of the best ways for a writer possessing the aforementioned successes to get a good agent is to try to find a person who is starting their own agency, or a person who has just joined an established agency. This type of personnel information is routinely reported in the industry trades, and in the writer-based chat rooms of the Internet. Editors frequently lose editorial jobs, due to the volatile economic earthquakes that wrack the publishing industry, and many of these former editors set up shop as agents and are on the lookout for new clients. Also, prospective authors should ask other represented or published writers for agent recommendations. Try querying members of an organization such as the Association of Author's Representatives (AAR), though not all good agents are members. The AAR has rules about who can qualify as an agent, and it has a canon of ethics its members must abide by.

Another good source for potential agents is the *Literary Market Place* (also called the LMP), which also has rules about who can be listed as an agent in its pages. Lists of agents can also be found in Jeff Herman's *Guide to Literary Agents* and the Writer's Digest book *Guide to Literary Agents*.

Telling Good Agent from Bad Agent

The wrong agent, or a poor agent, will not help you at all, and that agent may even hinder you. They'll offer bad advice, make you work hard at the wrong things because they don't have the proper editorial skills, and then not expose your work to the best editors.

The right agent will be able to suggest the best audience for your work, and he can assist you in polishing your proposal to target that audience. He'll also know the editors who are looking for the kind of material you've written, and his reputation will definitely carry some weight with editors when it comes to looking seriously and quickly at a proposal. Perhaps the best indicator of a successful agent is simply that he or she makes a living solely from commissions on sales. (In fact, you can't be a member of the AAR, the agent's "guild," unless you do.)

If an agent wants to charge you a "reading fee" or "editorial fee," my advice is to be very careful. The vast majority of reputable agents don't charge reading fees, nor do they provide "reader's reports." The whole concept of charging for reading creates a questionable conflict of interest if you think about it. How can someone give an unbiased opinion on an author's work if they're earning money by charging for editorial advice? This type of practice leads to authors buying their agent's time and attention, with likely little to show for their money at the end of the project, except hard lessons learned. The hard truth is that if you can't get an agent interested in your work without paying for some sort of "service," you're almost certainly not ready to be published, and you (and the agent, on your behalf) will have a hard time getting a publisher interested. Has the agent actually *read* your book or book proposal and can he talk about it intelligently?

Undoubtedly, a good agent will have editorial suggestions about making something clearer or more focused, or more commercially viable, but you should ask yourself: Does he really understand what I'm trying to do and sympathize with my efforts? And, particularly, is he enthusiastic about my idea?

Agents look for writers who have put together a terrific project, have paid their dues as professional writers, and are ready to be published. The agent then helps the writer polish the project and sell it, beginning, hopefully, a wonderful and enduring partnership.

Catching an Agent's Eye

There are basically three types of literary agents. One type is mainly composed of former editors and editorial types who develop and shape projects with the writers they enlist as clients. A second type includes agents who prefer spending their time and effort at selling writer's works rather than performing editorial work; these agents are into the "dance," as a friend of mine calls it; that is, they enjoy the hard bargaining that can take place during a book deal negotiation—the "I'll go there, and you go here, you give me this, and I'll give you that," kind of discussion. These agents prefer to represent "one-off" projects (often nonfiction and high-profile writer based) that look like commercial successes, and then they move on to the next author and the next deal, rather than concern themselves with developing a writer's career. Lastly, there are entertainment lawyers who basically just do the deal for the writer. Very successful authors (I'm talking very high six or seven figures) sometimes use lawyers because it's cheaper for them to pay an hourly rate than a 15 percent commission. This does not work well for less well-paid authors, for obvious reasons.

There's a common misconception that agents spend all their time developing new material and new clients for publishers. Unpublished writers think that if they just take their place in line agents will get to them eventually. Alas, it's another one of those publishing myths. You have to really catch an agent's attention through good writing and strong ideas.

Agents spend some of their time in the evenings and on weekends reading unsolicited, or slush, mail, but they do so only after they've finished reading the latest material sent to them by their clients. While they're always on the lookout for good new material by talented writers, they have plenty to do just keeping on top of their existing workload. This means your material has to be really special if you are an unpublished, prospective writer. However, if your idea is strong and attractive, you will attract the attention of agents and editors. The good news is that narrative nonfiction, if not a "hot" genre, is well regarded by editors, so the odds of being published, given a good job of putting together your nonfiction proposal, are better than average.

Unagented writers don't seem to realize that when an agent takes on a new client the agent is taking on a negative asset. The client will actually cost the agent money—in time, energy, mailing fees, telephone calls, photocopying proposals, and so forth before the agent ever sees a dime of the commission he will earn from a sale.

What Agents Do

Agents spend a lot of time developing new contacts with editors and publishers and maintaining and renewing old ones. They pitch projects by clients, write query letters on behalf of the client and the project, check on royalty statements, pursue outstanding royalty advances, go through the fine print of contracts, put out "fires," negotiate deals, come up with career plans and tactics to keep their clients published, keep in contact with foreign agents and movie and TV agents, if they don't happen to handle these rights themselves ... well, the list of the agent's duties is exhaustive.

Agents also take lunch meetings, attend book parties, speak at writers' conferences and make it their business to meet and get to know as many publishing-house acquiring editors as they can. The essence of the job is matchmaking—putting the right project with the right editor at the best house, so one of the definitions of a good agent is someone who consistently knows the right editor for a project and who knows that editor's needs, likes, and dislikes. Agents make it their job to keep up with the house at which particular editors are currently working, what type of ideas editors like, and what they looking for (not necessarily always the same thing), and in certain circumstances agents actually help to create book ideas for their authors that editors seem keen to try to acquire.

Each publishing house has its own personality and specialties and is continually reinventing itself in order to gain as large a share of the market as possible. These days editors move from house to house. Also, many mergers and acquisitions have taken place in the last couple of years, and the reshaping of giant companies such as Bantam, Doubleday, and Dell has had a serious effect on the rapidly changing publishing industry.

You can guarantee that in the next couple of years publishing won't much resemble what it looked like a few years ago. In the face of all this industrial volatility, agents provide a font of cutting-edge knowledge and a haven of stability for authors.

Figuring It Out

As I mentioned earlier, many new agents are not necessarily new to the publishing business. These days, many agents are former editors or publishing-house employees, and while they may not yet have placed many books as agents, they do know the business, how it's conducted, and a lot of the people in it.

If you make repeated calls to an agent and don't get a reply, it's a clue the relationship isn't working and that it won't work for you. Most agents will respond with 48 hours.

It is a common misconception that all good agents reside in New York City. While it's true that Manhattan is the heart of American publishing and most of the publishing industry is based there, there are many good agents based outside of the City. Some agents, not based in New York, usually make regular trips into the City to meet with editors. However, most of the work is done by phone and fax these days. It is better to have a good agent outside the City than a mediocre one based in New York.

Anyone can call himself an agent, take on clients, charge money for this and that, make outrageously optimistic claims, and never get anyone published. Thus, the Association of Author's Representatives (AAR) was formed to try to set standards and distinguish good agents from bad. The AAR is a not-for-profit trade organization of literary and dramatic agents. It was formed in 1991 through the merger of the Society of Authors' Representatives, founded in 1928, and the Independent Literary Agents Association, founded in 1977. The association's objectives include keeping agents informed about conditions in publishing, the theater, the motion picture and television industries, and related fields; encouraging cooperation among literary organizations; and assisting agents in representing and defending their authors' interests.

Membership in the AAR is restricted to agents whose primary professional activity for the two years preceding application for membership has been as an authors' representative or a as playwrights' representative.

To qualify for membership, an applicant must have sold ten different literary properties during the 18-month period preceding application. Member agents must adhere to the AAR's Canon of Ethics, and associate members are full-time employees of a sponsoring agent member.

For the most up-to-date AAR membership list, visit the website at *www.aar-online.org.*

The AAR's New Agent Questionnaire

The AAR publishes a list of questions that you may wish to pose to a new agent when the two of you are contemplating establishing a business relationship. Bear in mind that most agents are *not* going to bother to take the time to answer these questions unless they've decided to represent you. (The following is reprinted by permission of AAR):

1. Are you a member of the AAR?
2. How long have you been in business as an agent?
3. Do you have specialists at your agency who handle movie and television rights? Foreign rights?
4. Do you have sub-agents or corresponding agents in Hollywood and overseas?
5. Who in your agency will actually be handling my work? Will the other staff members be familiar with my work and the status of my business at your agency? Will you oversee or at least keep me apprized of the work that your agency is doing on my behalf?
6. Do you issue an agent-author agreement? May I review the language of the agency clause that appears in contracts you negotiate for your clients?
7. How do you keep your clients informed of your activities on their behalf?
8. Do you consult with your clients on any and all offers?
9. What are your commission rates? What are your procedures and time frames for processing and disbursing client funds? Do you keep different bank accounts separating author funds from agency revenue? What are your policies about charging clients for expenses incurred by your agency? (Commonly these days, book agents charge 15 percent for domestic sales and 20 percent for foreign sales, which are often shared with a foreign sub agent. An agent's commission is payable on anything the book earns as long as he or she is the agent of record on that project.)

10. When you issue 1099 tax forms at the end of each year, do you also furnish clients with a detailed account of their financial activity, such as gross income, commissions and other deductions, and net income, for the past year?
11. In the event of your death or disability, what provisions exist for my continued representation?
12. If we should part company, what is your policy about handling any unsold subsidiary rights to my work?

We'd Like to Make You an Offer...

If an editor makes you an offer, tell the editor you're very excited, but you need some time to consider the situation as you're in the process of getting an agent. It's a wise writer who, offer in hand, now returns to his list of "dream" agents and tells each of them he has an offer from publisher X. Is any agent interested in representing him? Most agents will respond quickly and positively to "he who has an offer in hand."

The best way for an author to secure the "best deal" is to use a reputable agent who has examined and negotiated the offer. This may not be a great deal compared to what other authors may have been offered, but it will be the best deal for you and your book at that moment in time. An agent is in a position to ensure that a contract is honored, saving the writer from pestering the publisher if a problem arises.

Whether an editor has made the offer to you directly and you've subsequently found an agent, or your agent comes back to you with an offer from an editor she showed your proposal to, you've reached a definitive stage in the process.

If your agent is lucky, she may be able to activate an auction, with editors bidding against each other to buy the book. If every editor but one drops out, the agent sometimes has a number of persuasive arguments she can make to get the editor to increase the proposed royalty advance.

Most deals operate from the guiding principles that the editor really wants to buy the book, and the author really wants to be published by that house and, ideally, through that editor. In speaking to an agent, in an effort to get the best deal for his house an editor may make the argument that the book he is seeking to buy may well not be a success despite a belief in the author's talent. He will argue that he's going out on a limb for an untried author, he has colleagues he must convince, and because of this risk the editor needs to get as many rights as possible to try to maximize the opportunities to earn back a royalty advance.

The agent will argue the author's case, saying, "How can you say the book isn't worth X? Surely, you wouldn't want to publish it unless you saw merit in it, would you?" Besides, agents will argue that first-time authors are often a better bet than previously published writers because there are no sales records to impact how many books a bookseller will order. Also, the agent will remind the editor that people know when they are being "screwed," and it is not a wise move to treat an author poorly from the outset but to give them the respect that will allow the relationship to grow in a healthy manner and provide many future books with that editor. The principle that an author should be allowed to reap the benefits of his work, if the book performs well, is one that good editors have no problem honoring. The success of a book should be indicative of everyone's success. The agent will badger the house, saying, "Give us this; show some good faith so that the author will really know how important he is to the company, etc." Of course, if there is a good sales track record, an agent will argue this fact very strongly as well.

Having negotiated the deal in broad measure, once the publishing contract arrives, the agent now turns into a paralegal and examines the contract closely. She'll discuss technical details with the editor as well as with the publishing company's contract staff in an effort to get the client the best deal possible, taking care of contingency disasters that almost never happen, but nevertheless need to be prepared for.

When Things Go Wrong

Publishing relationships between agent/writer and editor/writer suffer many of the same problems that sink romantic relationships: unrealistic expectations for what an agent can or should do for you; poor communication, as when writers (or agents) are inconsiderate and disrespectful of editors, forgetting to say thank you occasionally, and so on (or, of course, the other way around). Remember, everyone has other demands put on their time and resources. Respect each other's need for privacy but also expect that your agent will respond quickly if there is a problem that needs to be fixed. Both writer and agent must learn to trust each other.

Your agent will often be someone you like, but he or she is not your "friend," nor is friendship a good basis for a business relationship. Agents are not shrinks, nor should they be considered a source of emotional or psychological support, or even a personal editor. A good agent may exhibit some or all of these abilities because it is a job that involves nurturing, but don't expect it and don't ask for it, especially at the beginning. If you have personal problems, figure them out before you get together with your agent. Her job, remember, is to sell your work. If you have nothing to sell, there isn't much she can do for you.

A major area of conflict that can arise between writer and agent is over editorial revision. Many agents these days have editorial backgrounds (many were editors at one time in their career) and, increasingly in recent years, the onus of editorial work on a manuscript has fallen more on the agent's shoulders as publishing houses have abrogated that responsibility. Many editors today are not as skilled at line editing as editors once were, and they also don't have the time to work on manuscripts the way they once could. Consequently, editors are looking for manuscripts that are in near-perfect condition. Of course that's rarely the case, but agents know that in order to stand any chance of getting a book published it needs to be in good editorial shape.

However, there's no point making editorial changes to your manuscript just because someone says you should make those changes, regardless of whether or not those editorial comments are insightful. If the changes don't make sense to you, don't make them. You'll never please anyone if you can't please yourself first. But that is not the same thing as saying you shouldn't try to develop as objective a view as possible of your work, particularly when it comes to genre and structure. If an agent or editor has suggested a change, you've got to figure that whatever it is you've been trying to do in your manuscript at that point may not be working. The suggested solutions may not be right, but there's clearly some kind of problem, and it needs a solution, or, at least, consideration.

Ten Reasons You Should Get a Good Agent

The following are ten reasons why you should get yourself an agent rather than try to represent yourself:

- Your agent's enthusiasm and professional reputation will count for something in selling your book. An agent is well-versed in the tools of getting a book out into the marketplace, including the best timing for a submission and developing a little industry buzz about your book.

- It's an agent's job to know which editor at which house is interested in projects like yours, or which editor is looking for projects like yours. If you have already made the wrong approach to an editor, you may well have closed a door at that house that can't be reopened.

- An agent commonly submits a project to several editors at the same time (called multiple submissions). Editors accept this, but they sometimes don't like authors trying to do the same thing.

- Until you're published, you're not the best judge of your own work. An editor knows that if the agent sees something commercially viable in your work, he or she should pay attention to that submission.

- An agent can nearly always get a better deal for your book than you can, even if the initial contact is yours.

- Even if you're a lawyer, unless you know publishing law, publishing contracts can be a pain to understand and negotiate. Agents earn their commission by negotiating good contracts with publishers for their clients. Many agents have already agreed to changes in publishing houses' boilerplate contracts because of previous deals they've cut for other clients at that house.

- The agent makes money when you make money, so your interests are intertwined. Agents will get you the best deal, and their sub-agents may be able to earn you extra money through foreign and translation markets, and through the movie and TV arena.

- An agent can run interference for you with a troublesome editor or publishing house employee. If you don't think this means much now, wait until you learn your editor was fired and that your new editor is too busy or too cavalier to pay attention to you, particularly when the proofreader rewrites your book just as it going into galleys. (This really happened to a client of mine.)

- Your agent keeps track of who owes you money, how much, and when it's due to be paid.

- A good agent will be a career manager and adviser and will encourage and guide you in your literary endeavors.

Who Do You Know?
What Can You Do?
Marketing and Promotion

The market came with the dawn of civilization and it is not an
invention of capitalism.... If it leads to improving the well-being
of the people there is no contradiction with socialism.
　　　　—Mikhail Gorbachev, Soviet political leader
Writing ought either to be the manufacture of stories for
which there is a market demand—a business as safe and
commendable as making soap or breakfast foods—or it should
be an art, which is always a search for something for which
there is no market demand....
　　　　—Willa Cather, author, *On the Art of Fiction*

For the moment let's not even worry about what format your
book will be published in, be it hardcover, trade paperback, ebook,
or as a mass market original. That's a decision that the publisher
will make, anyway, and you won't have much say in the matter.
So, answer this question, and be brutally honest with yourself:
"Do I honestly believe that 10,000 people will buy my book over
the course of a year?"

If the answer is "No," then the odds of your book being
published by a reputable, established publisher diminish con-
siderably—maybe to one in five. If, prior to publication, a book
is expected to sell 5,000 copies or so, we enter the realm of university presses and regional presses, who tend to offer small advances and stringent publishing contracts. I made up that sta-
tistic based on my twenty years of experience in book publishing

as an editor, writer, and agent, but before you throw away this book in outrage for not being more sensitive to your aspirations and efforts as a writer, consider this: You may quite rightly believe that *someone else*—say a publishing marketing and sales professional—*should* be able to sell 10,000 copies of your book. But how many could *you* sell if you had to? What if the publishing company professional assigned to your book, for whatever reason—perhaps overwork, perhaps incompetence, perhaps exhaustion, perhaps indifference to your book's subject—screws up the promotion and marketing of your book?

How do you fix that? You should pay attention to this question because your career as a writer of books is ultimately dependent on two things: sales figures and review acclaim, in that order. And do you really want to have your career as a writer completely in the hands of someone else if you can learn to do some of that person's job yourself or if you discover that you have your own capability to market your book?

The truth is, these days the most successful authors aren't necessarily the best at writing, or even the most creative—they are the most effective in finding and developing an audience for their work, and helping to move their product—that is, their book(s)—off the bookshelves.

Most of us who try to make a living in the arts are faced with balancing this difficult dilemma: We want to be the best writers, actors, singers, whatever, *and* sell well. We soldier on, ever the optimist, pulling the handle of the great slot machine of life, believing that next time those three spinning wheels will line up three perfectly matching fruits, and our reward will come chug-chugging out of the slot as bells ring and lights flash. And, for some of us, given a degree of staying power, growing confidence and command of our craft, good advisors, and an ability to increasingly mature and improve our choice of material means that we create books with "legs" (i.e., slightly higher sales each time), so that our careers progress forward, if not as flamboyantly as we might like sometimes but at least healthily in the right direction.

A writer friend of mine, for example, who is pretty successful in his own right, is still stuck in the low to mid six-figure range
of advances despite writing five relatively successful novels and
a couple of screenplays. To put his situation into perspective, not
so long ago, a writer friend of his received a million-dollar advance for his new book.

"OK," my friend John said to his friend Jeff, voicing both
admiration and some professional frustration at his own lack of
similar success. "Now I'm officially jealous."

"Wait a minute," Jeff said. "This is my seventeenth book.
I've paid my dues."

And he was right. Jeff had labored hard for 20 years, not
just as a writer who improved his books with each one published,
but also at helping to promote those books. And he'd also been a
little lucky. Hollywood had finally come knocking, and that had
helped to tip him over the edge.

The fact is, authors these days must embrace not just the
Holy Grail-like quest of profound creativity and mastery of craft,
but they must also dance with Mammon without falling under
his corrosive spell. That's a tough balancing act to pull off.

Taking Advantage of Trends

Writers sometimes think that rushing books on a topical subject
into print is a way to fame and fortune. This confuses magazine
publishing with book publishing and, even then, there's usually
a minimum three-month lead time. The big problem with following "hot" trends in book publishing is that by the time you've
responded to them, it's too late; they're already cooling off. The
following is a crude timetable to give you some idea of how things
work in book publishing:

- From idea to research to book proposal: two months;

- From book proposal to literary agent: six months;

- From agent to editor and book contract: six months (if
  you're lucky);

- From contract to delivery of manuscript to editor: six months;

- From transmission by editor to finished book on the shelves: nine months.

Total Time: two years.

Part of the problem with rushing a book is that publishers have monthly "slots" for books, and sometimes it takes a while for a slot to open up for a book. If a publisher publishes a book early, then someone else's book is going to be bumped from its allotted publishing slot. Meanwhile, the sales and marketing process for that book is already underway and suffers if it is tampered with, while the sales and marketing plan for your book may not have yet begun and you'll be published into a void, with little or no attention from reviewers, who typically need books at least three months ahead of publication date.

Considering the previous mentioned aspects, you might think it would benefit you to go straight to the editor yourself (rather than working through an agent) and gain some time, but the truth is, an agent knows exactly who in a publishing house is looking for material and what his or her tastes are, so the agent will probably shorten the time it takes to get an editor to accept the book. They can also submit your idea to more than one editor at a time. It's tougher for an author to do this. Your proposal could languish in an editorial "slush" pile for months before it gets rejected and you have to start the process all over again.

Audience, Audience, Audience

Okay, so your book has been sold, written, accepted, and it's coming out soon. Your job now is to focus on what you can do to help it become a success.

Apart from the obvious need for the author to make the reader care about the characters in a story, whether they are the doomed sailors of *A Perfect Storm* or the unhappy children of *Angela's Ashes,* it should be realized that narrative nonfiction books sell well because they touch some sort of cultural nerve. Of course, divining what that communal nerve will be is largely guesswork, although some degree of good conjecture can be made, based on honed intuition, objective observations of the culture, experience studying the topic you want to write about, and the kinds of books this audience has previously been attracted to. Nevertheless, catching a reader's attention isn't just a function of how well you write your book. It's about somehow making sure your story is told in such an emotionally gripping way that it will appeal to as wide an audience as possible beyond the previously anticipated core audience.

At the beginning of this book, I spoke about the need to be aware of the audience appeal of your book. This is a defining aspect of whether or not an idea you feel passionate about can be written in a commercially successful way. Does the area you want to write about have a fan base? A sub-culture? Could you tap into that base somehow?

You should objectively compare your idea against what has already been published on the same subject or on a closely related subject. For example, why write another book of military history? Can you really re-create another *Black Hawk Down*? If so, the odds are high you will have a winner. Is there really room for another biography of Ben Franklin? What does your book add to the field? If it's only your thoughts and philosophies and particular perspective, unless you're an expert whose opinion is sought by colleagues in your field, the likelihood is your book will be a tough sell. If, however, you know your subject well enough that you realize there's a "hole" (i.e., something about your subject that hasn't been considered or written about yet), you're probably onto a good thing. And, now, long before your book hits the bookstores, is the time to start working all these leads.

We come to the big question: What will my publisher do to promote and market my book? The short answer is, "Not much." However, publishers will usually follow where you lead.

Mining Resources

Rachel Donadio summed up the limbo period between handing in your manuscript and seeing your book on the shelves nicely when she wrote in her *New York Sunday Times* Book Review essay, "Waiting For It," "The sudden change in cabin pressure from writing to waiting can be jarring—and can last a very long time." She quoted the Irish writer Colm Toibin, whose first novel, *The South*, appeared in 1990, a year and a half after he turned it in. "It was all slow and strange," he said. "It comes as a huge shock when it happens the first time."

The problem is that however advanced technology becomes in producing books, the books themselves still need to be hand-sold into the accounts—that is, to the bookstores—and it takes time to create a buzz and encourage harried bookstore owners to pay attention to a book that may not, on first look, stand out from the crowd in some way.

"It's not the technology that's the problem; it's the humans that are the problem," says Jonathan Karp, the publisher of Twelve, an imprint of Grand Central Books (formerly Warner Books) which releases one title a month.

Donadio quoted several industry insiders in her essay on this topic. For example, David Rosenthal, the publisher of Simon & Schuster, told her, "It's not only buzz, it's a product introduction—but with nothing like the advertising or marketing budget that a piece of soap would have."

The Internet offers many opportunities to hand-sell books directly to the audience who will find it appealing. Glenn Yeffeth, at Ben Bella books, bases a great deal of his sales and marketing strategy on information obtained from the Internet.

However, from a marketing standpoint, the down side is that there's a cacophony of voices that must be broken through in order to get out the message, so publishers plan months in advance when and how to release a book.

"We live in an impatient society and have a throwaway, Kleenex culture, so it takes time to get over the noise barrier," Nan Talese, the publisher of Nan A. Talese/Doubleday, told

Donadio. "With an established author whose work is known and [whose] sales patterns [are] reliable, less time is necessary," Talese said.

Karp added, "If it's a book by someone who people aren't familiar with, on a subject that people don't necessarily [feel they] need to have, it will take nine months to a year for people to figure it out."

As each new season of books moves toward publication, publicity and marketing teams create plans to get their company's books noticed—and sold. Publishing is an innately creative and inventive industry, so these plans can include not only traditional ways of pitching titles, but also targeted campaigns to reach niche audiences. At pre-sales and launch meetings, sales, publicity, and marketing staff get together with editorial staff to explore ways to maximize each book's sales potential.

"One of the challenges at a big house is making choices about which books will receive an extra push," Tracy van Straaten, director of publicity at Simon & Schuster Children's Publishing told *Publishers Weekly*. "Usually, the list [of books for that season] tells us what to do; many publicity and marketing opportunities just present themselves. But it's also fun to come up with creative things to do."

A publisher's anticipation of how a book will perform is determined by the initial print run and by the popularity and sales history of an author. Each season's list contains clear choices for which book will get niche treatment, and publicity and marketing staff must be careful how they allot limited financial resources on targeted campaigns. To help with that decision, they research markets, do targeted mailings, and talk with sales reps around the country who can tap into potential outlets. While the success of targeted campaigns is hard to measure, they can deliver incremental sales for a book. The numbers may not be overwhelming, but like water dripping into a cup, eventually it fills up. Everything helps, particularly over the long term. Van Straaten added, "Sometimes an author is our best resource. If they are knowledgeable enough about a topic to write a book on it, chances are they have great contacts."

Lissa Warren is director of publicity at DaCapo Press, and also happens to be a client of mine. Commenting on what authors can do to help publicize their books, she said, "The sad truth is that most editors, reporters, and producers do not like to be approached by authors directly. Some of them will humor you. Many of them will be rude to your face or hang up on you. Even if they take the bait and decide to interview you, your book is less likely to get a mention if you approach the media directly (they'll just use you for your expertise; if the publicist books it, they'll feel like they owe her a mention of the book). So it's far better for you to let your in-house or freelance publicist approach the media on your behalf. But if that's not an option, by all means, you should do it."

But what does an author do if he or she is approached directly by the media? "My instinct is to say, [talk to my] publicist," said Warren. "However, if the reporter is on deadline or the producer is pressing you for a commitment, forwarding them to your publicist could jeopardize the booking. So use your best judgment. If you do decide to handle it yourself right then and there, be sure to notify your publicist as soon as possible so that they can e-mail press material to the media contact and get a book right off to them. That will increase the chances that they'll mention [your book]."

The most common method publishing house publicists use in niche marketing is to cold-mail the book to a specialized media list. Each publisher will have a database of sources and will also use resources like Bacon's *Media Directories,* as well as other mailing-list services. Books that appeal to a particular culture, such as Asian, African-American, Hispanic, etc., will be mailed to the book review of feature department of special-interest magazines and newspapers, so they can let their readers know a new book that may appeal to them is about to be published.

At some of the larger publishing houses, the marketing departments create brochures or newsletters that are mailed to

reviewers, teachers, librarians, veterans, amateur and professional associations—any one, in fact, who may be interested in
knowing the book is coming out.

Authors Are the Best Resources

With established authors, or with writers with a column and a
following in a magazine, fan mail can be very useful. The simple
answer to selling books is publicity, Reap as much as you can get
for yourself and your book. Start with local publicity, and then
expand to regional publicity, and finally to national publicity.
How many people live in your town, your county, your state, and
how might you contact groups of them with information about
your book? What organizations might be interested in your
book? How many members do they have? What's the best way to
reach them?

If you can influence the sale of 5,000 copies regionally, you're
already beating the odds big time and getting the system to work
for you. Remember, even though all 5,000 copies were sold in
the Barnes &Noble stores in and around your hometown in the
north, a B & N in Florida or in Texas consults the company's
computer base numbers and sees total figures nationwide. With
some encouragement, if a book looks like it's moving, booksellers
may well want to jump on the bandwagon and provide a hot new
property for their customers.

It's helpful to know what the publishing company's publicity and marketing plans for your book will be, and you may have
to make inquiries to determine this. Also, ask if an author's tour
is planned, although you will likely be made aware of this fact
early in the marketing process. You should determine who's going to pay for an author tour, at least in terms of hotel and traveling expenses, and you are well advised to make sure it's the
publisher. If you do go on tour, create a space in your schedule to
accommodate your publisher's plans. If you anticipate or encounter any problems, get your agent involved immediately (although
he or she should be involved in the entire marketing process already). It's okay to ask your publisher's publicist for a copy of the

press release for your book before it's sent out. You need to make sure your book is being represented accurately and well.

"Just keep in mind that it's the publicist's name that goes at the top of that release, and [the publicist] needs to feel comfortable with it too," cautioned Warren. "Besides, she knows the media's likes and dislikes better than you do, and sometimes a publicist can lend a healthy perspective—one that's quite different from your own."

You can also ask how many galleys she's sending out. "The more review-driven your book, the more galleys that need to be sent out.... Biographies, memoirs, novels, short-story collections, and poetry are very review-driven," Warren said.

Be aware that some publicists prefer not to share their media lists, considering their Rolodexes to be proprietary information. "A publicist's greatest asset is her contacts, after all, so you can understand why she may be a bit hesitant to share them," Warren added.

If it's possible, and certainly after you've had a couple of books published that give you a decent track record (say, sales of 20,000 copies or more), try to choose a publisher who is known for strongly marketing books like the one you are currently attempting to sell to a publisher. Check bookstores, the Internet, writers' conferences, etc. for information on various publishers and for insights into which publishers perform most successfully with book similar to the one you are attempting to sell. You should also develop your own marketing plan (obviously, it needs to be down-to-earth and practical) suggesting how best to market your book. Can the book be marketed directly to your audience rather than being sold solely in bookstores? What contacts do you have that you can exploit in marketing your book?

Niche marketing can be more effective than aiming for national coverage. However, the big problem with niche marketing and publicity is that it is very time-consuming, and you may find that niche marketing becomes your own personal priority, following the release of your book. Publicity departments are often small and overworked, they have limited and finite resources, and those resources are generally earmarked for the books that a committee has determined will most successfully benefit the company's bottom line. The publicity department will get out copies of your book to reviewers and others who can help in the promotion of the book. They'll also help you get local signings, and arrange interviews. After that, you may well find yourself on your own in terms of marketing.

The Seasonal Lists

Until the 1990s, most bookstore business in the United States was done through independently owned and operated stores who were served by a publishing house sales force that ranged in size from about ten to thirty sales representatives. Each rep would attend to an account personally, operating like a door-to-door salesman, but needing perhaps as much as four-months' lead time to service each store. The reps in turn needed sales kits to present new titles to their accounts, so this meant that a publishing house had to create a time frame for the production of new sales packages, such as catalogs and other print sales material.

Today, following the demise of many of the small independent bookstores in the last decade, and the current near monopoly by several huge bookstore chains, the role of the publishing house sales rep has changed. Several times a year, sales reps for the company touch base with bookstore accounts. Some reps have large geographic areas, such as New England, or the Pacific Northwest, and others have large volume clients, such as the bookstores chains such as Barnes & Noble. The larger publishing companies have full-time sales forces, while the smaller houses use commissioned reps.

The problem with commissioned reps is that they often represent more than one publisher at a time, and they only earn money on the books they place. The inherent problems of the system are obvious. If the rep is selling your first book at the same time that she's promoting Bob Woodward or Richard Preston's new book, guess who's going to get the short end of the stick?

Sales conferences take place two or three times each year in order to give the sales reps the information and materials they needed to sell the upcoming titles. These sales conferences have become the central organizing force behind book marketing.

Book production deadlines are created by working backwards from the sales conference date. As a result, both the editorial staff and the publicity and marketing staff know when a manuscript has to be delivered, when catalog copy, flap copy, and publicity material need to be written, etc., so that a seasonal list can be closed in preparation for the up-coming sales conference. If, as an author, you miss your deadline for the submission of your finished manuscript, you mess with the schedules and your book will be bumped to the next list, or it will get very little attention from the sales and marketing staff at the most current sales conference

Publishers try hard to have just the right number of "big" books in a list, often separating into different seasons books that might otherwise compete for shelf space with each other. As the door-to-door salesman has been replaced with the telemarketer, so too, the larger book chains have replaced the independents. While the sales reps continue to service accounts, accounts are also sold by a sales staff working from the publisher's home office, and titles are often presented in monthly, rather than seasonal, groupings. The problem with the list system these days is that it forces publishers to rush or delay the publication of a book for no reason other than to hit a particular seasonal list. What were once Spring and Fall seasonal sales catalogues, have now become Spring, Summer, Fall and Winter seasonal lists, or variations thereof, each with its own sales catalog.

Some publishers are more laid-back about this "seasonal list" aspect than are others. Nevertheless, the focus on making a list means that a book won't get any formal marketing involvement until the book's list comes up. All of this means that guerrilla marketing, from a publisher's perspective, such as interactive marketing on the Internet, is frowned upon, or at least ignored, because it can distract from and interfere with marketing efforts for more immediately forthcoming books. Yet guerilla marketing is where an author can be most effective. The Internet takes time to develop an audience, but it is a grass-roots medium, and like other grass-root media, such as local organizations, word will travel in an ever-expanding web. While many publicists don't have the time or the resources to exploit these factors properly, authors do.

The best way for an individual author to successfully use guerrilla marketing is to develop the "ripple in a pond" strategy (drop a pebble in water and watch the ripples move out from a central point in ever-widening circles). The central point of your marketing and sales strategy, the point where the pebble hits the water, so to speak, should be local stores and local media outlets. If you can get local bookstores to stock your book, with the help of your publisher, and if you can imaginatively get the book to the attention of a local audience, through, say, the local newspaper and local radio and TV (the story would be both what the book is about and the fact that you are a local personality), then this success will soon create growing local interest, and as the ripples move out and widen, statewide interest, then regional interest, and eventually national interest.

One of the big problems with huge book superstores elbowing out independent bookstores is that the superstore book buyer is often based in a headquarters office, far removed from the point of contact with customers on the bookstore sales floor. Nevertheless, the superstore book buyer is responsible for buying books for a number of stores in the chain, and he is not often interested in addressing, or appealing to, local interests. He's more interested in promoting a handful of "name brand" authors and homogenizing his customers' taste because he feels this will make books sales more predictable.

The buyer for an independent store is often the store's owner, and she very often reads voraciously, loves to meet authors, and hand-sells books in her store to customers who often ask her advice on what to read next.

The chains seem to carry a wide variety of books. In fact, they often buy fewer titles overall than would several smaller independent stores, each with its own buyer reflecting his tastes and those of his customer base. Several independents catering to customers in the same location will buy a broader range of titles, though the stores will stock fewer copies of each title, while the chains may keep books on the shelves longer and stock more copies of individual titles. It becomes a battle between volume of books and quantity of titles.

Here's an interesting dilemma. Who knows better about what will sell? The author, who wrote the book and is considered an expert? Or, the publisher, who's taken the gamble to create and promote the book because the house staff believe it's a valuable addition to a particular genre, or may even revitalize the genre? Or, the guy who deals every day with the book buying public?

The truth is, the buyers for the chains rarely meet their customers, unlike the owners and staff of an independent bookstore. But the mechanics of big business, obsessed as it is with the bottom line, can seriously impact the number of copies your book could sell. The local Barnes & Noble, for example, may not order many copies of your book because it's perceived as too "niche." In some cases, a book buyer based miles away will make determinations on books to be sold in a store that have little to do with local dynamics, despite a local store manager's recommendations.

Rachel Donadio comments that, "Chain stores like Barnes & Noble and Borders generally buy books at least six months before the publication date and know about particular titles even farther in advance. Much to the anxiety of midlist writers clamoring for attention, chain stores determine how many copies of a title to buy based on the expected media attention and the author's previous sales record. Which is why publishers say it's easier to sell an untested but often hyped first-time author than a second or a third novel."

"It's one of the anomalies of our business that you have to reinvent the wheel with every title, virtually," says Laurence

Kirshbaum, a literary agent and former chairman of the Time Warner Book Group (now Grand Central Publishing). "For all the weeks and months that go into the gestation of the book, we're up against the so-called lettuce test once we get into the stores, If we don't get sales fast, the book wilts."

Donadio adds, "Some stores like Target and Wal-Mart reserve room in advance for mass-market paperbacks by authors like Janet Evanovich or Nora Roberts. If an author is late with a deadline and misses the target publication date, the stores won't have room on the shelf, since they're expecting next month's crop of projected bestsellers."

Matthew Shear, the head of paperbacks at St. Martin's Press (and Evanovich's mass market paperback publisher) agrees with Donadio: "Unless you have a major author, you probably have to wait another four to six months to publish that book."

Bookstores also make money these days by charging publishers for prime placement in their store. For several thousand dollars, a publisher can get a particular book placed near the front of the store. In many cases, bookstores also charge the publisher thousands of dollars to have their books included in the store's mail order or book club catalogs. What can an author do about this?

"Publishers have to pay—handsomely—for that kind of 'real estate,'" says Lissa Warren. "...And, even if your publisher is willing to pay, the buyer won't offer them the option unless they feel your book would be appropriate for this kind of treatment. Amazon.com has a similar program, but it's for space on their home pages rather than table space. The best thing you can do [as an author] is speak with your marketing manager about all of this. The good news is, for the independents, front table placement is at each store's discretion—which means it's something you can influence by contacting the store yourself."

The small guys are at a disadvantage. The big publishers won't usually bother to spend this kind of money on your book unless you're seen as a new Tom Wolfe, Jon Krakauer, Tracy Kidder, or whatever. Even if it is written into a publishing contract, authors have little control over what a publisher decides to spend their money on, or if they will spend any money at all on your book beyond publishing it. Yes, it may be a breach of contract—but what can you do about it, in any real sense, if the publisher "forgets" to honor that clause? Get into a legal fight? Get a reputation for being litigious? Who will want to publish your next book with that kind of reputation, particularly if you also have weak sales figures? These are tough questions to deal with.

Once all the advance orders are in, the publisher will have the warehouse ship the books to the stores. These days, publishers try to keep print runs low (a print run is the number of books a publisher prints in total when the book is published). With narrative nonfiction this is usually between 10,000 and 15,000 copies, on average, although the book may be restocked by going back to press as demand merits. Returns (that is, unsold books shipped back to the publisher by the bookstore) will also end up in the warehouse, so publishers may wait through critical marketing periods if they think copies of a book will be returned, and when copies are returned the publisher redistributes these copies, rather than printing more copies immediately. This can all affect the dynamics of book sales.

Self Aggrandizement or Publicity?

Obtaining publicity is one of the most effective things an author can do on her own behalf, especially if she works in conjunction with her publisher. It's not about telling everyone how wonderful and fabulous you are, but letting them know you have something to say that might interest them.

It's almost never too soon to start working on publicity for your book—with this proviso: If you get people excited about the book before it's available in the stores, you will lose the momentum you began, and will have to work twice as hard to get it back later on. With publicity, timing is critical.

Once your manuscript is completed and handed in, draw up two lists. The first list contains the names of half a dozen people whom you can approach to ask for a quote or "blurb" once they've read the book. These people should be both well known and relevant to your endeavors. The second list should be a wish list of famous people (obviously, they must all still be alive and approachable) whom your agent and/or editor might be able to help you reach, with the same objective—to get a quote. These should be writers or experts in the field you've chosen to write about whose work you genuinely admire. Once you have the backing of a publishing contract, many authors and experts you contact will say agree and say simply, "Send me something when it's ready."

It's your job to ask, and it's their job to say "Yes" or "No." But it's business, so don't take rejection personally. Many authors have their own deadlines to meet, and many are simply burned out from the process of being asked for quotes based on their celebrity.

Your publisher's publicity department staff members will promote your book for about three months before they move on to a new book by another author. If you ask nicely, they may give you a copy of their marketing plan, and a copy of the press kit they have prepared for your book. If you have a problem obtaining these marketing items, ask your editor or your agent to get them for you. No marketing plan? There's an answer for you right there, albeit a very troubling answer.

In general, advertising an unknown book by an unknown author is expensive and often achieves little. Advertising for books tends to work in only two ways: It boasts of a book's success in prizes and sales, essentially telling its audience, "Don't miss out on this hot property everyone else has read!" and it tells the eager fans of famous authors (or those interested in the specific things the book is about) that the author's next book is imminent. Tracy Kidder's fans, or Mark Bowden's fans, eagerly await the next book, and the adverts tell them it's on the way. Before you take the step of attempting to take over the publicity for your book, make sure you take advantage of anything your publicist puts your way. A good publicist is expensive, but a bad or mediocre one probably can't do much more than you can do for yourself. Thus, at some point in the marketing of your book, it is far better to learn the lesson of the *Blair Witch* filmmakers and use the power of the Internet to target your ideal audience.

A great deal of publicity and promotion involves knocking on doors and getting them politely slammed in your face. What you get with a good publicist is her Rolodex of sources, sources she knows personally and whom she can call up and often talk into giving you an interview. This means a publicist will be picky about any book and author she takes on, because her credibility is riding on the author's ability to come across with "the goods" for her contact.

If you're going to do interviews, you have to learn how to get your point across quickly and succinctly, and, well, sexily. I'm obviously not referring to overt sexuality, but about your making sure that you know what it is about your book that's going to whet people's appetites to hear more and get them to pick up a copy of your book the next time they're in their local bookstore.

Learning to Become Media Savvy

The best way to become media savvy if you have no experience at all is to take an evening class in media communications. Media trainers are available, but they're expensive, although I certainly recommend using a media trainer if you're in a pinch and you can find a good one. The media trainer will help you quickly develop an ability to think fast on your feet.

Before you start doing interviews, jot down on a "cheat sheet" (a 3"x 4" index card, ideally) what ideas, or promotional aspects, you want to get across. Come up with at least four major points of conversation. Always, if you're able, turn an interview question into something that will allow you to promote your book.

Acquire a small library of witty stories and practice using them. Even if your topic is deadly serious, make yourself a fun, energized guest. If you can accomplish this, then you'll help a potential publicist by giving them someone that TV and radio talk shows hosts and their producers will always want to have on their shows, regardless of the book you've written.

Before you cringe at the thought of repeat appearances on talk shows, consider this: What's more important, that the talk show audience remember the title of one book or that they remember the name of an author who may have written several books that are available?

It's good to get comfortable with this fact: Marketing and publicity are not about art—they're about selling. You need to learn to get strangers to pay attention to you and your book, despite the noise and chaos of their lives, and then *fork out money* to read it. We watch interviews with authors not to hear them talk about their latest book, but because they are interesting thinkers and witty raconteurs.

How Can I Get Myself on TV?

If you want to appear on TV or radio in an effort to promote your book, start locally, and convince producers you've got something interesting to say and that you'll be an entertaining guest. Study and research what works on camera and what doesn't. You need to learn how to present yourself, how to sit, how to make the camera like you, because the camera can be a pretty cruel and unforgiving instrument. Think about the image you want to project. Make sure it doesn't detract from your ability to talk seriously about the topic you've been asked to discuss.

In much the same way that you got yourself an agent and a book deal, you need to sell yourself to TV producers when you contact them. Send a photo to demonstrate how photogenic you are, plus a list of topics upon which they might base a show, and include a list of thought-provoking and "sexy" questions they might want to talk with you about. Consider any news item or current event that you might tie into an interview? Perhaps you could take questions from the audience or directly from your interviewer that test your knowledge of your subject in an entertaining way?

Don't expect anyone at the studio, other than maybe a research assistant, to actually read your book. It is up to you to use every opportunity to promote and sell your book, from an on-air display of your book cover, if that's possible, to setting up book signings at local bookstores that will correspond to the time you fly into a new town to give your interview. Make sure the bookstore personnel know you're going to be a "celebrity" on local or regional or national TV. Milk it, sell books.

Some Things to Do to Help Publicize Your Book

Several months before the book is due to be published, publishers usually send the author a questionnaire, called the Author Questionnaire. This is usually several pages long and your answers provide your publisher with basic background information about you and your book. It also gives you a chance to mention any ideas you have about promoting your book. The publisher's publicist will be particularly interested in any media contacts you may be able to call upon. Try to provide as much information as possible as your media contacts, including whether they've covered your work in the past, and, if so, when.

Push to meet your publicist even before you book is released, perhaps over lunch or drinks. Try to develop a good working relationship, and use your relationship so that you're up on the publisher's marketing plan, the marketing timeline, and what's going on in general with the publishing house, All of this information will help put you in a position to pick up any slack on your end.

If the publisher doesn't plan to do so, try to create some sort of book tour for yourself if, even if it's only local and unfunded. Remember that timing is important, because bookstore calendars fill up fast.

Ask to see, and try to help craft press material. No one knows your book and your accomplishments better than you. Develop some provocative, "newsy" questions an interviewer might want to ask you.

Consider hiring a freelance publicist. Sometime publishers will do this for books that, for one reason or another, require more time or attention than in-house staff can give. This is a major decision and a major investment but it can be well worth it, particularly in the case of nonfiction. You can try to get the cost of a freelance publicist written into your contract, or at the least, try to convince the publisher to cover half the cost.

Write an op-ed article for a newspaper or magazine that's tied to your book and, if you have an article published, be sure to include it in your bio.

Ask other authors who they've used for publicity and who they've contacted for interviews. Search the Web for additional contact information that might be of use.

Consider hiring someone to create a Web campaign for your book. Check with your publicist first, because some publishers include Web campaigns in their promotional efforts. There's no point in you paying for something that the publisher is already doing.

For three months or so around the publication date of your book keep yourself available to promote your book.

Try to be generous with your time and gracious to your interviewers. Most interviewers will probably not read your book and may ask you foolish questions or misrepresent what you've written. Deal with it. Politely, and using self-deprecating humor if you can, correct them. The point is not to worry about whether or not they have done their job properly, but to come across as a nice guy who has written an interesting book. Take advantage of reaching the audience you are being presented to, for free. Who knows who may be tuned in to the show?

When you call someone in reference to your book, first ask them if they have time to talk; don't just launch in with your pitch.

Make it easy for your publicist to contact you, so that you're not likely to miss an opportunity for coverage of your book.

Be prepared to research likely media contacts for your publicist. Help her help you.

Have your photos scanned in digitally as bitmaps—(.bmp), jpegs (.jpg), or tiff (.tif) files—so that you can e-mail them as attachments to whomever wants them.

Put together a tape of any previous TV and radio interviews you've done.

Send low-key, "Just checking in, did you get the book" follow-up e-mails to everyone who got a galley or finished copy of your book. Remember that quotes relating to this book may not make it to the book's cover, but they will help in selling and promoting the next book.

Don't burn bridges, if you can avoid it. This is a networking business, and you never know who knows who, or what they will say about you, so try to keep things as professional, positive, and upbeat as possible, regardless of how frustrated you sometimes feel. "Publishing" and "frustrating" can sometimes seem to be synonyms for one another.

Writing a Book Proposal

…The secret of success would seem to be to choose something that no one has ever thought about for long enough to write a book proposal [about] without dropping into a sudden narcolepsy. Once you have discovered a subject so obscure that no other publisher has come across it before, all that remains is to prove that it holds the key to universal understanding.
—Andrew Brown, in a review of *Universal Foam: The Story of Bubbles from Cappuccino to the Cosmos* by Sidney Perkowitz

I've left the chapter on how to write a book proposal for last because it's really a separate task and skill from writing the book. They are related, of course, and the proposal is actually written before the book, but the proposal is a description of, and sample of, a proposed book. It's primarily a sales and marketing tool—for you, and for your book. It needs to be focused and accompanied by supporting materials, and, above all, it needs to be dynamic. You need to impress the editor and the sales and marketing staff, make them feel they must have your book at all costs—but do it without being too cute, or arrogantly obnoxious, or obviously trying to make a silk purse (the proposal) out of a sow's ear (the subject of the proposal).

In considering your proposal, you should start with the following four thoughts in mind:

• What's the book about?

- What's so important and special about this book? Why would a publisher want to publish it? (Aren't there enough books out there already without adding another to the pile?)

- Why are you the best person to write this book?

- Who's the core audience for the book, and why will they care about it enough to buy it?

Are we back to audience, audience, audience? Afraid so, and I make no apologies for it.

Jim Srodes says, "The book proposal is a separate item from the book. You can't be too enthusiastic in a book proposal, you can't gush enough to an agent or a prospective editor, because if you don't show your enthusiasm, why should they? I [once] lost a sale because an agent was diffident with what I thought was a great proposal. It doesn't really matter, (all you agents close your ears now and all you editors do, also) if [the proposal actually] looks anything like the final book. Sell the book, then write the book."

Proposals not Manuscripts

I would disagree with Jim on this point alone: Much advance work on a new book is done by a publisher who is drawing ideas from what was included in a proposal, so the clearer and more focused the proposal, the more likely that book will be better represented when it's published.

Almost all nonfiction books are sold on proposal. It's unusual for a nonfiction book to be written on spec and then sold, and for this reason, crafting a proposal requires a skill that is separate from, but not independent of, your ability to write the book. You may think that the work you've begun on your book should be enough to sell it—but publishing, as you've probably gleaned by now, is a cooperative venture between author and publisher, and your job as author is to provide an editor with the ammunition he needs, at least initially, to get this book into the marketplace and sell the hell out of it.

The upside is that the more you become involved in the entire process, the more control you can exert on how well—or how poorly—you'll eventually be published. A word of warning: the more you rely on your belief that your skill as a writer alone should be enough to get you that book contract, the more you put yourself in the position of being just another pretty face in a lineup of many other pretty faces. If you refuse to take the time to practice your audition pieces and do the equivalent of merely stepping forward from the line to sing, dance, act, and otherwise demonstrate what you have to offer, you are unlikely to successfully grasp the brass ring—be it a role in a play or movie, or a book contract.

This may sound harsh, because many authors tend to struggle with the concept and principles of writing a book proposal. It seems unnatural, false, a con job in some way. Nothing could be further from the truth. No proposal is, or should be, cast in stone, but you would not consider building a house without blueprints, or consider preparing a particular dish without a recipe that you can refer to from time to time in order to keep yourself focused and on track. So a book proposal, in a sense, is the blueprint of the book.

There's a common argument I hear from authors who are unhappy about having to beef up a usually meager proposal for their book. "How can I commit to paper something I won't know about until I've done the research? It'll obviously change as I start writing it, so won't I be misleading the editor? Cheating her in some way?"

Editors hear this all the time, and it's not something they worry about unduly. Most editors expect a book to change as you write it. Books are, after all, organic creatures. Editors form and maintain a confidence in a writer based on the strength of his or her proposal regardless of difficulties the author may have during the writing process. An editor anticipates problems. It's part of an editor's job, just as it is part of the agent's job to help fix problems encountered during the writing process. However, a book will almost always improve from the original proposed idea, and it will seldom deviate completely. If you get into trouble, you always have your blueprint to fall back on. In a worst-case scenario, you and your agent and the editor can discuss writing another book and abandoning the one they bought based on the proposal. But it will be a joint decision, based on discussion of a better, more commercial idea and the difficulties you're having with this book, not a unilateral decision on your part. And, the new book will still need to have an outline and description for you to work from, that is, a proposal.

What's more, the better your proposal, the more likely you are to get a higher royalty advance. The reason is obvious: The more something is an unknown quantity, and therefore more of a gamble on a publisher's behalf, the smaller the amount of money they are going to risk on the project, if they decide to risk any money at all.

Publishers long for authors who write well and for authors who have strong concepts they know what to do with. Publishers will pay much more for this author, than for one who may have more innate talent, but who is less confident about what he selling and his ability to produce it. That is not to suggest you need to fake it—it is to suggest that you get enough of a grasp on your material, and thereby become so confident of your mastery of it and its appeal that editors immediately pick up on the fact. When an editor picks up a proposal and is immediately drawn in, you can bet your bottom dollar he realizes that other editors seeing that same proposal will no doubt feel the same way.

Brendan Cahill, while a senior editor at Grove Atlantic Press, was asked how a writer goes about creating an effective proposal that leads to a book contract. "...there are essential things that need to be in any proposal," Cahill responded.

> "Generally, [the book must] be about a topic that's broad enough for a general readership. The writer needs to be, if not expert, then well informed about the

given topic and to have done the initial thought work, legwork, that it takes to be able to render that experience in a thoughtful and intelligent way. And also [the author needs] to have the narrative techniques, skills, and ability to express the story in a way that will appeal to readers. There are books out there on how to write a book proposal that hone in on the specifics, but generally, once you have some sort of journalistic bylines under your belt, you can use the people who you know—agents, friends, friends of friends—to try to get your proposal into the hands of the right people who will be interested in it. Look at the books of the writers you admire, see who publishes them, find out who their editors and agents are. Find them and try to pitch them."

The basic philosophy behind writing a book proposal is to provide the editor with an enticing description of the book and with sufficient facts and figures that the editor will have enough ammunition to convince both editorial colleagues and sales and marketing staff members at an editorial board meeting that this proposed book is not only a quality piece of work, but it will make money for the publishing company. However, a prospective author should always realize that one of the best things writing the proposal can do is help a writer focus and organize a book idea.

What I'm going to do is outline some basic principles you should apply to writing a book proposal. Obviously, each proposal should convey the uniqueness of the particular book it's representing, so there is really no actual "formula" that can or should be applied. The proposal itself should have the form of a story or narrative, and it should be between 20 to 40 pages, but no longer, depending on the amount of sample material included.

A commonly accepted structure for a nonfiction book proposal broadly follows the following outline:

- Title Page. Name of book, name and contact info for the author.

- A one-paragraph, in-a-nutshell description of the project or idea. That is, the project in a "hook" format.

- A one-to-two page overview of the project, presented in a dynamic narrative style.

- A marketing analysis, consisting of approximately half a page, explaining who the audience is for the book, and why the book will appeal to that audience.

- A brief description of competing books, with emphasis on recent commercially successful books in the field (if there are any), and a brief explanation of why your book offers new material or perspective, not currently met by books in this field.

- An up to one-page biography of the writer(s), emphasizing writing experience, any expertise on the proposed subject, and explaining why he/she/they are the best people to write that book.

- A Table of Contents (TOC) that is quite literally a list of chapters and their subheadings. (In other words, an at-a-glance description of the book.)

- A half-page to one-page narrative description of each chapter listed in the TOC.

- A sample chapter or two from the book.

- Accompanying material, such as reviews of previous books, supporting documentation for the book, copies of photos that might be used in the book, etc.

Make sure that every page of the proposal is bylined and tagged in some fashion and easily recognizable through continuous numbering (except for the first page). If an editorial assistant drops the pages by accident, he or she should be easily able to reconstruct the proposal. Keep pictures and graphics to a minimum and don't include them if the quality is poor.

This structure of the proposal can be viewed as two broad categories: Features and Benefits. Simply put, features are concerned with what an object is; benefits are concerned with why you need it. Many writers put together proposals filled with features, but they forget to include any of the benefits. To be effective, a proposal should be balanced with both.

The Features Part of a Proposal (The "What" of Your Proposal)

• *The Cover Letter*

This should be brief, warm, and it should present the "hook," a one- or two-sentence summation of your story and why it's so compelling. It should include your address and phone numbers, relevant information, such as that you're a prize-winning writer, a member of this or that group, an expert in the topic you propose, that you were referred by or mentored by someone significant, whatever. Mention the book's title and what kind of book it will be, and then let the accompanying proposal do the rest of the work.

Always include a stamped, self-addressed envelope (SASE) if you are submitting a hard copy of the material.

• *The Title Page*

Center your title and the subtitle of the book proposal. Under the title, add your name, your address, your e-mail address, and your telephone numbers, voice, cell, and fax (if you have a fax number). Make yourself easy to reach. Be certain that your answering machine is working. Have a professional-sounding message on the answering machine. These things definitely count, and they will certainly affect the image an editor or agent develops concerning you and your ability to produce high-quality work.

• *The Table of Contents*

A TOC provides an at-a-glance guide to the book's content and organization, and perhaps a glimpse of the degree of wit or seriousness you intend to bring to the project, through your sub-titling of each listed chapter. (E.g., Chapter 1: I Am Miserable and Broke; Chapter 2: I Meet Elvis: The Man Who Will Change My Life; Chapter 3: I Attend Astronaut School; Chapter 4: Elvis Is Accused of Murdering My Sister, etc.)

At least 75 percent of a book proposal's success lies in its organization. You may have a great idea, but if you present it poorly, it shows not only a poor writing ability, but also a poor thought processes. In nonfiction, beyond the originality of the idea in question, what you're offering is a logical exploration and understanding of the importance of your subject. Agents and editors look for books that are logical, well-written, and well-organized. It's a good idea to begin working up the TOC early on in the project. As you develop the proposal, you'll find you'll continually revise it, but it will provide an excellent overall map to the project while you're working, as well as a guide to its final form when completed.

• *Chapter-by-Chapter Descriptions*

Once you've nailed down the overall structure of your book in the TOC, you should write at least a couple of paragraphs, if not more, expanding on what you plan to cover in each chapter. The key here, as throughout the proposal, is your ability to write succinctly, yet dynamically, about your subject.

• *Sample Chapters*

This is pretty self explanatory. A nonfiction book needs a mixture of narrative, emotion, and logic to work well. It doesn't matter what chapters you include, but you should aim at an overall sample of about fifteen to twenty pages. No more than two chapters need to be included. If you use partial chapters, make sure the person reviewing your proposal will know this is not the complete version of the chapter.

• *Author Biography*

Who you are is important in selling the project. Why are you the best person to write this book? It's less true in narrative nonfiction, but it's worth bearing in mind that it's highly advantageous to be an expert on something, or work in collaboration with one, because you will be competing with others who are experts, even if their books aren't very well written. Establishing your credibility may mean getting articles published in magazines on the subject you propose well before you start querying editors and agents with your book idea. You should write this biography in the third person, rather than first person, unless you have a life experience that makes your view of the world particularly valid.

The Benefits Sections of the Proposal (The "Why" of Your Proposal)

• *The Hook Overview*

The "hook" statement (for you book) should be a one- or two-sentence, in-a-nutshell description of the book that absolutely nails the book and its appeal. (In fiction, this can often be determined by thinking "What if ..." or "Suppose ...") The "hook" helps the editor sell the book to colleagues in 30 seconds or less. Down the line, a good "hook" may end up helping the sales rep sell your book to a bookstore buyer. In general, make sure that your passion and interest for your subject comes through in your "hook." An effective second person voice can work here: for instance, "Have you ever thought about how you would survive if you were attacked by modern day pirates and set adrift at sea? Joe Bloggs didn't, until it was almost too late. And it cost him his family and a leg."

• *The Larger Overview*

This overview is an expansion of the first, "in-a-nutshell" overview. If, after hearing the "hook," an editor's colleagues say, "That sounds interesting, tell us more," you can now provide the editor with broad facts and figures (if applicable) and a general overview of the project. This overview is a much stronger sales tool than your manuscript, because it allows you to state not only what the book is about (features), but also why it's important (benefits).

The following are some general things to consider in the development of an overview:

• What's the book about?

• Why is there a need for this book? What hole in a genre can this book help fill?

• Who's going to read this book?

• How will your readers be entertained by this book? State your case as dramatically as you can without being overly sensational. Startle us from the outset and make us consider your topic with fresh eyes.

• How is your book different from others in the field?

• Why are you the best person to write this book?

• How long will the manuscript be, and how long will it take you to write it?

Don't answer these questions with hype or rhetoric. Nobody's interested in your opinion on how great this book idea is; what you really have to do is convince us of this fact, using solid content summed up in a paragraph of two.

Close your overview with something that sums up the benefits or merits of the book, something that reminds the reader of the book's importance.

Try and do all this in no more than four double-spaced pages, and, ideally, do so in two pages.

• *Marketing Analysis*

In this section, you need to explain who the audience is for your book. That is, who's going to go into a store and plunk down $7 for a paperback (or $14 for a trade paperback, or $25 for a hardcover) version of your book. What evidence can you offer that your assessment is accurate? In this section, use facts and figures you have obtained from diligent research. How many people belong to organizations or subscribe to magazines that deal with this topic? What other books are out there with sales figures that prove there is a successful and eager audience for your proposed book? Why will members of this potential audience still be interested in reading about your topic in two years time, or five years time (what publishers call a book's backlist life). Give us statistics about groups who may be interested in buying copies of the book in bulk. It won't help to be sloppy or too general in your assessment.

If you have experience or knowledge in selling, marketing, or promoting, mention this information here. Do you have a seminar that you present from time to time in various locations, or do you lecture to specific groups of people regularly? What can you do to translate your experiences into book sales? Are you a member of organizations who will help publicize your book, and ideally, who will buy lots of copies?

Could you help sell bulk quantities of your book to organizations that might want to give them away as gifts to members? Do you have a connection to well-known members of you targeted audience who might endorse your book and help increase book sales in this way? A strong marketing plan, accompanying a book proposal, will go a long way in helping to sell it.

• *Competing Books*

The identification of competing books includes compiling a list of the half dozen most successful and most recently published books in the same field or concerning the same topic you propose to write about. Do not feel disturbed in tackling this chore, as nothing breeds success like success, particularly if you have a new take on a successful idea. When listing the competitive books, give title, author, year of publication, publisher, a one- or two-sentence description of the competing book, and provide a sentence pointing out the difference between your proposed book and the previously published book. Every competing book gives you an opportunity to make a new point about your book idea, so take advantage of the opportunity. Use the library and the Internet for researching competing titles. Browse the bookstores in your area, befriend bookstore owners, and chat with book people in general. If there's nothing in the field to compare with your book, make certain you convince editors and agents that there really is a market for the book, and you're just the first person to have spotted a hole and decided to fill it.

Some Closing Thoughts

The following are some closing thoughts on writing a book proposal:

- It's worth remembering that on average it can take perhaps two years from the time a nonfiction book contract is signed to the book appearing on the shelves, so your book idea must be appealing enough that in two or three years time people will still be excited about it.

- Your proposal should be tightly written, with style and verve. It should offer just enough information, presented in an accessible and hopefully entertaining manner, to convince an editor that you have a good project idea, that you know your subject, and that you can write well about it. The proposal should be well organized, it should be presented in a logical progression of ideas and facts, and, ideally, it should reflect the tone and style of the final book.

- Research the competing books section as early as possible in your endeavor, because what you discover may save you a lot of work, disappointment, and aggravation if you discover there's no viable market for your book idea, for one reason or another, e.g. someone with better credentials has just published a book exactly like the one you propose.

    Another book recently published on your subject may not necessarily be a fatal blow to your book idea, because you may find once you've read the published book that the author treats the subject differently from the way you intend to treat it.

    It is very useful, however, to apprise editors and agents of the fact that you know this other book is currently in the marketplace and that you explain why it won't be a problem for your book idea.

    If an editor is in ignorance of this other book because you failed to mention it in your proposal, and he puts forward your idea in an editorial meeting, and someone at the table says, "But so-and-so just published a book exactly like this," that editor will have been made to look foolish and ill-prepared. Your chances of getting published will have just plummeted drastically.

- Propose one idea at a time. Don't inundate an editor or agent with a shopping list of ideas at one time, on the basis of, "*If you don't like this, then try that.*" This is an unprofessional approach, and it shows a lack of commitment and passion to the project.

Included in the appendix are sucessful sample book proposals that were prepared by clients of mine.

Sample Book Proposals

Below are parts of four successful proposals. The formatting of these proposals has been altered somewhat to fit this book.

Heart So Hungry by Randall Silvis (Knopf Canada/Lyons Press)

Heart So Hungry was sold in auction to Knopf Canada, and later was republished by The Lyons Press in the United States under the title *North of Unknown*. It grew out of a discussion that the author and I had about a change of pace and rhythm for him as a writer, because up to this point he had been writing novels and nonfiction articles for magazines like *Discover*, but he had written no book-length nonfiction pieces.

The lack of a great deal of primary source material was a problem which I think the author handled imaginatively and effectively, and certainly he handled it to the original editor's satisfaction. And, the fact that he changed editors in midstream while he was writing the book didn't help the process much at the time, although it all worked out pretty well in the end.

A Note on the Writing of *Heart So Hungry* by Randall Silvis

A few years ago I made a trip to the Arctic Circle in Alaska for the Discovery Channel. Upon my return, I was talking about the trip with an acquaintance who had also been to Alaska. He mentioned another trip he had made, this one to Labrador. He made the place sound so interesting that I did a bit of Internet research, and there I came across the stories of Leonidas and Mina Hubbard.

After I had done a fair measure of research I came to the conclusion that a part of this story had never been adequately told—Mina's "internal" story; that is, the psychology behind her expedition. To me it was the most intriguing aspect of the Hubbards' story, because I like nothing better than to examine the demons and desires that drive an individual. This story contained love, tragedy, adventure, and revenge—how could I pass it up?

After I came across the Hubbards' story, every reference led me to a new article or other publication. Each of these in turn led me to others. Like any good hunting dog, a writer has to first find the scent. Then just keep your nose to the ground all the way.

The biggest difficulty I faced turning the research into a narrative with a beginning, middle, and end was that my task was to intertwine three separate expeditions—one in 1903 and two in 1905—into a single narrative. It's like trying to force together 1,000 pieces of a jigsaw puzzle into a straight line. Fortunately my book is a hybrid of fact and fiction, which allows me to extrapolate certain connections; by re-creating Mina's thoughts and conversations, I can use them to draw the story away from and then

back to the main narrative. The trick is not to be arbitrary in the use of this device, and certainly not to stray from what I perceive to be Mina's essential character.

The hard part for writers tackling narrative nonfiction is finding the story. Sometimes a good one will drop into your lap, but this is rare. A writer has to be vigilant—reading, talking, listening, traveling—in order to come across a story worth telling. The rest, assuming one possesses the proper storytelling skills for language, characterization, dialogue, and so forth, is all a matter of structure.

HEART SO HUNGRY:
A proposal for a nonfiction book
by Randall Silvis

"Stars so beautiful. Heart so hungry, so hungry, oh so hungry." —from the diary of Mina Hubbard

PROLOGUE

In 1953, at 83 years of age, Mina Hubbard is a small woman, not frail but petite, an expatriate American living in a small village in England, a quiet village of neat homes with hedge-rowed yards and well-tended gardens. Even now there is evidence in the quickness of her gait and in the angle, not quite imperious, at which she holds her chin, of a certain brashness of character, a headlong spirit. When she crosses one of the narrow streets, for example, she does not pause to study the traffic, she strides on, eyes straight ahead, arms extended to hold the cars at bay. Her eccentricities are well known by the locals, and accommodated with affection, because Mina herself is an affectionate and generous woman, notwithstanding her unyielding attitude toward traffic. Moreover, she is not merely a local character, but a woman of international reputation. The car and lorry drivers are happy to slow or swerve to let Mina Hubbard pass.

But a locomotive is not as maneuverable as an automobile. A train can not swerve to avoid an unswerving woman. And when Mina Hubbard strides across the local railroad tracks, she is confronted, for the first and last time in her life, with an opponent that her own strength of will can not deter.

Or could it be that Mina has been waiting most of her life for just such an unswerving opponent? Has she, possibly, been trying for half a century to silence the awful memory of her husband's final days, been hoping for relief from that memory every time she stepped headlong onto a busy street? Has she, all along, been challenging those cars and lorries and buses, and finally a train, to bring her peace at last?

It seems unlikely that Mina Hubbard could have failed to hear the train rumbling toward her. Unlikely too that, even if she failed to hear it or failed to glimpse it looming into the corner of her vision, she would have failed to feel it, so close, shaking the earth beneath her feet.

On the other hand, Mina Hubbard lived a very unlikely life indeed. Her own small footsteps caused a fair amount of earth-shaking. So maybe she *had* fully expected that train to get out of her way.

And maybe she hoped it would not.

Who was this woman who remained headstrong and heedless to the very end? She was not always so obdurate. By all accounts, this stubborn streak did not show itself in Mina Hubbard until the unfortunate year of 1903, the worst year of her life, the year her beloved husband died of starvation in the frozen wilderness of Labrador. That was the year her determination was hardened in the forges of grief and was later alloyed with outrage. That was the year an unflinching devotion to her husband's memory began to transform Mina Hubbard into the most celebrated female explorer of her time.

THE STORY

1902: In the Staten Island Hospital, the young Leonidas Hubbard Jr., recuperating from typhoid, restlessly wanders the hall. He encounters another young man, a stranger named Dillon Wallace who has been visiting the hospital daily, where his bride of one year, a patient there, is dying of consumption. Hubbard strikes up a conversation with Wallace. In their shared miseries—Hubbard has lost a good job as a journalist because of his illness, and he worries how he will provide for his own young wife—they find some comfort, and in the fondness they share for hunting and fishing.

After the death of Wallace's wife, Wallace relies more and more on Hubbard's friendship. On one of their many hikes together, Hubbard reveals that he has talked his new employer, the editor of New York City's prestigious *Outing Magazine*, into sponsoring a canoe expedition into Labrador to chart 500 miles of the last unexplored wilderness in North America. Hubbard is desperate to make a name for himself, to secure his and Mina's future by joining the ranks of men like Peary and Roosevelt and Amundsen, men whose recent exploits have spawned a national fervor for exploration. Indeed, there is more to his proposal than a desire for financial security.

"I am haunted by a craving for adventure, Dil. By a desperate need to see what has never before been seen. To walk where no white man has ever walked. Few such places remain."

Wallace is reluctant. It would not be easy, he says. Not like one of their fishing trips.

"But you are haunted too, Dillon; you know you are. We are both of us haunted men. Come with me into Labrador. We will confront our ghosts together."

Despite his misgivings, Wallace eventually agrees.

#

From this point on, the proposed book, *Heart So Hungry,* becomes a two-pronged narrative. The principal narrative begins in 1904, when Mina Hubbard is living quietly in Massachusetts, a grieving widow. To those who know her, her life seems over already, a woman only thirty, petite and pretty. She has attempted to distract herself from grief by returning to high school, completing her degree, and by starting her training as a nurse. Even so, it seems to Mina Hubbard that there can never again be laughter and sunlight in her small cottage, no room for any emotion but despair.

But then the book arrives. *The Lure of the Labrador Wild* by Dillon Wallace, her husband's best friend and fellow explorer. The book contains several photographs of her loving husband Laddie, so dashing and young, so full of life. Seeing them, she is reminded of how it had all started—how, with the brightest of hopes, the tragedy had begun....

And now we flash back to the preparations for Leonidas Hubbard's 1903 expedition. Despite numerous setbacks, Hubbard is unflinchingly optimistic—too optimistic, in the view of Dillon Wallace. But in every argument, Hubbard's eagerness carries the day. He is responsible for outfitting and planning the expedition. Unfortunately his preparations mirror his editor's notion that a canoe trip into unknown Labrador will be hardly more demanding than a picnic in the Catskills. As a result, the expedition is poorly provisioned; Hubbard expects to find plentiful game all along the journey. But he fails to pack a shotgun. Nor does he deem it necessary to secure a reliable set of maps. And, when he can convince no local guide to lead them into the wild, Hubbard hires a Canadian named George Elson, a quiet, half-breed Scotts-Cree Indian, who has never been to Labrador.

In the summer of 1903, these three men, accompanied by Mina, sail by freighter from New York City to Halifax. It is already mid-July, and far too late to start a journey into the northern latitudes. Perhaps because of her sense of foreboding, Mina finds the crossing dismal, her accommodations cramped, the ship tossed by storms and plagued by icebergs. The only thing that keeps her spirits elevated is her husband's boyish enthusiasm. He enjoys every miserable moment of the trip.

"What great fun this is!"

On the bleak Labrador coastline, where not a glimpse of tree or bush can be seen, nothing but a boggy and wind-scoured flatness, Mina bids her husband "Godspeed" and sends him off to his adventure.

#

A year later, as Mina reads Dillon Wallace's chronicle of the expedition, she comes to a passage that causes her to feel something other than the numbing chill of grief that has been her only emotion since the previous October. She reads, not once but several times throughout the book, Wallace's implication that the expedition failed because of Hubbard's incompetence, that if Wallace had been the expedition leader, success would have been guaranteed.

How, she wonders, could Wallace say such a thing? And why? For mere self-aggrandizement? She was well aware of the drama with which he played up his own brush with death, his almost miraculous survival. But she had never expected that he would stoop so low as to blame the tragedy on her husband and his own best friend. Were it not for Leonidas Hubbard's vision and ambition, Wallace would not now be enjoying such fame as a speaker and writer. Nor would Mina have moved there to Massachusetts, to the village next to Wallace's, so as to help him with the production of that odious book!

For days Mina strides around town seething, unsure of what to do with all this outrage. The only thing she knows for sure is that she can not let this insult to her husband go unanswered.

Then, the final humiliation: Wallace announces that he will undertake the expedition again, ostensibly in the memory of his friend. Mina knows better. She knows that, given his own success, Wallace intends to establish her husband as a fool.

She can not allow this to happen. And the only way to prevent it is to humiliate Wallace himself. This she will accomplish by mounting her own expedition and beating Wallace to the finish line. But of course she must keep her plans secret. She would be laughed at and ridiculed, discouraged at every turn.

There is only one man she can trust—the half-breed George Elson, who always spoke with great affection for her husband. She asks Elson to guide her into the wilderness. He considers the scheme hare-brained and impossible. But ever since he left Hubbard alone in a tent in 1903, Elson has been wracked with guilt. And so, he agrees to guide Mina, if only to prevent her from a fate similar to that of her husband.

Months later, in the summer of 1905, Mina Hubbard and George Elson journey to Halifax. As far as the public knows, Mina intends only to investigate the details of her husband's earlier expedition. She seeks out the three men who, in 1903, rescued Dillon Wallace. Their stories strengthen her conviction that Wallace had failed to do his utmost to save her husband.

Before Mina departs Halifax, word gets out that she suspects Wallace of hastening, if not precipitating, her husband's death. Wallace hears the gossip and notes in his journal that he intends to have Mina Hubbard arrested for slander. The controversy is reported in the New York City newspapers, and passions are soon inflamed. Nearly all public sentiment, however, as well as that of Hubbard's own family, is aligned against Mina.

In the midst of this animus, the rival expeditions are forced to share the steamship *Harlow* as they sail up the Labrador coast to the Northwest River Post, where they will take to their canoes.

Aboard ship, Mina and Wallace have only one brief and tense encounter. Otherwise they do their best to avoid one another.

At the Northwest River Post, Elson recruits two young Eskimos to accompany Mina Hubbard's expedition. There are five men in Wallace's party. Neither team wastes any time launching their canoes on Grand Lake. And on the night of June 27, 1905, the teams camp on opposite sides of the lake.

Wallace's team appears organized and professional; Mina's seems little more than a ragtag band of ne'er-do-wells led by an inexperienced woman. But Mina is relentless, haunted by the spirit of her husband, driven by love. When, on the Naskapi River at the northern end of Grand Lake, Wallace's team pulls out to portage around a rough spot in the river, Mina's team remains in the water, and thereby gains its first advantage.

This early lead is Mina's first small victory, but it brings her no joy, for it comes at the site of her husband's first mistake. It was here, in 1903, when Leonidas Hubbard mistook the mouth of the Susan River for the Naskapi, and consequently directed his team up the wrong river. When the Susan narrowed to a stream, barely navigable, Hubbard was forced to dump some of the team's provisions. Next day, their canoes capsized, and even more provisions were lost. Still, they forged ahead. Unfortunately, the game they had thought would be bountiful was hard to find, and since Hubbard had failed to bring along a shotgun, it was obviously even harder to shoot. They had no reliable maps of even chartered territory, and, once they entered uncharted land, they could only wander aimlessly, using up their precious provisions and losing too much time....

#

Each of these incidents and the many to follow from the 1903 expedition will be juxtaposed against those of the principal narrative of Mina Hubbard's expedition. Mina's ordeal is far less dangerous than her husband's, and far less demanding. Aided by George Elson's unflagging loyalty and the admiration they come to feel for one another, she is able to find moments of joy in the wilderness that so delighted her husband. But every day also brings another painful memory. Sometimes she notices something in the landscape that reminds her of an entry from her husband's journal, and this catapults us back to a recreation of that moment during her husband's trip. Sometimes the flashback is triggered by a comment from George Elson, the unifying factor in both Hubbard expeditions. Dramatic tension is maintained by occasionally looking at Dillon Wallace's journey as he and his team race to beat Mina to the finish line.

Wallace's expedition, by comparison to Mina's, is beset by pitfalls. They capsize and lose provisions; they get lost; Wallace injures himself with an ax.

The real poignancy, however, is captured as we watch Mina experience, through her own expedition, the agonies faced by her husband during his expedition:

The early Labrador winter of 1903 closes in on Hubbard and Wallace and Elson. Tensions rise; fears increase. Hubbard falls ill. Finally, only some 33 miles short of Lake Michikamau, the midpoint of their journey, Wallace and Elson turn back to get help for Hubbard, who is dangerously ill and incapable of travel.

Hubbard spends the next few days alone in his tent as the snow accumulates around him. On Sunday, October 18th, 1903, he writes a hopeful entry in his journal:

"Yesterday at an old camp we found the end we had cut from an old flour bag. It had a bit of flour sticking in it. We boiled it with our old caribou bones....

"The boys have only tea and one half pound pea meal. Our parting was most affecting. George said, 'The Lord help us, Hubbard. With his help, I'll save you if I can get out.' Then he cried. So did Wallace. Wallace stooped and kissed my cheek with his poor, sunken, bearded lips, and I kissed his. George did the same, and I kissed his cheek. Then they went away.

"Tonight or tomorrow perhaps the weather will improve so I can build a fire, eat the rest of my moccasins and have some bone broth. Then I can boil my belt and a pair of cowhide mittens. They ought to help some. I am not suffering. The acute pangs of hunger have given way to indifference. I am sleepy. But let no one suppose that I expect it.... I think the boys will be able with the Lord's help to save me."

Eventually Elson and Wallace make their separate ways to civilization. Wallace, who started the trip at 170 pounds, now weighs 90. Rescuers are sent for Hubbard, but too late; he has died of starvation. As soon as they are able, Wallace and Elson, in the dead of a Labrador winter, return for their friend's body.

#

On August 1st, 1905, George Elson and Mina Hubbard leave the river to climb a wooded hill. From that hill they see Lake Michikamau, which her husband never reached. Mina is well ahead of schedule and has had a fairly easy time of it. But she can not find much pleasure in her accomplishment. She wonders if, for the sake of her husband's memory, it wouldn't be better if she does *not* succeed where he had failed. Wouldn't it be better if, somewhere along the way, she should be killed "by heat and flies and effort and most of all thoughts(?)"

Despite reservations, Mina holds to her plans. And on August 10th, she reaps the reward of an encounter with the Montagnais Indians who live along the coast. The Indians are initially frightened of Mina's party, and especially of the first white woman they have ever seen, but they soon invite the explorers to stay and feast with them. Mrs. Hubbard is inclined to accept this invitation until the men in her party are extended the hospitality of "many fine wives until you leave." Mina then deems it appropriate that they should leave at once.

Farther north, on August 20th, Mina's party encounters the Naskapis, the elusive Barren Ground Indians. From them, George learns some wonderful news: Ungava Bay, their end-point, lies a mere 200 miles north.

To Mina's eyes, the Naskapis are in a wretched state, in short supply of provisions, with a long, hard winter looming. So, before taking to the river again, she has forty pounds of her own supplies unloaded for the Naskapis.

Again they are on the water. Mile after mile of thunderous rapids are braved and left behind. Mina begins to contemplate success:

"I dread going back.... But I mean to try to face the other life as bravely as I can and in a way that will honor the one I loved more than all the world and who loved me with such a generous love. Only what am I going to do? I don't know....

"I might possibly get back and get my story and some of my pictures in print before Wallace is ever heard from, and that would be the thing for me."

As for Dillon Wallace, his expedition continues to be troubled. Whereas Mina's party encounters so much game that she is sometimes forced to forbid the men from shooting or else the meat will go to waste, Wallace's team suffers so severely from dwindling provisions that he is forced to send three of his party back. Only he and Clifford Easton continue. But this makes their journey no easier.

On the unpredictable George River north of Michika-mau, their canoe capsizes in whitewater, and thirty minutes pass before the men can drag themselves out of the frigid water. Both men are hypothermic. Their struggle to build the fire that will save them is every bit as dramatic as Jack London's fictional tale.

But Wallace and Easton do survive, and on October 14 they manage to reach the Post at Ungava Bay, only to find Mina Hubbard and her party already there, having arrived not days but a full month and a half before Wallace.

#

Unfortunately, the triumph brings Mina Hubbard no lasting peace. Though she later marries again, the marriage does not last, for she remains haunted by the memories of her beloved Laddie. Though heralded as an explorer, she finds little satisfaction, as indicated by this entry in her diary: "Had to laugh a good many times and very heartily, but when laughing hardest was hardest to keep from crying...."

Morever, it is as if her husband's restless and impetuous spirit has come to possess Mina, for although she lives a long life, she moves back and forth between England and America, always searching for something that no longer exists...until, at the age of 83, headstrong to the end, she strides across the railroad tracks in an English village and is struck down by the train.

SOURCES

This story would draw its information from the unpublished diary of George Elson, the unpublished diary of Leonidas Hubbard, and the unpublished diary of Mina Hubbard (all available on microfilm from the Public Archives in Ottawa), the unpublished diary of Dillon Wallace (held privately in Beacon, New York), as well as from any additional correspondence or unpublished materials that can be discovered. Further, there exist three excellent accounts of the explorations written and published by the principals: first, the book that so inflamed Mina Hubbard's passions, *The Lure of the Labrador Wild*, by Dillon Wallace, published in 1905 by Fleming Revell; Mina's account of her subsequent expedition, *A Woman's Way Through Unknown Labrador*, published in 1908 by McClure Company; and Wallace's account of his second expedition, *The Long Labrador Trail*, published by the Outing Publishing Company in 1907.

Additional insights into the character of Leonidas Hubbard, his preparations for the expedition, and on the harshness of Labrador itself will be gathered from William Brooks Cabot's book *Labrador*, published in 1920, as well as from Cabot's private journal, slides, and lecture notes, all held at the Smithsonian Institution.

A more recent account of the Hubbard-Wallace adventure also exists: *Great Heart*, by James Davidson and John Rugge. This book was published by Viking Penguin in 1988, but although Mina Hubbard's expedition is recounted in the second half of the book, it is told primarily from the point of view of her guide, George Elson. What I propose is a narrative told from Mina's point of view, the drama of how this small, indomitable woman was driven by love to become the first Caucasian to traverse the wild heart of Labrador. It is, unlike her husband's ill-fated and romantic adventure, very much a love story—a tragic love story, yes, but one that lifted Mina Hubbard and George Elson into the realms of human greatness.

STYLE AND APPROACH

By making use of the aforementioned sources, it will be possible to assemble a complete, if skeletonic, chronology of the three separate expeditions to be related here. We know, for example, that Mina Hubbard met with Wallace after reading the manuscript of his book, and that her reaction to this manuscript was the genesis for her own expedition. What we do not know is what Mina and Wallace said to one another at that meeting, whether the conversation was heated or restrained, if Wallace fidgeted in his chair as Mina pointed out the traitorous passages, or if Mina spoke in a timid whisper and could scarcely bring herself to look at him.

Yet these unknown details are the very essence of human drama. Without them we have no story, only a dry delineation of facts.

In the tradition of Truman Capote's *In Cold Blood* and Mailer's *The Executioner's Song*, I will use the tools of creative nonfiction to give life to this drama by re-creating dialogue, setting, nuances of a character's movements and body language, all the while striving to remain well within the truth of the real character and the actual events.

ABOUT THE AUTHOR

Randall Silvis is the author of seven books of fiction to date. His most recent novel, *On Night's Shore* (Thomas Dunne/St. Martin's Minotaur, January 2001), a historical thriller featuring Edgar Allan Poe, received a starred review from *Booklist*. Historical novelist Maan Meyers said of *On Night's Shore*: "Move over, Caleb Carr. Randall Silvis' writing is exquisite and true." *The New York Times Book Review*, in a glowing review of *On Night's Shore*, praised its "vibrant panorama" and "pungent impressions," while the *New York Daily Post* said "Silvis has created an evocative backdrop, brilliantly capturing the sights and sounds of 19th century Manhattan.... *On Night's Shore* drips with descriptive power."

Silvis's eighth novel, *Disquiet Heart*, also a historical thriller featuring Poe, will be released in 2002.

Randall Silvis's first book of fiction was chosen by Joyce Carol Oates to win the prestigious Drue Heinz Literature Prize. He has been a Thurber House Writer-in-Residence, a Fulbright Scholar, a finalist for the Hammett Prize for Literary Excellence in Crime Writing, and the recipient of two fellowship awards from the National Endowment for the Arts.

As a writer of nonfiction, his work includes numerous cover stories and feature articles for *Destination Discovery*, the magazine of the Discovery Channel. His historical features include nonfiction narratives about Blackbeard, Tecumseh, and the Alaskan Highway. His two-part series about the real Pocahontas was used to launch The Discovery Channel Online.

Randall Silvis will bring to *Heart So Hungry* the stylistic and dramatic skills of an acclaimed novelist and award-winning playwright, plus the impeccable research skills of a historian.

SALES AND MARKETING
Audience

Heart So Hungry will be directed at the same mainstream audience that has enthusiastically supported numerous best-selling nonfiction narratives of personal adventure, such as *Into Thin Air* and *The Perfect Storm*, in which man battles against the forces of nature. It will appeal as well to readers of histori-cal adventures such as the Alexander and Hurley chronicle of Shackleton's *Endurance*, Niven's *The Ice Master*, and the forth-coming history of the Iditarod, which garnered an advance of $500,000. It will find another eager audience among readers of historical biography, such as Dava Sobel's *Longitude* and Alison Weir's *Eleanor of Aquitaine*.

All of these are fine books that have enjoyed widespread suc-cess. But nonfiction books in which intriguing moments of history are illuminated in a series of highly dramatic incidents, books in which compelling and endearing characters are pitted against na-ture *and* against each other, books in which the hero or heroine is willing to risk even life itself in the pursuit of an ideal, these books are rare. Indeed, the kind of people we discover in them are rare.

Heart So Hungry will slip neatly into each of three sub-genres of nonfiction: the biography, the historical re-creation, and the personal adventure narrative. As the story of a grand and dangerous adventure, it will appeal to armchair explorers of both genders. But *Heart So Hungry* will distinguish itself in two important ways. First, it is the story of a *woman's* triumph, of an ordeal voluntarily undertaken in the name of love—the story of a woman who triumphed where men could not, and in a pursuit that was, and for the most part still is, considered wholly mascu-line. As such, it is an inspirational story that resonates with deep emotional impact.

Secondly, *Heart So Hungry* is first and foremost a love story. The adventure, the challenge, and the danger all grow out of the love. A woman risks everything, including her own life, for one reason only—to prevent the memory of her beloved, if impetuous, husband from being besmirched. Love, loyalty, tragedy, personal danger and sacrifice, and triumph—all with a woman as central character.

For these reasons *Heart So Hungry* will hold a special appeal for female readers.

Marketing Points

Heart So Hungry will exemplify the qualities of human drama, perseverance, and triumph that appeal to television talk shows, from Oprah and Rosie and Leeza to Larry King, as well as to magazine-format shows, radio talk shows, and popular print publications.

The author has made extensive public appearances to promote his previous seven books, and he is comfortable in all the aforementioned formats; he is prepared to undertake a promotional tour of readings and book signings upon the publication of *Heart So Hungry*.

[A sample chapter was included with this proposal.]

Enemy of the State by Michael Scharf and Michael Newton (St. Martin's Press)

The proposal for *Enemy of the State* went through much editorial discussion between myself, as agent, and the authors, in a strenuous effort to make sure that while the book had strong substantive content, it nevertheless would read easily and appeal to audiences of narrative nonfiction who were looking for a story arc. This trial itself, and the work of the authors in telling its story, will likely prove to be one of the most substantive and lastingly worthwhile things we achieved in the Middle East after the invasion of Iraq, and it was soon clear to us all that it should take its place alongside the Nuremberg trials. I'm particularly proud to have been the agent on this book and to have found an editor who so clearly saw the book the way we all did.

The book was bought in auction by St. Martin's Press.

Enemy of the State:
Inside the Trial of Saddam Hussein
By Michael A. Newton & Michael P. Scharf

Book Proposal

Description

At 10:00 AM, on October 19, 2005, Saddam Hussein, the ruthless Iraqi leader accused of war crimes, crimes against humanity, and genocide, was led into the courtroom of the Iraqi Special Tribunal in Baghdad. Millions around the world tuned in to the televised proceedings of what has repeatedly been described as "The Trial of the Century" and the "Mother of All Trials." For high drama, this case had it all: a strident former dictator determined to turn the televised trial into a political stage; the backdrop of a coalition occupation struggling against a growing insurgency; raucous and disruptive defense lawyers whose chief strategy was to challenge the legitimacy of the proceedings and focus the trial on the legality of the U.S. invasion of Iraq; mysterious assassinations of key trial participants; controversial judicial rulings; and smoking-gun documents and videotapes of the worst atrocities imaginable.

Unlike Adolf Eichmann, who Hannah Arendt famously described as "the banality of evil," Saddam had a powerful animal magnetism that Professor Newton and other first-hand observers of the trial in Baghdad immediately recognized. One of the major themes of the Dujail trial was the battle of the wills between Saddam and a series of chief judges who unsuccessfully tried every trick in the book to maintain control of the proceedings. The legal processes formed the canvas against which an explosive mix of personalities, politics, power, and ego combined to produce the most important legal proceedings in the history of the region. Ironically, many of the decisions intended to increase the perceptions of fairness and to demonstrate the rebirth of an Iraqi judiciary dedicated to restoring the rule of law in place of a tyrant's will instead served to increase the cynicism of the population and feed popular misconceptions of the trial as an extension of American power.

The Dujail trial began in October 2005 against a backdrop of high drama and the pent-up expectations of the Iraqi people. Exactly twelve months earlier, in October 2004, the authors received calls from the U.S. Department of Justice requesting that they lead an elite team of experts who would train the judges and prosecutors of the Iraqi Special Tribunal. Professor Scharf, a former State Department official who helped create the Yugoslavia Tribunal back in 1993, had initially been an outspoken critic of the plans for the Iraqi Special Tribunal. He was therefore reluctant, but decided to accept the assignment based on assurances that he would be given full autonomy in training the judges and the right to candidly express his views about the process upon his return. Newton, then a professor at West Point, also had some concerns about the controversial tribunal, but felt that he could best contribute to the success of the endeavor from the inside. In the following months, Scharf and Newton shuttled back and forth between secret training sessions across the globe, culminating in a mock trial at Stratford upon Avon, England. Together, they helped prepare the judges to handle unruly defendants and tutored them about the developing body of law dealing with war crimes, genocide, and crimes against humanity. In the months leading up to the trial, Scharf and Newton also helped re-write the Rules of the Iraqi Special Tribunal and, with the help of their students, they provided legal analysis on dozens of issues that were expected to arise in the course of the trial.

Braving the perilous security situation in Iraq, Professor Newton met often with the judges in their Baghdad chambers, answering their probing questions about international law and explaining the complicated interface between Iraqi and international law that would form the backbone of the work of the tribunal. Newton's first of four trips to Baghdad coincided with the public announcement of the promulgation of the Tribunal's Statute (which he had helped to draft) and he was just off-camera during the celebrated press conference in which Ambassador Paul Bremer announced Hussein's capture to the world. Professor Newton's last trip was in December 2006, where he was the only outside expert to read the appeals filed by Saddam and the other defendants and met for many hours with the Appeals judges prior to the issuance of their decision.

Professors Newton and Scharf are among the world's leading experts on the law in this area, but more importantly they can bring unique insights into the temperaments and tactics that permeated Saddam's trial and ultimate execution. Scharf and Newton jointly created the world's most visited Internet website devoted to the Saddam Hussein trial (law.case.edu/saddamtrial). They have been among the most prominent worldwide commentators on the trial processes and have between them served as expert commentators on over 300 broadcasts, including NBC *Nightly News* with Brian Williams, NBC's *The Today Show*, ABC News *Good Morning, America*, Fox news special: "The Saddam Hussein Trial," Court TV, Fox & Friends, CNN *American Morning*, CNN National News, CNN International News, The BBC, The Greta Van Susteren show, *The O'Reilly Factor*, and *NewsHour* with Jim Lehrer. They have been quoted in dozens of stories in *The New York Times*, *The Wall Street Journal*, *The LA Times*, and *The Washington Post*, and in other leading papers around the world. Scharf and Newton were involved in every phase of the development, training, preparation, and conduct of the trial. They can tell this story using insider quotes and previously untold stories in a manner that will capture the essence of this process in an understandable and gripping narrative.

Based on their unique inside perspective and expertise, the authors will tell the real story behind the trial of Saddam Hussein. The trial was a complex mixture of explosive personalities, political overtones, and lingering doubts from the wider world, as the lengthy Arabic proceedings were often portrayed only as sound bites or caricatures in the Western media. More than anything else, *Enemy of the State* will permit the average reader to understand what really happened in the Dujail trial, and why those developments are important for the world today. Scharf and Newton can also provide insights into the text and significance of the judicial opinion that no other authors could provide.

The book, written to appeal to a mass audience, will examine the political and legal issues that shaped the course of the controversial trial. Readers will learn of the deep paradoxes that were intertwined within the trial. Even as the United States and other Western nations were amending their legal procedures to curtail the access to judicial forums and personal freedoms given their enemies, the Iraqis built a process from scratch designed to give leading Ba'ath Party officials more protections and rights than ever before in the history of Iraq. The Agency for International Development translated the leading opinions from other tribunals into Arabic for the first time, and Professor Newton delivered those translated copies to the judges of the tribunal, which in turn spawned deep conversations about their principles and predicates. The Iraqi judges, prosecutors, and defense counsel crammed a lifetime of learning about international humanitarian and international criminal law into a few months. The inevitable mistakes they made as they applied this body of law for the very first time in the Arab-speaking world were magnified by gavel-to-gavel television coverage. Meanwhile, more than any other of the leading trials in world history, the insurgency outside the courtroom was linked to the legal battle being televised every day across the region. Part of the defense strategy was to deliberately incite the insurgency in the hopes that those who sought to overthrow the rule of the democratically elected government would succeed in derailing the legal processes inside the courtroom.

Enemy of the State will focus on the people themselves who made this achievement possible and illustrate the legal principles that were put into practice. The questions that will be addressed include:

Why did the negotiators decide to pursue a domestic-based trial rather than an international trial for Saddam Hussein?

Why did the drafters of the Tribunal's Statute decide to include the death penalty and the crime of aggression over the objections of the United States, United Kingdom, and United Nations?

How were the judges and prosecutors selected and trained, and were they really up to the task of trying one of the greatest cases of all time?

Why did the tribunal decide to begin with the trial of the Dujail incident, a minor atrocity in comparison with the Anfal campaign, the destruction of the Marsh Arabs, and the invasion of Kuwait?

Did it make sense to begin the trial while the security situation in Iraq was still unsettled, with suicide bombing and drive-by shootings a daily occurrence in the country?

Was it really possible for someone like Saddam Hussein to get a fair trial?

What prosecution and defense strategies and tactics were most effective, and what were the major missteps made by each side during the trial?

What was the relationship between the judicial processes inside the courtroom and the raging insurgency outside the Green Zone?

Was the judgment fair and just, and was the tribunal's legal analysis above reproach?

Will the trial be remembered as a success story or a train wreck, and what effect will it have on the peace process and transition to democracy in Iraq?

What really happened inside the room when Saddam was executed?

Will the criticisms and perceptions of the flawed execution ultimately undermine the entire process?

We envision *Enemy of the State* as a reasonably priced book of about 200 pages, with an index, glossary, bibliography, and a dozen photos and maps. We have some superb original behind-the-scenes photos of the trial participants, for which we will not need to obtain copyright permission. This book will be in the style of such classics as Hanna Arendt's *Eichmann in Jerusalem* (1964) and Telford Taylor's *Anatomy of The Nuremberg Trial* (1992). The book will be of keen interest to the general public, and can also be marketed for adoption as a supplemental text for undergraduate political science, justice, and foreign relations courses, and for international law and criminal law courses. It will be completed by the fall of 2007 so that it can be in print during the run up to the U.S. presidential election, which is likely to turn on American perceptions about the U.S. involvement in Iraq. Saddam's capture still ranks as one of the most successful aspects of the counterinsurgency campaign in Iraq, and the Iraqi High Tribunal has been one of the most highly visible components of the resurgent Iraqi sovereignty. The controversies behind the tribunal's creation, operation and sentencing, as well as America's overall Iraq policy, will drive sales of the book.

Chapter Outline

Prologue: The Take-Down (5,104 words as drafted) [attached]

Paints the picture of the actual events surrounding the capture of Saddam. His capture spawned optimism across the region that what Iraqis referred to as "the entombed regime" could really be put into the past. This chapter seeks to grab the reader's attention by describing the first explosive moments of the trial and setting the context for this enormously complex and important criminal trial.

Chapter 1: Introduction—The Genesis of Justice (7,000 words)

This chapter provides an introduction to the trial of Saddam Hussein by describing the events in al-Dujail that formed the basis for the charges and ultimate conviction of Saddam and his co-defendants. This chapter will also preview the structure of the book and highlight the thematic strands that will guide the reader to a deeper understanding of the entire process.

Chapter 2: From Nuremberg to Baghdad—The Dujail Trial in Historic Perspective (4,200 words as drafted) [attached]

This chapter traces the history of major war crimes trials, from Nuremberg and Tokyo, to the Yugoslavia and Rwanda tribunals, to the Pinochet prosecution, to the decision to create the Iraqi Special Tribunal to prosecute Saddam Hussein.

Chapter 3: Hammurabi Was an Iraqi—The Creation of the Tribunal (5,000 words)

This chapter tells the story of the negotiation of the statute of the Iraqi Special Tribunal and the drafting and re-drafting of its rules of procedure and evidence. It discusses the key provisions of the law that governed the trial of Saddam Hussein. Many of the decisions intended to increase the perceptions of fairness instead served to increase the cynicism of the population and feed popular misconceptions of the trial as a form of American power. This chapter will focus on the personalities and challenges faced by the judges and explain why they adopted the provisions that sowed the seeds of later controversies.

Chapter 4: Proving Incredible Events with Credible Evidence (7,000 words)

This chapter describes the investigation into the Dujail case, and explains why the decision was made to begin with such a relatively minor incident, rather than greater atrocities like the genocidal Anfal campaign, the 1991 massacres, or the attacks against the Southern Marsh Arabs. In addition, this chapter will detail the battles surrounding the ultimate decision to televise the trial as well as the logistics surrounding such a new development in the Arab-speaking world. This decision was one of the most fateful for the entire trial and readers must understand its reasoning using the insider information available to the authors.

Chapter 5: Trial and Error (7,000–10,000 words)

This chapter tells how the judges were selected and trained, and examines whether they were competent to face the challenges of the Saddam Hussein trial. It opens with the first explosive moments of trial and details the core of the evidence against Saddam and his co-accused. This chapter will reveal some never-before available information about the processes behind the trial and the reasoning behind some of the more controversial aspects. It will also explain for the reader unfamiliar with Iraqi procedural law why the trial unfolded as it did.

Chapter 6: Deception, Distortion, and Distraction (7,000–10,000 words)

The "Mother of all Trials" was full of twists and turns that left many outside observers unaware of what was really happening inside the case. This chapter contains a narrative of the key moments in the trial, surprising revelations by witnesses, legal missteps by the prosecutor and defense attorneys, and controversial rulings from the bench. In particular, it will focus on the defense strategy and why it ultimately failed. Extensive dialogue taken from trial notes will be included in both chapters 5 & 6.

Chapter 7: Judgment Day (7,000 words)

This chapter analyzes and critiques the Trial Chamber's decision, focusing on the critical findings of fact and conclusions of law. It will include eyewitness descriptions of the events in the courtroom as the verdicts were announced. Even the events surrounding the announcement of the opinion had surprising ramifications for other trials and for the Iraqi goal of restoring the rule of law in place of the tyrant's whim.

Chapter 8: Appeal and Execution (7,000 words)

This chapter describes the process of the appeals and discusses the role of the appeals in the complex polticial circumstances of the time.

Chapter 9: Conclusion (7,000 words)

This chapter examines the lessons learned from the Dujail trial and makes some predictions about how the future trials of leading Ba'athists will unfold over the next several years. It also examines whether the Saddam Hussein trial merits the label "Trial of the Century" and what the precedent will mean for the future of international accountability.

Glossary
Bibliography
Index

Marketing and Promotion Information

Enemy of the State is likely to be the first published book that discusses the processes and people behind the Saddam Hussein trial. There is a recently published book from Carolina Academic Press entitled *Saddam on Trial: Understanding and Debating the Iraqi High Tribunal* [2006, 438 pp, paper, ISBN-10: 1-59460-304-9, ISBN-13: 978-1-59460-304-4 $29.95], which constitutes a series of scholarly essays on discrete issues from a variety of perspectives. *Enemy of the State,* in contrast, will be the first book to detail the proceedings with any particularity in light of the actual events inside and outside the courtroom. Timely books of this type about major war crimes trials tend to be critical and commercial successes. This book will be in the style of Hanna Arendt's *Eichmann in Jerusalem* and Telford Taylor's *Anatomy of The Nuremberg Trial*. Michael Scharf has had a great deal of success writing in this genre. His book *Balkan Justice* (Carolina Academic Press) was nominated for the Pulitzer Prize in 1998; his book *The International Criminal Tribunal for Rwanda* (Transnational Publishers) won the American Society of International Law's Book of the Year Award in 1999; his book *Peace with Justice* (Rowman and Littlefield) won the International Association of Penal Law's Book of the Year Award in 2003, and his most recent book, *Slobodan Milosevic on Trial* was described by the book editor of the *Times* (London) on October 22, 2005, as "The best account of the Milosevic trial."

The authors are nationally recognized as the leading experts on the Saddam Hussein trial. They have appeared frequently as expert commentators about the trial on such television news programs as NBC *Nightly News* with Brian Williams, NBC's *The Today Show*, the Fox news special: "The Saddam Hussein Trial," CNN National News, CNN International News, The BBC, *The O'Reilly Factor*, and *NewsHour* with Jim Lehrer, and they have been quoted in *The New York Times*, *The Wall Street Journal*, *The LA Times*, and *The Washington Post*. In addition, Scharf, who was nominated for the 2005 Nobel Peace Prize for the work he has done assisting in the prosecutions of Slobodan Milosevic, Charles Taylor, and Saddam Hussein, has recently been profiled in *Continental In-Flight Magazine* (October 2005 issue), *The Legal Times* (August 2005 issue), *The American Lawyer* (November 2005 issue), and the *Plain Dealer Sunday Magazine* (July 10, 2005 issue).

The public's intense interest in the Saddam Hussein trial and the unfolding situation in Iraq, the authors' expertise and high media profile, and their journalistic writing style will command attention for this book and drive sales. The book would be marketed primarily as a trade book, but it could also be marketed for adoption as a supplemental text for undergraduate political science, justice, and foreign relations courses, and by law school international law and criminal law courses. Because this is just the first of a series of trials involving leading Ba'athists that will take place over a period of as long as five years, the book should have a fairly long shelf life. Scharf and Newton are also highly visible in the international legal community and in media appearances outside the United States. The subject matter and candor of this text presage strong international sales as well.

Delivery

The 70,000-word manuscript will be delivered on disk and in hard copy by the second week of September 2007. The text will include a number of descriptions of people and events that will also be featured in the original photos submitted. An index, bibliography, two maps, and fifteen to twenty photographs [including some original photos of the trial participants and the courtroom under construction] will complement the text.

Author Biographies

[The authors' biographies were included here using about five paragraphs each.]

Sample Chapter

[The prologue and Chapter 2 were included as sample chapters along with the extensive notes section for the prologue and the footnotes for Chapter 2.]

The First Copernican by Dennis Danielson (Walker)

This proposal was clearly in the tradition of Dava Sobel's *Longitude,* and it was a particular source of pride to me that Dava's editor and publisher, George Gibson, someone whom I consider one of the best publishers and editors in the industry, saw the merit of this book and published it under the title: *The First Copernican: Georg Joachim Rheticus and the Rise of the Copernican Revolution* (Walker).

It is presented here using its original title. The author included some illustrations from material of the time, which I've omitted.

Son of Copernicus: How a Man Who Loved Stars, Triangles, and Beautiful Ideas Launched Modern Science by Dennis Richard Danielson

A Book Proposal

In a Nutshell

In the same way that Simon Winchester's *The Professor and the Madman* is the story of two men who loved words and helped to create the *Oxford English Dictionary*, the projected work *Son of Copernicus* is the story of how two men who loved mathematics brought about the dawn of the scientific age.

Georg Joachim Rheticus, a gifted but troubled intellectual adventurer, was "adopted" in his youth by the aging Nicolaus Copernicus. *Son of Copernicus* tells the story of how Rheticus saved the great astronomer's work from oblivion and proclaimed Copernicanism—the foundation of modern science—to the world.

Rheticus was faced with universal rejection of his late master's teaching, and so, to defend the "absurd" yet deeply beautiful theory of a moving earth, he forged new observational and geometrical tools still in use today.

Son of Copernicus is the story of a man whose passion for science and commitment to the beauty and poetry of mathematics provides a unique prism through which the radiance of the Copernican Revolution can be seen anew.

Overview

In his early teens, after his father was beheaded, Georg Joachim Rheticus embarked on a quest to make sense of the world, starting with mathematics and astronomy—and to find someone else he could call father. By age 25 he had become one of the youngest professors of mathematics in Europe. Intrigued by reports from Frauenburg in the far north of an elderly country doctor and amateur astronomer's proposal that the sun—not the earth—stood in the center of the universe, with the earth moving around it, Rheticus set out on a pilgrimage to meet the author of this absurd idea, a man whose name was Nicolaus Copernicus.

Copernicus's dream of publishing his stunning cosmological announcement had all but faded by the time he met Rheticus. But the young Protestant professor from Wittenberg adopted Copernicus as his teacher and father figure, falling in love with the intellectual achievements of the aging Catholic astronomer. Alone among his peers, Rheticus appreciated both the beauty and the profundity of Copernicus's new vision of the universe. He published a brilliantly written Copernican trial balloon, the first book to proclaim "heliocentric" theory to the world, and he persuaded his teacher to finish his great work, *The Revolutions*. Rheticus then personally delivered the manuscript of this epoch-making treatise to Nuremberg, the leading center for scientific publication, and as soon as it was in print rushed a copy to Copernicus in Frauenburg. Copernicus finally beheld it on the day that he died.

For the next three decades, Rheticus remained the sole apostle of Copernicus, doggedly nurturing the legacy of his intellectual father. In the process, he founded the "science of triangles" (later dubbed trigonometry) in support of Copernican astronomy.

While later teaching and studying in Leipzig, Rheticus was forced to flee for his life rather than face charges that he had sodomized one of his students. He abandoned academia and migrated eastward, studying medicine, as Copernicus had done, and, like Copernicus before him, almost allowing his astronomical and mathematical mission to be swallowed up by the overwhelming demands of a busy medical practice.

After Rheticus had spent two decades in exile, an enthusiastic young mathematician named Valentin Otto arrived on his doorstep as unexpectedly as Rheticus had, years before, appeared at the door of Copernicus. And just as Rheticus had done for Copernicus, so Otto now rekindled the scientific career of *his* teacher—who soon after died in his arms. It took a further twenty years and many more struggles before Otto was finally able to publish Rheticus's masterpiece, the *Opus Palatinum*, which became the cornerstone of modern trigonometry.

* * *

Drawing from original archived documents and previously untranslated source material, *Son of Copernicus* will recount the colorful life of Rheticus, a story never before told in English, one that freshly illuminates how the advent of modern science had its beginning in two men's passion for the beauty of mathematics.

The story spins together two differently shaded strands. Boldest of these is the biographical, with significant elements from the lives not only of Rheticus and Copernicus, but also of other vital contemporaries such as Melanchthon, Lemnius, Ramus, Giese, Gasser, and Cardano. The second strand—accessibly woven for the intelligent general reader—is cosmological: an account of the fascinating interconnected issues of geometry, celestial mechanics, and aesthetics with which Rheticus grappled. The reader's sense of direct access to these two strands is enhanced by fresh readings and translations of the words of Rheticus and his contemporaries. The resulting narrative fabric not only conveys a grasp of how Rheticus discovered, disseminated, and supported the scientific work of Copernicus, but also offers a moving glimpse of how one man's enthusiasm, character, and sheer determination—not merely the impersonal forces of culture and history—have decisively shaped our world.

The argument of *Son of Copernicus* can therefore be summed up in four words: "No Rheticus, no Copernicus." From Copernicus's death in 1543 until his own in 1574, Rheticus was heliocentrism's lone public and scientific torchbearer, single-handedly creating a bridge between Copernicus himself and the next generation of Copernicans (Maestlin, Kepler, Galileo) that arose at the end of the sixteenth century to take up that flame once more. The story's essence, however, is less contention than exclamation: How astonishing to see how Rheticus's courage, love, entrepreneurial skill, quirks of character, mental brilliance, and human sorrows combined to launch and sustain the seemingly ridiculous idea that ignited the Scientific Revolution.

Although it is biography, this book thus opens onto wider vistas of human history. Like Simon Winchester's bestselling *The Professor and the Madman*, *Son of Copernicus* offers readers an intriguing, up-close biographical experience that bleeds directly and vividly onto a larger cultural canvas, in this case the origins of modern cosmology and the Scientific Revolution.

The Market, and Other Books in the Field

Almost none of the story of Rheticus has ever been told in English. The only stand-alone biography of him appeared in German in the late 1960s (see Burmeister, below). *Son of Copernicus* also differs from most other books about the history of science in its depth of textual scholarship and intensity of biographical appeal. Its intersecting scientific and story-telling dimensions position it in a similar category with the immensely successful works of Dava Sobel—*Longitude* and *Galileo's Daughter*. Moreover, *Son of Copernicus*, like *Galileo's Daughter*, uses original translation to unveil potentially distant and arcane writings—which, once rendered in familiar idiom, bring alive the characters and their stories as well as the ideas that they engaged.

The following books (listed chronologically by date of publication) deal, at least in part, with the Copernican Revolution:

The World of Copernicus (by Angus Armitage, Signet, 1947; rpt. Dover, 2004) is a popular, unfootnoted but responsible, and slightly bland overview of Copernicus, his context, and his achievement. Contains only a brief summary of the contribution of Rheticus.

The Copernican Revolution: Planetary Astronomy in the Development of Western Thought (by Thomas S. Kuhn, Harvard UP, 1957) is the classic English-language scholarly text on the technical aspects of Copernicanism.

The Sleepwalkers: A History of Man's Changing Vision of the Universe (by Arthur Koestler, Macmillan, 1959). A very influential book containing some account of Rheticus, but predating the work of Burmeister (below) and the scholarly discoveries connected with the life of Rheticus that emerged in the last four decades of the twentieth century.

The Copernican Achievement (by Robert Westman, University of California Press, 1975). One of the best collections of scholarly articles on the announced theme.

The Genesis of the Copernican World (by Hans Blumenberg, MIT Press, 1987; original date 1975). A daunting 800-page tome translated from German, embodying a fascinating but decidedly "heavy" approach to Copernicus and related issues. Some account of the contribution of Rheticus, but idiosyncratic and not popularly accessible.

The Eye of Heaven (by Owen Gingerich, American Institute of Physics, 1993). A collection that reprints scholarly papers on issues related to the Copernican Revolution.

Moving Heaven and Earth: Copernicus and the Solar System (by John Henry, Icon/Totem, 2001). A useful but short (less than 40,000-word) and somewhat colloquial rack-size paperback original from the British publishers of the *"Introducing ..."* series.

Of these titles, only Koestler and Blumenberg pay any substantial attention to Rheticus. However, they take into account neither the scholarly, three-volume *Georg Joachim Rhetikus: Eine Bio-Bibliographie* (Pressler-Verlag, 1967–69), by Karl Heinz Burmeister, nor the numerous articles by Burmeister that have appeared since his biography, nor the treatise by Rheticus *On Holy Scripture and the Motion of the Earth*, discovered and edited by R. Hooykaas (North-Holland, 1984). Beyond this list, the eminent Copernican scholar Owen Gingerich has recently published a popular and highly respected book on the publication history of *De Revolutionibus* (*The Book Nobody Read*, Walker and Co., 2004), which includes a brief account of the contribution of Rheticus. Rather than competing with or preempting *Son of Copernicus*, however, Gingerich's book has in fact broadened interest in the whole field of Copernican history, as has the recent republication in English translation of *De Revolutionibus* in Stephen Hawking's astronomical landmark series, *On the Shoulders of Giants*. Growing recognition of the importance of Rheticus himself is further evidenced by the purchase, for $1.5 million, of a first edition of his *Narratio Prima* (*First Account*) by the Linda Hall Library (Kansas City) in early 2004.

Although, as already indicated, *Son of Copernicus* has a solid scholarly foundation—primary historical and textual research, with a strong sense of relation to secondary literature in the field—it is intended as a trade book: It delivers the unique story of Rheticus together with some bracing history of ideas in a fast-paced, accessible manner to a wide audience of intellectually curious readers. Nor is that audience limited to North America or the English-speaking world. *Son of Copernicus* will also appeal to European readers, especially those in Italy, Poland, and

Germany, nations that are vitally connected with the origins, education, and legacy of both Rheticus and Copernicus.

The Author

[The author's bio was included in four paragraphs.]

Schedule

As of April 2005, ten of the projected twelve chapters (including an appendix) of *Son of Copernicus* are complete, as is all of the research for the entire book. The full manuscript (80,000 words) will be available for delivery, in hard copy and on disk, by mid-August 2005.

Supporting Materials Included with this Proposal:

Blurb sheet for *The Book of the Cosmos*
Table of Contents for *Son of Copernicus*
Chapter summaries
Sample chapters:
Prologue

Chapter 1	No Rheticus, No Copernicus
Chapter 2	Patrons and a Poet
Author's Afterword	A Day in Krakow

Table of Contents

Prologue

Chapter 1 No Rheticus, No Copernicus
The visit
Fanning the flames
Why triangles matter
Copernican legacy
Chapter 2 Patrons and Poets
Feldkirch

Zurich, and back to Feldkirch
Wittenberg
  i. Luther
  ii. Melanchthon
  iii The sweetness of things
  iv. The Lemnius affair

Chapter 3 Roundabout Road to Frauenburg
The southern circuit
  i The Nuremberg connection
  ii. Ingolstadt, Tübingen, Feldkirch
The journey northward

Chapter 4 Vita Copernici
Frauenburg
The uncle of Copernicus
Copernicus the Humanist
Copernicus the economist
Copernicus the doctor
Everything is connected with everything else

Chapter 5 Joachim from Sun City
What Rheticus knew
The search for a system "pleasing to the mind"
"The desired harmony"

Chapter 6 Copernican Sunrise
"To the verge of disbelief"
"God's geometry in heaven and on earth"
Farewell to Sun City

Chapter 7 Copernican Afterlife
A stranger returning
Copernican dean
Songs of angles
Sabbatical projects

Making a world: Aristotle
"Saving the appearances"
Orchestrating the world: Claudius Ptolemy
"These are real difficulties"
Moving the earth
Nicolaus Cusanus

Chapter by chapter summaries

[A chapter-by-chapter summary was included. Each chapter's summary ran about 2 paragraphs or 200 words. I've included the Chapter 1 summary here.]

Chapter 1—summary

No Rheticus, No Copernicus

Banished from Germany for 101 years, Georg Joachim Rheticus has now also left his longtime residence in Poland and, at the invitation of a powerful general, moved to Cassovia in Upper Hungary. Here he is vaguely hoping to fulfill his thirty-year obsession: forging mathematical tools to defend the strange but beautiful new theory he had single-handedly brought to the world's attention, the cosmology of his late teacher Nicolaus Copernicus. But, unexpectedly, one day early in 1574 a passionate young man named Valentin Otto arrives all the way from Wittenberg and asks to be Rheticus's student. Remembering his own youth, the startled scientist welcomes him, and just as Rheticus had done for Copernicus, so now Otto rekindles the career of *his* adopted teacher and reinvigorates his dream of founding a new science.

In these intense early weeks together with Rheticus, Otto deepens his grasp of why progress in astronomy demands a better science of triangles (later dubbed "trigonometry"). He discovers how others, including a famous mathematician in Vienna, have urged Rheticus to finish his triangles project. Otto also learns just how bound up that project is for Rheticus, with his enduring commitment to fulfill the legacy of his revered teacher, to deliver "fruit from the most delightful gardens of Copernicus."

And yet, with these intimate glimpses into his new teacher's momentous scientific and personal career, Otto's introduction to the amazing life of Rheticus has only just begun.

The Butterfly Garden by Chip St. Clair (HCI)

This proposal is a memoir by Chip that again followed much discussion between the author and myself over the development of the book. Chip came to me with an idea for his book and with ample notes, but he had no real understanding of what was needed to create an effective proposal, although he eventually worked hard and diligently to get it into shape. Chip's is a powerful story of overcoming adversity and using that adversity to fuel a desire to do something for others, and to "give back." It all kind of fell into place once we got a title—*The Butterfly Garden,* which came from something Chip had said to me about a special safe place he went to recover from the brutalizing experiences he had suffered at the hands of his father. I had a hand in the line-editing of the proposal, but not the finished book, which garnered attention even before it was published and has gone from strength to strength since then.

The author had received a lot of TV and media attention by the time we met, and he spliced together a DVD of some of his more memorable appearances that accompanied the proposal when it was sent around to editors. The book was pounced on by Chip's eventual editor, who has been a champion of it from the beginning, seeing it very much in the tradition of *A Child Called It,* which had been a big success.

Once Chip and the publisher came up with the subtitle: "Growing Up on the Run with One of America's Most Wanted," we knew we had pretty much nailed this baby.

The Butterfly Garden

PROLOGUE

The unexamined life is not worth living.
        —Plato (469–399 B.C.), Greek philosopher.
        Attributed to the character called Socrates in
        Plato's dialogues

There is for all of us a profound "Moment of Truth" that lies in wait—a moment that transfixes our attention and forces us to confront the essential questions in life: Who am I? What is my purpose?

For some, this moment begins enlightenment: a process of personal evolution that comes through introspection. For others, it is a blip on the radar that is soon ignored, a wayward stroke of philosophy, never again considered.

My Moment of Truth came in the form of a large, black trunk with a brass lock, when I was 22. I remember the day I found it, in the residence of my parents, tucked away in a place forbidden to me as a child. It was my own Pandora's Box.

My fiancée Lisa and I entered their apartment, and although no one was home, nor would there ever be anyone at home again, my heart raced with anxiety and fear. I was looking for something, but I wasn't sure what.

I traced my way through rooms I had been in a hundred times, searching through drawers and closets, finding nothing. We eventually made our way to the staircase to inspect the upper level, and as we ascended, my legs became very heavy, my steps became slow and deliberate. I realized if anything was to be found at all, it would be in the room at the top of the stairs—my parents' bedroom. Reaching the upper landing, I quickly grasped the handle of the door before I had time to lose my nerve, and with a look to Lisa, I turned the knob and walked in.

The air was stale and musty, and the room was filled with dark shapes and shadows, for the curtains were drawn at the back, blotting out all light save that which spilled in through the doorway. And, there before me, catching the light, placed neatly at the foot of my parents' bed, was the trunk. It was not hidden. There was no lock, nor any need for one. My father ruled by fear, and fear can be more powerful than any lock. I trembled as I stood there staring at the trunk, feeling very small. Years of being told as a child never to inquire about my childhood made me reluctant to approach, yet I forced myself to kneel before it and a moment later Lisa joined me. The seconds before I opened it seemed like hours, as I rested my hand on its latch. A rustling quiet hung in the air, reminding me of the stillness before a storm.

I might have seen the trunk a couple of times over the years; it's hard to recall. But I had before never dared to open it for fear of the cruel wrath of my father.

I had no concern for him now. After 26 years on the run, he had been sent back to prison for murdering a three-year-old child almost thirty years before. And my mother was sitting behind bars facing charges of theft and embezzlement.

When my father's true identity was finally revealed to me, I somehow had lost my own. Everything I believed about my life had been a lie, and I searched desperately for answers. I had spent all of my 22 years of life with my parents on the run, always moving, yet never knowing.

With great expectation, I undid the brass latch and raised the lid of the trunk. Inside, however, I found not answers but more questions: forged birth certificates, pictures of other children with my name on them, falsified school records, locks of hair and baby teeth, all clues that alluded to an even greater mystery. This revelation left me reeling with doubt, confusion, and emptiness. I had opened the trunk hoping to find answers to who I was, and instead I discovered that I didn't know my own name or my own birthday. I didn't know if the people I had called "Mom and Dad" were even my parents, for now there was a horrifying suspicion that I might have been kidnapped. And perhaps there had once been other children in their care, children who may not have survived my father's brutality.

I had been presented a unique opportunity to face the questions we all must ask ourselves. In a very literal sense, this was my Moment of Truth, the beginning of the quest for my identity.

Those who have looked within and found the answers they've been seeking have discovered they are somehow transformed, gaining a renewed sense of focus, of peace, and of freedom. They gain a freedom that flies beyond confusion, anger, and doubt; a freedom that flies to new heights of understanding, of hope. And, as my journey gradually unfolded, I realized I didn't simply wish to fly. I wanted to soar....

MARKETING ANALYSIS

Since the moment I decided to share my story publicly, I realized through the reaction of others the profound impact it had on their lives, and I pondered the possibilities should they see not just a snapshot of my story in a local news article or national interview, but view the whole picture as I lived it, in my memoirs. For despite the multitude of interviews where the media examined the mystery, intrigue, and compelling circumstances of my life, it was the personal triumphs, the endurance of character, and the inspiration of hope for change that most viewers and readers were actually drawn to. This is the basis for the anticipated success of *The Butterfly Garden*.

AUDIENCE

As regional director of the Michigan chapter of Justice for Children, I am fully aware that nearly 100 million Americans have suffered some sort of trauma or abuse as children. And even more staggering, over 90 percent of the prison population report having been abused as children. So not only is there a vast market for those who relate directly to some of the issues in *The Butterfly Garden*, but the need for inspiration and change is great. And while I believe those individuals and members of groups who survived some level of suffering will make up a large majority of readers of this book, I believe the outreach of my message truly knows no bounds.

Today, people are increasingly searching for answers, about the world and about themselves. I believe they can find these answers where I did, in their own personal "Butterfly Gardens."

The Butterfly Garden, being a story of inspiration, hope for the prospect of change and personal enlightenment, will appeal to a vast array of readers, organizations, and book clubs. To name a few:

Rotary clubs
Optimists clubs
Self-help groups
Corporate groups
Parent groups
Teachers' organizations
Psychology/sociology networks
Recovery groups/workshops
Self-esteem groups/workshops

* Many of the the above-mentioned groups already have established book clubs.

The Butterfly Garden is perfect for all media audiences, including local and national magazine and newspapers, radio, and talk-show format audiences, i.e. Montel and Oprah—and it will be a natural fit for Oprah's Book Club.

With interest from professors at various universities in integrating *The Butterfly Garden* into the curriculum, ultimately numerous doors could open in the academic world. The book could be studied by psychology and sociology students across the country, which would not only translate into additional presentations and book sales, but would prove *The Butterfly Garden*'s message as timeless. As long as we are forced to confront tragedy in one form or another, as long as we must face that defining Moment of Truth, people will look for a story of inspiration and of hope for the dawn of change.

PUBLICITY AND PROMOTIONS

The fact that I've appeared on the front page of newspapers over 40 times shows the versatility of my story, and of my relationship with the media. And, having developed excellent working relationships and a mutual respect with those in the media, I've been offered their special attention should I run across a story of interest or be in need of assistance in following up on, or assisting in, a particular case or project.

I am confident I can rely upon the media relationships I have built to promote and publicize *The Butterfly Garden.*

Since testifying before Michigan's House and Senate, alongside Mark Lunsford, concerning Jessica's Law, he and I have formed a close bond and have been in constant collaboration. His national presence has earned a great deal of respect, as he has at his disposal the personal cell phone numbers of Bill O'Reilly, John Walsh, and Nancy Grace, among others. Obviously, Mark's influence is far- reaching, and he has offered me the opportunity to take advantage of his contacts and his assistance.

I am constantly being engaged to be a guest speaker at conferences, panel discussions, seminars, benefits, and school presentations, telling my story to literally thousands of people—most of whom request a copy of my book, (including state legislators, as I've testified before Congress on four separate occasions).

From Optimist and Rotary clubs, with total memberships in the millions, to the AT&T Michigan headquarters, I'm being asked to share my story purely for the inspirational value and to offer the prospect of change. I'm confident that these groups would be willing to help promote, publicize, and sell *The Butterfly Garden.*

Through Justice for Children, I have access to even more extensive lists of organizations who would likely aid in the promotion of the book.

Currently, I am being booked several months in advance to share my story before various groups. The Oakland Town Hall, which has a local membership of 300, has booked a speaking engagement next November and it has offered to promote my book to its members and within its book club.

I have a strong relationship with the University of Houston and local universities (i.e. University of Detroit Mercy, Wayne State University, etc.) who provide my office with interns. I am certain the professors I work with in these institutions would be interested in integrating *The Butterfly Garden* into the curriculum, ultimately drawing consideration from other universities.

Now, not just adults, but children will now begin to reap the benefits of my message as a local school district is in the process of writing my presentation into the high school curriculum.

MEDIA
Coverage of Personal Story:

Television:
Good Morning America - 1/2/03
The John Walsh Show - 2/19/03
Dateline NBC - 7/29/03, 3/04
Montel Williams Show - 10/7/04, 2/05
CNN - 4/8/06
MSNBC - 5/05, 4/06
Shelby T.V. (Macomb Today) - 11/03
Positively Positive - 4/05
Out of the Ordinary - 4/05
WXIX (Cincinnati) - 7/8/04, 7/21/04
WNDU (NBC affiliate) - 7/7/04, 7/21/04, 4/5/06
Michigan Government Television - 10/21/03, 3/06, 5/06

WDIV (NBC affiliate) - 2/27/04, 7/9/04, 7/21/04, 4/5/05

WXYZ (ABC affiliate) - 1/2/03, 4/4/06, 4/5/06, 4/7/06, 4/30/06, 5/1/06

Print:

Detroit News - 9/8/04, 5/06, 7/06

Indianapolis Star - 7/8/04, 7/21/04

NWI Times - 7/8/04, 7/21/04

Fort Wayne Journal Gazette - 4/6/06

Courier-Journal (Louisville, KY) - 7/8/04, 7/21/04

Detroit Free Press - 12/17/02, 7/7/04, 7/21/04, 4/27/05, 4/5/06, 4/6/06

The Associated Press - 12/18/02, 7/8/04, 7/21/04

The Elkhart Truth - 7/6/04, 7/20/04, 4/5/06, 4/14/06, 4/16/06

The Oakland Press - 7/8/04, 7/21/04, 7/22/04, 9/8/04, 9/12/04, 5/12/05, 8/13/05, 4/5/06, 4/7/06, 5/11/06, 7/06

The South Bend Tribune - 7/8/04, 7/21/04, 3/1/05, 4/5/06, 7/2/06-7/15/06

Radio:

The Mitch Albom Show - 9/8/04

NPR - various times

The Warren Pearce Show - 4/9/06

Metro Magazine w/Ron T - 4/05, 10/05

Lloyd Jackson - 4/5/06

WJR - various times

WKRK - various times

WRIF - various times

Annie Armen Live - 11/18/04

The Frank Beckman Show - 5/05, 4/5/06, 4/7/06, 5/06

I've had to develop a keen marketing sense as regional director of a nonprofit organization, finding creative ways to raise our level of visibility and catapult us into the public eye. To that end, I'm experienced in local and national press releases, on-camera and radio interviews, and in crafting the all-important sound byte. While continuing developments in my life spark an interest in updates by producers and reporters, I'm also sought after as a resource for child abuse and identity theft related topics.

COVERAGE OF RELATED TOPICS:
Television:
Inside Edition—5/19/05
Virginia Local T.V. - 10/2/06
CN8 News - 12/14/05
Michigan Government Television - 10/21/03, 3/06

Print:
The Associated Press - 4/27/05
Detroit News - 10/25/05
The Oakland Press - 3/1/05, 8/06
The Daily Tribune - 3/2/05
Lansing State Journal - 3/1/05
Observer & Eccentric - 11/6/05
Birmingham Eagle - 4/05, 3/06, 4/06, 5/06
"O" Magazine - 9/06
Rochester Post - 4/05, 3/06, 4/06, 5/06, 8/06
Suburban Lifestyles - 4/05, 3/06, 4/06, 5/06

Radio:
NPR - various times
Metro Magazine w/Ron T - 4/05, 10/05
WWJ - various times
WJR - various times
WKRK - various times
WRIF - various times
The Frank Beckman Show - 5/05, 4/5/06, 4/7/06, 5/06

Montel has requested I return for future shows as a child abuse expert, and *Dateline, Inside Edition*, and *The O'Reilly Factor,* among others, have expressed their interest in using me as a resource to discuss current child abuse cases and related topics. In addition, I've been in contact with producers from the shows below, producers who have expressed interest in doing an interview about my story and/or related topics:

HBO
CNN News
Lifetime TV
20/20
Fox News
Oprah
ABC World News Tonight
ABC Primetime
The O'Reilly Factor
On The Record With Greta
Nancy Grace
America's Most Wanted
NBC affiliate in Florida NBC affiliate in Michigan ABC affiliate in Michigan

CURRENT MEDIA

As my profile increases, I find myself as the center of many requests. I have been asked to make introductory remarks at a press conference held by the Oakland County sheriff before the local viewing audience in the metro Detroit area, with a population of approximately 4 million, and most recently I have been requested to do both statewide and national commercials for a U.S. senatorial candidate.

After tracking a known child predator across state lines for months, I launched a full scale investigation at Justice for Children when I learned this monster, who already served 13 years in prison for sexually assaulting children, had written a children's book and was targeting his young, unsuspecting readers at school presentations, camp outings, and book signings. The investigation revealed he faced 19 charges of child sexual assault across six states, and his most recent crime of sodomizing a five-year old in Florida had been pled down to probation. Determined to not allow him to slip through the cracks any longer, I began working with the local NBC affiliate in Florida to expose this man and the flaws in the system. As word of this story has spread, many local and national media outlets wish to interview me and cover this breaking news. A list of current interest is as follows:

> The O'Reilly Factor
> Nancy Grace
> CNN News
> ABC National
> Fox News Channel
> America's Most Wanted
> Local NBC
> Detroit Free Press
> Associated Press

Similar coverage is expected for another case involving an Atlanta hospital that failed to report a four-year-old boy who had been admitted for a broken arm, a dislocated hip, and six broken ribs within a three-week period. A week after being released, the boy was found strangled. The *Atlanta Journal Constitution* has already requested I write an op-ed piece on the case.

Advisory board member Mark Lunsford, who became a national spokesperson and child advocate after the abduction and murder of his daughter Jessica two years ago, will begin the trial of his daughter's killer in the coming months. Below is a list of outlets that showed interest in interviewing me as a panelist during the trial:

> Nancy Grace
> The O'Reilly Factor
> On the Record,

As my father looks to be released in the fall of 2007, despite the fact he is a suspect in the deaths of at least five other children, John Walsh of *America's Most Wanted* has expressed interest in covering the story. He hopes to flush out any new leads or tips which could result in a new conviction.

I recently invited *Dateline*'s Chris Hansen to attend a Nov. 10th Benefactors Event where we will be honoring him for his special investigations on child predators. Chris graciously accepted, and upon issuing a press release, I have been swamped with media interest.

Soon I will be unveiling ground breaking-legislation aimed at improving the Child Protective Service system. As I prepare to testify before the legislature, I am already drawing media attention.

Hour Detroit magazine is currently working on a story involving our upcoming Benefactor Reception and is also interested in doing a feature article on my story in a future issue.

THE BUTTERFLY FOUNDATION

Based upon the anticipated success of *The Butterfly Garden*, I hope to form The Butterfly Foundation—an organization designed to help children of abuse find the path to transition from caterpillar to butterfly, and to become a resource for adults looking to make a change in their lives - to make the transformation. This could be enormously popular for self-help groups (i.e. AA, Narc-Anon, etc.) and self-esteem building organizations, along with any of the previously mentioned groups.

Other aspects of the foundation would include an annual $25,000 scholarship awarded to the high school student who wins an essay contest on how literature made a profound impact on his life, as it did mine. This would obviously raise the visibility level of the foundation and, in turn, the book, as the contest would be offered to nearly every school district in the country.

MERCHANDISE POTENTIAL

Typically, there is no merchandise potential for a book in this genre. However, I believe if a butterfly symbol were created, something signifying change or overcoming adversity or perhaps surviving child abuse, this symbol could be sold with proceeds benefiting The Butterfly Foundation. Whether it be key chains, stickers, charms, or stuffed animals, people would purchase this symbol of change to remind them that hope always lies within.

THE BUTTERFLY GARDEN

TABLE OF CONTENTS

PROLOGUE: Pandora's Box

The book opens with my wife Lisa and me exploring my parents' empty apartment. My father is in jail for child murder after 26 years on the run; my mother is in jail for embezzlement. I find an old trunk in their bedroom. My hands shake as I open it up and begin to rummage around inside. But instead of answers as to who I am, the contents of the trunk plunge me into profound questions about my identity and origin.

1—THE TRUTH SHALL SET YOU FREE

I arrive at a prison in Indiana where a parole hearing is being held to determine if my father should be released. I prepare to relay horrific examples of his brutal abuse during my childhood prior to learning of his secret past.

2—RIDING OUT THE STORM

In recounting one of my earliest childhood memories, I describe the fear and anguish in witnessing one of the many vicious attacks on my mother.

3—UNCONQUERABLE SOUL

On a rare family trip to northern Michigan, I stumble across a poetry book, and I encounter the poem "Invictus," which ultimately sparks my love for literature. After a simple boat trip on the lake with my father turns sour, I find myself clinging to the words of the poem as I struggle to survive in the cold water of Lake Michigan.

4—SANCTUARY

In recalling one of my birthdays as a child, the reader is introduced to the only safe place I knew - a small wooden gazebo. Lying beneath the structure for hours, I absorb the peace and serenity of my secret spot, finding it a tiny oasis from the hell I call a childhood.

5—A WINTER FORSHADOWING

During the week leading into Christmas, I recount to the parole board the events centered on a question my dad posed to me when I was child: *What would you do if you found out you were kidnapped?* It's a question that will haunt me for years.

6—INTO THE WEST

My family and I move to California in the mid 1980s, where many revelations await me. At 11 years old, I refine my passion for literature, devouring everything from Hemingway to Shakespeare to Plato. Yet the fire of hope inside me is dwindling following a horrific incident. In another one of his sick, dangerous games, my father forces me onto a 28th floor balcony, threatening to send me over the railings, laughing, while I am in terror of falling to my death.

7—PRELUDE OF A DREAM

I bring the reader through my teenage years after returning to Michigan. I attempt suicide shortly after creating the self-portrait I call "Anonymous." The reader then meets my future wife, Lisa. Confusion and restlessness torment me as a struggle ensues for my soul between my father and Lisa. A struggle of a love I have never known and don't understand, and of fear and submission to my father.

8—RITE OF PASSAGE

I am finally out of the house and into college, and Lisa helps me to begin the process of breaking free of the chains my parents placed around me, never realizing the extent or strength of those chains. As I gain more independence, I begin to build a life with Lisa, and I grow ever more confident and more defiant of the hold my parents try so desperately to maintain with each passing day.

9—REVELATIONS

I finally recount to the parole board the night everything in my world fell apart: the night I discovered my father's dark, secret past—as a child murderer and as a fugitive on the run for 26 years. I describe how and why I turned him in, and I recall the pain, misplaced guilt, and anger I experienced over the following weeks. In an effort to find answers, I look to the past, to the night he committed the murder.

10—THE MOMENT OF TRUTH

Following my father's arrest, I uncover a trunk in his apartment containing so many more mysteries: forged birth certificates, doctored documents, strange photographs, leading not the answers for which I was desperately searching, but to more questions. In finding out my father's identity, I have lost my own. And the seemingly insignificant questions posed to me as a child return. *What would you do if you had been kidnapped? What would you do if you found out I had been in prison?* Thus begins the quest we must all face at some point in our lives, the quest for our identity. Yet mine is forced upon me in a very literal sense. My Moment of Truth has begun.

11—A NEW SOLACE

As I sift through clues and search for answers, Lisa and I grow closer. Her resilience, her unwavering love for me, teaches me ways of compassion, of love, and of peace.

I bring Lisa to the gazebo—my sanctuary as a child— and propose to her—making *her* a part of my safe place.

12—OPEN WOUNDS

Ten days before our wedding on February 14th, 1999, Lisa, her father, and I travel to prison. Only nine months after I turned in my father, he has been granted the opportunity of parole despite 26 years on the run after being convicted of killing a three–year-old child. I reveal to the parole board what my life had been like with Michael Grant, ultimately compelling the board to keep him locked away—until the next hearing.

13—SHROUDED IN DARKNESS

This minor victory unlocks a torrent of emotions inside me that I have tried to keep at bay for years. Mysteries still loom. I begin to realize the only way I can have a future is to reconcile the past. I need to find peace and try to understand the darkness inside my father.

14—THE BUTTERFLY GARDEN

Then one day I have an epiphany in a most unexpected place. Lisa and I visit a facility known as the Butterfly Garden, which houses hundreds of butterflies in various stages of life. This offers me a chance to gain insight and understanding through the comparison of butterflies to people. Through a deep examination I begin to understand my father, myself, and ultimately the world around us.

15—MASTERING DEMONS

With this newfound insight, I find I am able to master my demons, through understanding the past. I gain the ability to enter parts of my mind without fear, but rather with peace. And, at Lisa's urging, I begin to write poetry again, which inspires me to share my story in an effort to help others make the transformation from caterpillar to butterfly.

16—MASTER OF MY FATE

After appearances on various media outlets, I find many of the answers to the mysteries in the black trunk. Upon hearing my story, the national nonprofit organization Justice for Children asks me to be the regional director of a new chapter in Michigan, and so I make the transition from victim to victor, saving children from the very nightmare I once faced.

17—THE BUTTERFLY WITHIN

Returning to the Butterfly Garden, I examine many thoughts about our society, people like Lisa, and people like my father. Although many challenges still lie in the road ahead for us, I feel a sense of peace and understanding of my fate, and I take comfort that I can help others master their own.

Sample Chapters

[Chapters 1 to 3 were included as sample chapters along with extended summaries of subsequent chapters.]

A Highly Opinionated and Totally Subjective Reading List

Okay, no one expects you to read all these books. However, if you're looking for a place to start to figure out what's good to read or you're looking for potential models to use for your book, this is a pretty decent place.

All the President's Men by Bob Woodward and
   Carl Bernstein

Allen Dulles: Master of Spies; and *Franklin:
   The Essential Founding Father* by Jim Srodes

Angela's Ashes by Frank McCourt

The Arcanum by Janet Gleeson

The Best and the Brightest by David Halberstan

A Bright and Shining Lie by Neil Sheehan

*Band of Brothers: E Company, 506th Regiment,
   101st Airborne from Normandy to Hitler's Eagle's
   Nest* by Stephen E. Ambrose

Barbarians at the Gate by Bryan Burrough, John Helyar

Black Hawk Down by Mark Bowden

The Butterfly Garden by Chip St. Clair

*Cinderella & Company: Backstage at the Opera With
   Cecilia Bartoli* by Manuela Hoelterhoff

A Civil Action by Jonathan Harr

Common Ground by J. Anthony Lukas

Communion by Whitley Streiber

Dead Certainties by Simon Schama

Den of Thieves by James B. Stewart

The Diving Bell and the Butterfly: A Memoir of Life in Death by Jean-Dominique Bauby

Dispatches by Michael Herr

Eleanor of Aquitaine: A Life by Alison Weir

Executioner's Son by Norman Mailer

The Founding Fish; The John McPhee Reader (ed. William Howarth) by John McPhee

Fatal Vision by Joe McGinniss

Fermat's Last Theorem by Simon Singh

Fingerprints by Colin Beavan

Flags of our Fathers by Jim Brady

Generation Kill by Evan Wright

The Glass Castle by Jeanette Walls

Greed and Glory on Wall Street by Ken Auletta

Green River, Running Red by Anne Rule

A Heartbreaking Work of Staggering Genius by Dave Eggers

The Hot Zone by Richard Preston

Heart So Hungry (aka North of Unknown) by Randall Silvis

House; The Soul of a New Machine; Among School Children by Tracy Kidder

In Cold Blood by Truman Capote

Indecent Exposure by David McClintock, James B. Stewart

Into Thin Air by Jon Krakauer

The Informant: A True Story by Kurt Eichenwald

Jarhead by Anthony Swofford

John Adams by David McCullough

The Killer Angels by Michael Shaara

The Kiss by Kathryn Harrison

Kon Tiki by Thor Heyerdahl

Last Man Down by Richard Picciotto

Longitude by Dava Sobel

Low Life by Luc Sante

Lucky by Alice Sebold

Marley and Me by John Grogan

Max Perkins: Editor of Genius by A. Scott Berg

A Murder by Greg Fallis

Midnight in the Garden of Good and Evil
    by John Berendt

Nickel and Dimed: On (Not) Getting By In America
    by Barbara Ehrenreich

*Our Story: 77 Hours That Tested Our Friendship and
    Our Faith* (ed. Jeff Goodell), the Quecreek Miners

Paper Lion/Confessions of a Last-String Quarterback
    by George Plimpton

Paula by Isabelle Allende

The Perfect Storm by Sebastian Junger

The Professor and the Madman by Simon Winchester

Riding The Iron Rooster by Paul Theroux

The Rape of Nanking by Iris Chang

The Right Stuff by Tom Wolfe

Rivers of Blood, Years of Darkness by Robert Conot

Seabiscuit by Laura Hillenbrand

Schindler's Ark by Thomas Keneally

Sleepers by Lorenzo Carcaterra

Shadow Divers by Robert Kurson

Silent Spring by Rachel Carson

Small Sacrifices by Anne Rule

South by Ernest Shackleton

Sputnik: The Shock of the Century by Paul Dickson

Spy: The Inside Story of How The FBI's Robert Hanssen Betrayed America by David Wise

A Trial by Jury by D. Graham Burnett

The Von Bulow Affair by William Wright

Walking the Bible by Bruce S. Feiler

A Year in Provence by Peter Mayer

Notes

The quotes and interviews in this book come from four essential sources:

- Interviews I carried out for the book;
- Public discussion panels I was on;
- Research in Lexus-Nexus;
- Remarks by authors in their books about how and why they wrote the way that they did.

In most instances, I have indicated in the text the source of quoted information. When I say, "In an interview...", the interviewer was myself unless otherwise stated. However, I thought it appropriate to also annotate here the source material for the comments quoted in each chapter. Practicing, I hope, what I preach.

Introduction

Opening Quote: brainyquote.com/quotes/quotes/t/q110841.html.

Kirn: The state of narrative nonfiction writing, Nieman Reports; Cambridge; Fall 2000.

Dickson: 2002 Washington Independent Writers Conference, Spring Conference, May 171/N dash---JDM18, 2002 Washington, D.C National Press Club taped round table on narrative nonfiction, Rubie moderator.

Chapter 1

Opening Quote: brainyquote.com/quotes/quotes/t/q111095.html.

Vare: The state of narrative nonfiction writing, Nieman Reports; Cambridge; Fall 2000.

Gethers: Iinterview with Peter Rubie, Fall 2002.

Galassi: Interview with Peter Rubie, Fall 2002.

John: Quoted in *The Independent* (London) March 10, 1999.

Lister: *Science Mania: Read All About It.*

Hart: Interview with Peter Rubie, Fall 2002.

Gibson: Interview with Peter Rubie, Fall 2002.

Dunow: Quoted in *The New York Times* October 21, 2002.

Goldstein: *A Dark First Novel Suddenly Soars to the Top.*

Rabiner: *Thinking Like Your Editor.*

Goodwin: brainyquote.com/quotes/quotes/d/q113581.html.

Krakauer: *Into Thin Air.*

Winder: Quoted in *The Independent* (London) April 12, 1998.

Morrison: *Too True.*

Spicer: Quoted in *Editors On Editing,* (Ed. Gerry Gross).

Chapter 2

Opening Quote: The Columbia World of Quotations. 1996.

Hughes and Irving: Wikipedia; Irving's web site www.clif-fordirving com.

Irving: *The Hoax.* Crimelibrary.com (Rachael Bell).

Selzer: *The New York Times,* several editions, March 2008; *Entertainment Weekly (ew.com).*

Wolfe: *New Journalism.*

Sheed: *The New York Review of Book,* Oct 27, 1988.

McGinniss: *The Last Brother.*

Galassi: Interview with Peter Rubie, Fall 2002.

Spicer: Quoted in *How To Write and Sell True Crime,* by Gary Provost.

Olsen: Quoted in *How To Write and Sell True Crime,*
by Gary Provost.

Powers: *Bush At War,* by Bob Woodward, reviewed in *The New York Times* Sunday book review section, December 15, 2002.

Fry: Quoted in *Tom Wolfe's Revenge,* American Journalism Review, 16 Oct. 1994 by Chris Harvey.

Woodward: Quoted in *Tom Wolfe's Revenge,* American Journalism Review, 16 Oct. 1994 by Chris Harvey.

Hart: Ethics of narrative nonfiction, roundtable, reported by *Editor & Publisher,* Nov 28, 1998, confirmed in an interview with Peter Rubie, Fall 2002.

Hart: Interview with Peter Rubie, Fall 2002.

Gethers: Interview with Peter Rubie, Fall 2002.

Eissler: Quoted in Seligman article: Craig Seligman, *Salon.com,* Feb 29, 2000.

Seligman article: Craig Seligman, *Salon.com,* Feb 29, 2000.

Keith: Judge Damon J. Keith, US Court of Appeals for the Sixth Circuit, 2002.

Fink: Quoted in *The New York Times,* Sept 2, 2002.

Cahill: The Age of Creative Nonfiction, *nidus* Roundtable Discussion, 2001, online publication supported by the Writing Program at the University of Pittsburgh's English Department. (pitt.edu/~nidus/archives/fall2001/rt1.html).

Gutkind: The Age of Creative Nonfiction, *nidus* Roundtable Discussion, 2001, online publication supported by the Writing Program at the University of Pittsburgh's English Department. (pitt.edu/~nidus/archives/fall2001/rt1.html).

Chapter 3

Opening Quotes: The Columbia World of Quotations. 1996.

Stewart: *Follow the Story*.

Galassi: Interview with Peter Rubie, Fall 2002.

Krakauer: *Into Thin Air*.

Conaway: Interview with Peter Rubie, Fall 2002.

Gethers: Interview with Peter Rubie, Fall 2002.

Gibson: Interview with Peter Rubie, Fall 2002.

Twain: Quoted by science reporter James Burke, Voices from the Smithsonian Associates, June 28, 1999 at the Smithsonian Institution (http://smithsonianassociates.org/programs/burke/burke.htm).

Hart: Interview with Peter Rubie, Fall 2002.

Beavan: *First Success*, Colin Beavan, *Writer's Digest*, May 2001.

Bowden: *Black Hawk Down*.

Dickson: 2002 Washington Independent Writers Conference, Spring Conference May 17–18, 2002 Washington, D.C , National Press Club taped round table on narrative nonfiction, Rubie moderator.

Srodes: 2002 Washington Independent Writers Conference, Spring Conference May 17–18, 2002 Washington, D.C , National Press Club taped round table on narrative nonfiction, Rubie moderator.

Ehrenreich: "PW Talks with Barbara Ehrenreich." *Publishers Weekly*, May 14, 2001.

Chapter 4

Opening Quote: The Columbia World of Quotations. 1996.

Krakauer: *Into Thin Air*.

Chang: *The Rape of Nanking*.

Rhodes: *How to Write*.

Eichenwald: *Rewriting the Rules of Nonfiction*, by Kurt Eichenwald, published on booksense.com Jan/Feb 2001.

Burke thumbnail: Adapted from James Burke, Voices from the Smithsonian Associates, June 28, 1999 at the Smithsonian Institution. Streaming audio (http://smithsonianassociates.org/programs/burke/burke.htm).

Junger: *The Perfect Storm.*

Srodes: 2002 Washington Independent Writers Conference, Spring Conference May 17–18, 2002 Washington, D.C , National Press Club taped round table on narrative nonfiction, Rubie moderator.

Kidder: As quoted in *How to Write*, by Richard Rhodes.

Conot: *Rivers of Blood, Years of Darkness.*

McPhee: *John McPhee Reader, (*ed. William Howarth).

Bowden: *Black Hawk Down.*

Chapter 5

Opening Quote: The Columbia World of Quotations. 1996.

Krakauer: *Into Thin Air.*

Burnham: Quoted in *The New York Times*, May 20, 2002. Warren St. John: *The Talk of the Book World Still Can't Sell.*

Coady: Quoted in *The New York Times*, May 20, 2002. Warren St. John: *The Talk of the Book World Still Can't Sell.*

Cahill: The Age of Creative Nonfiction, *nidus* Roundtable Discussion, 2001, online publication supported by the Writing Program at the University of Pittsburgh's English Department. (pitt.edu/~nidus/archives/fall2001/rt1.html).

Conot: *Rivers of Blood, Years of Darkness.*

Eichenwald: *Rewriting the Rules of Nonfiction*, by Kurt Eichenwald, published on booksense.com Jan/Feb 2001.

Chang: *The Rape of Nanking.*

Rabiner: *Thinking Like Your Editor*.

Burnett: *A Trial by Jury*.

Mondale: Quoted in *The Rhetoric of Film*, by John Harrington.

Sayles: *Thinking In Pictures: The Making of the Movie Matewan*.

Dickson: 2002 Washington Independent Writers Conference, Spring Conference May 17-18, 2002 Washington, D.C , National Press Club taped round table on narrative nonfiction, Rubie moderator.

Chapter 6

Opening Quote: The Columbia World of Quotations. 1996.

Hirst: Nathan Edwards, *The Damien Hirst Website*. (geocities.com/ SoHo/Museum/4686/hirsthome.html).

Rule: *Small Sacrifices*.

Capote: *In Cold Blood*.

Krakauer: *Into Thin Air*.

Dickson: 2002 Washington Independent Writers Conference, Spring Conference May 17-18, 2002 Washington, D.C , National Press Club taped round table on narrative nonfiction, Rubie moderator.

Srodes: 2002 Washington Independent Writers Conference, Spring Conference May 17-18, 2002 Washington, D.C , National Press Club taped round table on narrative nonfiction, Rubie moderator.

Sobel: *Longitude*.

Preston: *The Hot Zone*.

Junger: *The Perfect Storm*.

Franklin: Quoted in *Tom Wolfe's Revenge, American Journalism Review*, 16 Oct. 1994 by Chris Harvey.

Bowden: *Black Hawk Down*.

A. Scott Berg: *Max Perkins: Editor of Genius*.

Schama: *Dead Certainties.*

Stewart: *Follow the Story.*

Chapter 7

Opening Quote #1: The Columbia World of Quotations, 1996.

Opening Quote #2: *Writing the Breakout Novel,* Donald Maass.

Chapter 8

Opening Quote #1: Mikhail Gorbachev, Soviet political leader. *The Guardian* (London, June 21, 1990).

Opening Quote #2: The Columbia World of Quotations. 1996.

Donadio: "Waiting For It." *New York Times*, Feb 3, 2008.

van Straaten: Tracy van Straaten, director of publicity at Simon & Schuster Children's Publishing in *Publishers Weekly,* Nov 19, 2001.

Warren: Q&A for Peter Rubie, Fall 2002.

Chapter 9

Opening Quote: *The Guardian* (London), April 21, 2001.

Brown: *Universal Foam: The Story of Bubbles from Cappuccino to the Cosmos*s by Sidney Perkowitz.

Srodes: 2002 Washington Independent Writers Conference, Spring Conference May 17-18, 2002 Washington, D.C., National Press Club taped round table on narrative nonfiction, Rubie moderator.

Cahill: The Age of Creative Nonfiction, *nidus* Roundtable Discussion, 2001, online publication supported by the Writing Program at the University of Pittsburgh's English Department. (pitt.edu/~nidus/archives/fall2001/rt1.html).

Index

About the Author

Peter Rubie is currently the CEO of FinePrint Literary Management (www.fineprintlit.com), a Manhattan-based literary agency. He is a former BBC Radio and Fleet Street journalist and has been a member of the NYU faculty for over a decade. For ten years he taught the only university-level course in the country on how to become a literary agent.

Prior to becoming an agent he was a publishing house editor for nearly six years whose authors won numerous prizes and critical acclaim. He has also been the editor-in-chief of a Manhattan local newspaper, and a freelance editor and book doctor for major publishers. He was a regular reviewer for the international trade magazine *Publishers Weekly*, and is a published author of both fiction and non-fiction and has had pieces published in various magazines including the *New York Times*. He regularly lectures and writes on publishing and the craft of writing, and was once a professional jazz musician.

The Fast-Track Course

Nonfiction Book Proposal
by Stephen Blake Mettee

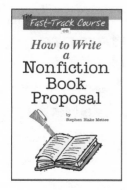

Mettee, a seasoned book editor and publisher, cuts to the chase and provides simple, detailed instruction that allows anyone to write a professional book proposal and hear an editor say "Yes!"

"...essential, succinct guideline. This is a must have reference book for writers...sets the industry standard."
—Bob Spear, *Heartland Reviews*

"Every writer needs a book like this. Mettee's sound, practical advice is just the ticket to make an editor welcome a writer's work! Keep the book close by, because you'll use it—guaranteed!"
—William Noble, author of *Writing Dramatic Nonfiction*

Both titles are Writer's Digest Book Club Selections!

Quit Your Day Job!
How to Sleep Late, Do What You Enjoy, and Make a Ton of Money as a Writer!
by Jim Denney

Resolution and perseverance are required to build a writing career and if you're going to succeed, you don't need the hype or hyperbole so often dished out in other writer's guides. You need a candid, no-nonsense appraisal of the daily grind of the writer's life, with the potholes and pitfalls clearly marked.

This book is your road map, written by someone who's lived the writing life for years, with more than sixty published novels and nonfiction books to his credit.

"While there are always a few charmed souls, most career-bent writers are destined to struggle. Jim Denney has been there, done that. Read his book and save yourself much of the anguish."
—James N. Frey, author of *How to Write a Damn Good Novel*

QuillDriverBooks.com • 1-800-345-4447